D0221013

# THE BRITISH POP DANDY

# The British Pop Dandy
## Masculinity, Popular Music and Culture

STAN HAWKINS
*University of Oslo, Norway*

ASHGATE

© Stan Hawkins 2009

Published by
Ashgate Publishing Limited
Wey Court East
Union Road
Farnham
Surrey, GU9 7PT
England

Ashgate Publishing Company
Suite 420
101 Cherry Street
Burlington
VT 05401-4405
USA

www.ashgate.com

**British Library Cataloguing in Publication Data**
Hawkins, Stan
   The British pop dandy : masculinity, popular music and culture. –
   (Ashgate popular and folk music series)
   1. Male singers – Great Britain – Psychology 2. Rock musicians – Great Britain
   – Psychology 3. Dandies – Great Britain – History – 20th century
   4. Masculinity in popular culture – Great Britain – History – 20th century
   I. Title
   782.4'2166'081'0941

**Library of Congress Cataloging-in-Publication Data**
Hawkins, Stan.
   The British pop dandy : masculinity, popular music and culture / Stan Hawkins.
      p. cm. — (Ashgate popular and folk music series)
   Includes bibliographical references and index.
   ISBN 978-0-7546-5858-0 (hardcover : alk. paper) 1. Popular music—Great Britain
   —History and criticism. 2. Dandyism in music. 3. Masculinity in music.
   4. Sex role in music. 5. Popular music—Social aspects—Great Britain. I. Title.

   ML3492.H38 2009
   306.4'84240941—dc22

2008023034

ISBN 978-0-7546-5858-0

**Mixed Sources**
Product group from well-managed
forests and other controlled sources
www.fsc.org Cert no. SA-COC-1565
© 1996 Forest Stewardship Council
FSC

Printed and bound in Great Britain by
MPG Books Ltd, Bodmin, Cornwall.

# Contents

# General Editor's Preface

The upheaval that occurred in musicology during the last two decades of the twentieth century has created a new urgency for the study of popular music alongside the development of new critical and theoretical models. A relativistic outlook has replaced the universal perspective of modernism (the international ambitions of the 12-note style); the grand narrative of the evolution and dissolution of tonality has been challenged, and emphasis has shifted to cultural context, reception and subject position. Together, these have conspired to eat away at the status of canonical composers and categories of high and low in music. A need has arisen, also, to recognize and address the emergence of crossovers, mixed and new genres, to engage in debates concerning the vexed problem of what constitutes authenticity in music and to offer a critique of musical practice as the product of free, individual expression.

Popular musicology is now a vital and exciting area of scholarship, and the *Ashgate Popular and Folk Music Series* presents some of the best research in the field. Authors are concerned with locating musical practices, values and meanings in cultural context, and may draw upon methodologies and theories developed in cultural studies, semiotics, poststructuralism, psychology and sociology. The series focuses on popular musics of the twentieth and twenty-first centuries. It is designed to embrace the world's popular musics from Acid Jazz to Zydeco, whether high tech or low tech, commercial or non-commercial, contemporary or traditional.

Derek B. Scott
Professor of Critical Musicology
University of Leeds, UK

# List of Dandies

Marc Almond (1957) – singer, songwriter and lead vocalist of Soft Cell

Adam Ant (1954) – singer, songwriter and lead vocalist of Adam and the Ants

Marc Bolan (1947–1977) – singer, songwriter, guitarist. Founder member of Tyrannosaurus Rex

David Bowie (1947) – singer, songwriter, producer and audio engineer

Jarvis Cocker (1963) – singer, songwriter and lead vocalist of Pulp

Ray Davies (1944) – singer, songwriter and lead vocalist of The Kinks

Pete Doherty (1979) – singer, songwriter and lead vocalist of Babyshambles

Paul Draper (1970) – singer, songwriter and lead vocalist of Mansun

Stephen Duffy (1960) – singer, songwriter, producer, and guitarist

Bryan Ferry (1945) – singer, songwriter and lead vocalist of Roxy Music

Neil Hannon (1970) – singer, songwriter, frontman for The Divine Comedy

Justin Hawkins (1975) – singer, songwriter and lead vocalist and guitarist of The Darkness

Mick Jagger (1943) – singer, songwriter and lead vocalist of The Rolling Stones

Jay Kay (1969) – singer, songwriter and lead vocalist of Jamiroquai

Steven Morrissey (1959) – singer, songwriter and lead vocalist of The Smiths

Robert Palmer (1949–2003) – singer, songwriter and member of Power Station

Robert Smith (1959) – guitarist, songwriter and lead vocalist of The Cure

Rod Stewart (1945) – singer, songwriter and lead vocalist of The Faces

David Sylvian (1958) – songwriter and lead vocalist of Japan

Neil Tennant (1954) – singer, songwriter and lead vocalist of the Pet Shop Boys

Sid Vicious (1957–1979) – rock musician and bass player of the Sex Pistols

Paul Weller (1958) – singer, songwriter and founder of The Jam and The Style Council

Robbie Williams (1974) – singer, songwriter and original member of Take That

# List of Illustrations

# List of Music Examples

**Example 5.5**
Robbie Williams: 'Millennium'
Transcr:         *Come and have a go if you think you are hard enough,*
                 *Millennium*
Location:        02:20
Tempo:           91bpm
Album:           *I've Been Expecting You*
Company:         Chrysalis Records
Released:        1998                                                    133

**Example 5.6**
Bryan Ferry:     'Don't Stop The Dance'
Transcr:         *Mama says the truth is all that matters, Lying and deceiving is a*
                 *sin*
Location:        00:27
Tempo:           128bpm
Album:           *Boys And Girls*
Company:         Virgin Records
Released:        1985                                                    135

**Example 5.7**
Pete Doherty:    'Albion'
Transcr:         *So come away, Won't you come away, We'd go to Catford,*
                 *Watford, Lincoln, Digberth, Liverpool, Anywhere in Albion*
Location:        01:19
Tempo:           101bpm
Album:           *Down in Albion*
Company:         Rough Trade Records
Released:        2005                                                    136

**Example 5.8**
Paul Draper:     'Wide Open Space'
Transcr:         *I'm in the wide open space, It's freezing, You'll never go to*
                 *heaven with a smile on your face from me*
Location:        00:35
Tempo:           106bpm
Album:           *Attack of the Grey Lantern*
Company:         Parlophone
Released:        1997                                                    137

**Example 5.9**

| | |
|---|---|
| Jarvis Cocker: | 'Common People' |
| Transcr: | *You'll never live like common people, You'll never do whatever common people do, Never fail like common people, You'll never watch your life slide out of view* |
| Location: | 04:38 |
| Tempo: | 138bpm |
| Album: | Single *(Different Class)* |
| Company: | Polygram |
| Released: | 1995                                            139 |

# Acknowledgments

The concept behind this book started as a course called 'Music and Identity' at the Department of Musicology, Oslo University in the late 1990s, and brings together my own disciplinary field of musicology with numerous fields that are engaged in subjectivity. This project would not have been possible without the encouragement and support of students and colleagues at my university. I also want to thank the Faculty of Arts, University of Agder, Kristiansand, where I hold an adjunct professorship in popular music.

Parts of this book are a logical outgrowth of other book projects I have been involved in, where the subject of gendered representation in popular music has been foregrounded alongside musical texts. The following editors and co-editors I have worked closely with have been sources of inspiration in my engagement with critical ideas and new theoretical directions in popular music studies: Andy Bennett, Ian Biddle, Freya Jarman-Ivens, the late Vanessa Knights, Jennifer Rycenga, John Richardson and Sheila Whiteley.

Numerous colleagues at home and abroad have leant support and useful feedback during a process that at times has seemed insurmountable in terms of its scope. At the beginning, the middle, and final critical stages of this project, I have been fortunate to receive advice and intellectual support from many of my associates working within the interdisciplinary field of popular music studies. I owe a special thanks to the following: Nicholas Cook, Thomas Hylland Eriksen, Susan Fast, Simon Frith, Richard Middleton, Allan F. Moore, Sarah Niblock, John Richardson, Derek Scott, Erik Steinskog, Robynn Stilwell and Steve Sweeney-Turner.

Many friends, colleagues, ex- and current students have provided stimulating discussions, constructive criticism, and a good deal of chuckles along the way. Special mention should be made to: Anne, Bendik, Bette, Cláudia, Dezi, Even, Eystein, Hans Thorvald, Kyrre, Marita, Mats, Michael, Moyra, Nishlyn, Odd, Shara, Ståle, Tellef and Tor. For help with my transcriptions and invaluable insights into techniques of guitar playing, sonic markers, and studio production, a special thanks goes to my current PhD student, Eirik Askerøi. Also thanks to Jon Mikkel Broch Ålvik for help with the proofs and a meticulous eye for detail. I also welcome this opportunity to express a particular gratitude to the Faculty of Humanities, University of Oslo, who support regular sabbatical leave and generous research funding for book projects of this nature. Short-term absence from teaching and administrative responsibilities during 2007 certainly helped make this book possible.

Close ones remain to be acknowledged. Without them this study would never have materialised. During my sabbatical year in France the dandy, a creature of fascination, became a compelling topic of conversation almost without exception: Monique and Francois, Marie, Odd, Christiane, Michel, deserve a hearfelt thanks for all the inspiring conversations on dandyism from a French perspective. In addition, Paul Jackson, from the BBC, was of invaluable help in pinning down the British pop dandy. Without his support, recommendations and feedback this book would not have felt the same. Ashgate continued to offer the best assistance and most professional support. Thanks go to the staff, Heidi May, Lorraine Slipper, Nick Wain, and Derek Scott, the series editor. Finally, to my close circle, Jacqueline, Helgs, and Martin, for being part of this process and making it all the more enjoyable I thank you. This book is for you as much as all the pop dandies I chose to write about.

# Copyright Acknowledgments

'Just Like Heaven' from *Kiss Me, Kiss Me, Kiss Me*, words and music by Robert Smith/Simon Gallup/Porl Thompson/Boris Williams/Lol Tolhurst © 1987 Fiction

*Chapter 4*

'La Belle et la Bete' from *Down in Albion*, words and music by Pete Doherty/Peter Wolfe/Robert Chevalley © 2005 Rough Trade
'Kitsch' from *Stardom Road*, words and music by Paul Ryan © 2007 Sanctuary
'Adolescent Sex' from *Adolescent Sex*, words and music by David Sylvian © 1977 Hansa
'Bamboo Houses/Bamboo Music', words and music by David Sylvian/Ryuichi Sakamoto ©1982 Victor

*Chapter 5*

'Slip Away' from *Heathen*, words and music by David Bowie © 2002 ISO
'Hideaway' from *Goddess in the Doorway*, words and music by Mick Jagger © 2001 Virgin
'At Last I am Born' from *Ringleader of the Tormentors*, words and music by Steven Morrissey/Michael Farrell © 2006 Sanctuary
'I Believe in a Thing Called Love' from *The Darkness – Permission to Land*, words and music by Justin Hawkins/Dan Hawkins/Ed Graham/Frankie Poulain © 2003 Must Destroy
'Millennium' from *I've Been Expecting You*, words and music by Robbie Williams/Guy Chambers/John Barry/Leslie Bricusse © 1998 BMG/EMI/Universal
'Don't Stop the Dance' from *Boys and Girls*, words and music by Bryan Ferry/Rhett Davies © 1985, Virgin
'Albion' from *Down in Albion*, words and music by Pete Doherty © 2005 Rough Trade
'Wide Open Space' from *Attack of the Grey Lantern*, words and music by Paul Draper © 1997 Parlophone
'Common People' from *Different Class*, words and music by Jarvis Cocker/Nick Banks/Candida Doyle/Russell Senior/Steve Mackey © 1995 Polygram

*Chapter 6*

'Children of the Revolution', single, words and music by Marc Bolan © 1972 EMI/reprise
'Heroes' from *Heroes*, words and music by David Bowie/Brian Eno © 1977 RCA
'Fashion' from *Scary Monsters (and Super Creeps)*, words and music by David Bowie © 1980 RCA
'Charmed Life' from *The Very Best of Mick Jagger*, words and music by Mick Jagger © 2007 WEA/Rhino

# Introduction

Yankee Doodle went to town,
A riding on a pony;
Stuck a feather in his hat
and called it macaroni.
Yankee Doodle,
Keep it up,
Yankee Doodle Dandy …

As part of the USA Bicentennial jubilations, a score of *The Disappointment: Or, the Force of Credulity* was reworked for a performance on 29 October 1976 at Washington's Library of Congress. Intended for an American audience, this two-act ballad opera by Andrew Barton ingeniously satirized the office of King George, poking fun at various Philadelphian individuals. Alas, in 1762 its first performance was cancelled, and five years later, just before its scheduled performance at the new Southwark Theatre in Philadelphia, it was shelved; the piece's personal reflections and comic barbs were deemed far too inappropriate. Incredibly, Barton's opera comedy would sit for two hundred years waiting for its first performance, during which time most of the musical arrangements and score parts were lost. In the early twentieth century the American musicologist Oscar Sonneck would unravel a number of interesting facts concerning this opera, not least the inclusion of the song, 'Yankee Doodle'. Allegedly this was played by troops marching from Boston to reinforce British soldiers in combat with Americans at Lexington and Concord. Soon the American militia appropriated the song, going into battle and forcing the British back to Boston, singing: 'Yankee Doodle, Keep it up, Yankee Doodle Dandy …'.

Reportedly written by a British army surgeon, Dr Richard Shuckburg, the tune would become known to most English speakers, resounding with the words, 'yankee', 'doodle', 'dandy' and 'macaroni'. Alternating accounts of the word 'yankee' (or Yankey) have suggested it came from the word 'Nankey', in a jingle about Oliver Cromwell, or from the Indian pronunciation of 'English' as 'Yengees'. Be that as it may, by the mid-1700s 'yankee' referred to English colonists, especially New Englanders, while the word 'doodle' dated back to the early 1700s, to the Low German, *dudeltopf*, designating a sorry, trifling person, a fool, a simpleton. Not entirely unrelated to doodle, 'macaroni' was a jibe at a group of young Britons in the mid-eighteenth century whose dress codes included large powdered wigs, with a little hat on top, indeed placed so high up on the head that it could only be removed by the tip of a sword. By sticking a feather in his hat and calling it 'macaroni', Yankee Doodle unwittingly proclaimed his naivety:

he believed this was all it took to be a 'macaroni'. Derisively, the colonists would employ 'macaroni' to ridicule the uniforms worn by the British, while 'dandy' would be used to mock the 'gentleman' of affected manner, dress and attitude. It needs to be emphasized, though, that much speculation surrounds the derivation of 'dandy'.

One version suggests its transference from France to Scotland in the sixteenth century. Meaning fool or 'nincompoop', the word *dandin* was used by the French soldiers in the war against England, where it changed gradually from a term of abuse to one of resentful respect. A second account suggests 'dandy', originally English, dated back to the 1490s when it referred to the silver half-groat of Henry VII; a coin of little value referred to as a 'dandiprat'. Over time this term (also spelt 'dandyprat') would be applied to worthless and contemptible people. Undoubtedly insulting for their time, the references to 'dandy' in 'Yankee Doodle' encouraged the Americans to add their own verses in ridicule of Washington's visit to the Provincial Camp at Cambridge, Massachusetts. Legacy has it that he rode in with flaming ribbons, gleefully slapping his stallion's sides: 'And there was Captain Washington, And gentlefolks about him; They say he's grown so tarnal proud, He will not ride without 'em.'

Revolutionary upheavals in Europe during the late 1700s seemed right for the emergence of dandyism. In particular, the open display of pretension – in the affectation of male costume and poise – became part of the dandy's contradictory mission as the reactionary and the revolutionary, so much so that by the dawn of the 1800s the dandy would stand for 'superiority, irresponsibility, inactivity' (Moers 1978, p. 13). By and large, though, this went against the grain of the rising majority's call for equality. Ideologically, dandyism fused disparate ideals of invention to provide a caustic commentary on the bourgeois spirit of the time, behind which lay the 'heavy earnestness of the Victorian prose' (ibid., p. 14) and a craving for anti-bourgeois values. As a satirical take on provincialism, then, 'Yankee Doodle' seems a fitting tune for situating the 'dandy' in a new context. After all, dandyism in France represented a social and cultural phenomenon of great consequence, with its roots firmly in the momentous historical events of the *Cent Jours*: the Battle of Waterloo, the fall of the emperor and the rule of Louis XVIII from 1814.

This was also a period of anglomania, as *le dandyisme*, integral to the intellectual community of France, would now be imported from the British Isles (Moers 1978, pp. 107–24). Figures such as Charles Baudelaire and Barbey D'Aurevilly would gain their inspiration from the alien temperament across the channel. For, as Ellen Moers points out, the 'ambiguous symbol of the dandy brought together ideas and attitudes of the most unlikely contemporaries in the two countries' (Moers 1978, p. 13). But this was 1816 and not 1952, when another group of dandies, the Teddy boys, took Paris by storm in much the same way as the first touring English dandies did in the early 1800s. Loud clothes of garish colours – the *fumée de Londres*, vert anglais, bronze anglais and *redingote lord Novart* – symbolized the transition from the austerity of the 1940s to the prosperity of the 1950s in Britain.

Part of this was instilled in the Teddy's attitude of pride that looked back to the Regency dandies, with displays of tame eccentricity, dry wit, vulgarity, comic excess and most 'troublesome' behaviour.

Passed down from the eighteenth century to the beginning of the twenty-first century, trends in dandyism are inextricably connected to the identification of eccentricity and peculiarity. One-upmanship, something quintessentially British, has always entailed conduct and imaginative refinement that panders to an intricately regulated coding of insiders and outsiders. During the second half of the twentieth century this formed the rationale for a consumer-based imperative. George Walden proclaims in his essay *Who's a Dandy?*: 'In a mass age we must expect our dandies to be mass-produced' (Walden 2002, p. 47). And so, the iconic status of the pop celebrity emerged, with the flaunting of personal pride, lifestyle and social protest.

Central to any discussion of the phenomenon of the British pop artist are the trademarks of social class, gender and ethnicity, confounded by the peculiarities of cultural identification. Interpreting who and what constitutes the pop dandy includes trawling through the idiosyncrasies of performance socio-musically. Replete with historic lineages, my study casts light on the emergence of pop performers in recent times, revealing the intangible notions of national ethnicity and male behaviour. One of the challenges has been identifying Britishness against the dominant undertow of Englishness. For since the end of the Second World War, momentous social and political changes have altered notions of nationality and belonging in the geographical space known today as the United Kingdom.[1] From the eighteenth century onwards, Englishness, an overriding ingredient of Britishness, has had troublesome points of reference. As Robert Colls debates in *Identity of England*:

> The state was British and dominated by England, but the Scots, Welsh, and Irish were not over-much expected to convert into English or even into something synthetic called British (…) The English sought Union for reasons of security, the Scots for economic advantage, some Irish tarried with it in the hope that it might yield to them what it had yielded to others. The Welsh were not consulted. (…) What this left was a set of British peoples with a sense of their own nationality but never quite sure of how to talk about themselves as a collective of nations.[2]

---

[1] In Grant and Stringer (1995) a wide range of essays take up the complicated historical chain of events and political circumstances that determine British history and identity. Among the many topics aired in this anthology is that of convergence and divergence and to what extent the groupings of various peoples within the British Isles can be integrated into one British people. In addition, the concept of the United Kingdom as an entity is problematized as a means for understanding the failures and successes of attempts at integrating the people of the British Isles. Also see Alibhai-Brown (2000) and Colls (2002).

[2] Colls (2002, p. 377).

In Colls's research employment of the term English is freely substituted for British, and vice versa. Ostensibly, Colls's arguments for a strong English identity appear to contest British citizenship. Yet, identifying someone as English or British is a complicated matter that evokes many sentiments attached to ideology, politics, social class and ethnicity. For this reason, I have been loath to entitle this book *The English Dandy*, for fear of omitting a whole range of artists and bands whose birthplace does not necessarily define their own notions of collective belonging. With only one exception, Irish-born Neil Hannon of The Divine Comedy, all the artists covered in this book are born in England. Notwithstanding the fine-tuning of definitions of citizenship, I cautiously advocate Britishness as a selective term that broadly encompasses the groups of interrelated people that reside in or originate from the United Kingdom and hold British passports. To be or feel British inevitably designates some kind of multi-layered identity, and as in the case of Hannon, like his band, he is remarkably English.[3] But this is not that extraordinary. Kari Kallioniemi verifies that dandyism is a split-personality syndrome of Britishness, extending from 'Coward's Scottish, English and Irish origins, Morrissey's Anglo-Mancunian-Irish identity, to the Yorkshiremen who made a living out of flaunting English-stereotypes (Neil Tennant, Bryan Ferry, Martin Fry and Jarvis Cocker)' (Kallioniemi 1998, pp. 91–2).

National identity, ethnicity, gender, sexuality and class are some of my focal points when deciding what constitutes the British pop dandy. Many other categories of course also objectify and complicate the dandy character. In earlier studies[4] I have maintained that general changes in male behaviour have had a strong effect on the formation of pop texts, opening up the necessity for scholarship in gender studies and representation politics. In the main, writings on gender have concentrated on the binarisms of the masculine and feminine, forming the basis for critiques of subjectivity. Intertwined with these debates are two principal areas of interest: musical performance and spectatorship, both of which are useful for addressing how bodies have changed and developed in their objectification, erotically, sexually and politically. Controlled by the onlooker, whose gaze constructs shifting positions, gender positioning not only naturalizes but also idealizes identity. Surely in musical performance gendered behaviour, as asserted in contested social and cultural spaces, requires de-naturalizing.

Judith Butler (1993) would agree. Her discourse of gendered performance and the notion of the subject as a cultural construction is applicable to this study, especially when asking: Who is the male pop dandy, and what is it that accounts for his appeal? The attention paid to these questions involves working out subjectivity and its annex to music, where the goal is to foreground the body. Emerging from many of my debates is the concept of performance as a strategic intent, where the mission is primarily to entertain. Voyeuristically offering himself up as an object

---

[3]   See Campbell (2007). Also see Garnett (2005) for a fascinating perspective on Britishness through her study of barbershop.
[4]   See Hawkins (2002, 2004, 2006, 2007b).

for spectatorship, the pop dandy is a phenomenon of the recorded form. Tantalizing the fan, and assuming many guises, he can be demure, sensual, sexually naive, or bold, cock-sure, rough and vulgar; or even passive, regressive, and a psycho-case. And mocking his own self-loathing, the dandy exhibits an outward expression of superiority, an embodiment of the Wildean idea of the self as a work of art.

Arrogance, conceit or rebellion? All, of course. For dandyism is a platform on which to stand and mask oneself. Unavoidably, selecting a group of pop celebrities opens up a critique of categorization that deals with personal agency in music. In one sense a reductive exercise, classifying the dandy is about making judgments and subjective assessments. Admittedly personalized, the criteria I have chosen for labelling selected performers as dandies cannot purport to be anything near a comprehensive list. I have sought out artists who have gained consensus in the community in which I work, and throughout this study I have been in dialogue with work associates, friends, students, scholars and journalists. As such, the nexus of this project is a mobilization of the musicalized character through selected recorded performances, reflecting my own deep-rooted curiosity in the peculiarity of male behaviour. Against the backdrop of specific styles and traditions, male performances are an integral part of the conventions and assumptions that shape them. From this it follows, then, that the male subject's adherence to language, mannerism and musical performances has enormous cultural significance.

In many ways an ideal forum for contemplating the enactment of gender, pop music provides a key to understanding the representational forces invoked by mediation. Bryan Ferry's persona, for instance, is conveyed through a soft, sexy crooning style that functions as a key factor in understanding the role of temperament. Moreover, his vocality can be contextualized culturally within an urban context. Addressing the wider issues of urbanity, Adam Krims (2000, 2007) reflects on music's mediation as part of relations that are formed, reproduced and negotiated. The bent of Krims's understanding of production is through an analysis of urban geography; the sum of human activity, where individual agency holds less significance than cultural situations. Rotating Krims's model around slightly, my study pinpoints music's function by primarily taking stock of individual agency. If music is under constant social change, then it stands to reason that it works dialectically across a range of situations; for just as individual agency is mediated through performance and production, so music draws its source from the historical and cultural context of its conception. Understood in this way, the social spaces that shape individual agency hold vital clues for comprehending musical performance.

Music-analytically, this study entails a flexible approach that aids the task of locating specific moments that are symptomatic of agency, style and idiosyncrasy. Pleasure, located in the familiarity of a song, I argue, is always style-dependent. The theoretical premise of this involves addressing the performance and how it achieves its aesthetic effect through stylistic and technical codes.[5] As I set out to

---

[5] For a discussion of stylistic and technical codes and their ramifications, see Chapter 1 in Hawkins (2002).

show, relating to a musical performance is about sensing the junctions between music, performer and listener. The music researcher's task, then, is one of working out the constructs of human behaviour in musical performance within the broader politics of cultural location.

While writing a book on male identity, I pondered long and hard over the issue of the female dandy. Acutely aware that the female is often shoved to the side of academic scholarship at the expense of the male, I grappled with the dilemma of exclusion.[6] There is little doubt that female dandies have been around as long as their male counterparts. During the period of Brummell's ascendancy there were enough dandified ladies (dandettes) who maintained *salons*, hosting elaborate affairs and defying the British custom of being sent out of the room after dinner to chatter while the men sat on their own and gossiped over brandy. Among these Regency ladies were 'Corky' (Lady Cork), a kleptomaniac who dressed in white and was highly rouged, Lady Holland, a proud, domineering woman who bore Lord Holland's son long before they were married, Lady Morgan, best-selling novelist and author of *The Wild Irish Girl*, and Lady Blessington, an author who accounted for the dandyism of Count D'Orsay.[7] Another obvious genealogy stems from the *demi-mondes*, such as Cora Pearl, and later on, after the First World War, Marchesa Luisa Casati, whose personae would pave the way forward for the superstars of the twentieth century: Patti Smith (Godmother of Punk), Siouxsie Sioux, Annie Lennox, Madonna, Kylie Minogue, Björk, Gwen Stefani, Beyoncé, and many others. That I have restricted my study to male pop artists[8] (choosing from now on to use the male pronoun when referring to the dandy) does not on any count preclude my recognition of female artists, whose impact on the rise of dandyism in pop has been tumultuous. Brett and Wood (2002, pp. 16–19), referring to the 'diva effect', identify an attitude more than a phenomenon that has appealed across wide audiences during the twentieth century. The notable offshoot of this is found in cabaret, from Judy Garland, her daughter, Liza Minnelli, Marlene Dietrich, Mae West, Bette Midler, Barbara Streisand and Edith Piaf to Zarah Leander. Qualities in these singer-performers – irony, camp and vulnerability – are mirrored in the

---

[6]    This point is debated in Freya Jarman-Ivens's preface to a collection of essays on masculinities and popular music, *Oh Boy!* (2007).

[7]    Fascinating accounts of female dandyism are taken up by Ellen Moers in her in-depth discussion of The Regency 1800–30 (Moers 1978, pp. 39–67).

[8]    Of the two main strains of critical studies of men and masculinities (the first emerging in the 1980s as a critique on hegemony and power relations by pro-feminist scholars, such as Connell and Kimmell), I am more preoccupied with the second, which is mainly influenced by post-structural theory and cultural studies, where the focus falls on performativity, sexuality and the politics of representation. When it comes to the debates around the 'crisis of masculinity' (that masculinity is threatened by the pressures of the workplace, education, the media and the family), I reject this anti-feminist backlash, and side with Tim Edwards's position (2006) that masculinity is not in crisis, but *is* crisis because it is a social construction, a fictive invention.

self-reflexive glamour of disco divas such as Donna Summer, Gloria Gaynor, Patti LaBelle, Sister Sledge, the Pointer Sisters and the Weather Girls. A dominant feature of popular culture, the diva effect is grounded in fashion, film, television and club culture, and is a celebration of excess and style. And finally, the queered performance that finds its way into every spectacle possible almost owes everything to the 'diva effect'. Queer pop acts, as we will see, ascribe meanings to texts that are fluid, free-floating and ephemeral in specific social and cultural spaces.

What then is the role of the popular musicologist in all this? Identifying subjectivity from a musicological perspective must involve working out textual orientation and discursive location. Shared views of codes, processes and structures mean music exists in all forms and guises. This is the basis, then, for my considering the ontology of the musicalized dandy and what best qualifies him for this role. Generally speaking, vast differences exist between experiencing an artist live or in recorded form, where the boundaries invariably come over blurred. As a domain in their own right, pop recordings interface with music and performance to mediate notions of reality and belonging. A main goal in this respect is to consider musical expression in the recorded form. Because the constitutive function of technology and creativity in music is produced culturally, experiences of any performance are dependent on shared responses to codes and processes. That said, listening in the absence of viewing can be easily taken for granted in terms of body language, gender and desire. Central to this study, then, is a consideration of the positioning of the body and its presence in recorded form. Thus, in line with approaches to performativity,[9] I am keen to interrogate the politics of visual display.

Koestenbaum (1993) insists that without the visual spectacle, listeners respond instinctively to the intensity of sonic *jouissance*. When contemplating sound as something disembodied, Koestenbaum suggests that feelings are evoked by pleasure as much as displeasure through the corporeality of sound itself. Acts of repeated listening, he discovers, are about reconstruction, as the memory of hearing music recorded in the past becomes part of a continual process of self-reflection and introspection in the present. In this sense, traces of the body in a visual performance involve gestures that are intended to make the sound more impressive than it is.[10] Seeking out the intricacies of the diva effect in opera, Koestenbaum positions himself not only as interpreter of musical experience, but also as subject and object of contemplation. Of the key narratives he presents, his homoerotic impressions and fantasies are omnipresent in all his interpretation. So, what makes opera *desirable* for him (and possibly for the reader) remains something mysterious and unfathomable.[11]

---

[9]   In particular the gender-oriented studies of McClary (1991, 2000), Walser (1993), Richardson (1999), Fast (2001), Garnett (2005), Middleton (2006), Jarman-Ivens (2007).

[10]   Thanks to Robynn Stilwell for this valid point and her affirmation that the English dandified body can be 'heard' through the singer 'putting on' a certain sound.

[11]   For an enlightening review of Koestenbaum's *The Queen's Throat* (1993), which also addresses some of these issues, see Kevin Kopelson (1994).

Possibilities for enjoying music performances, as Koestenbaum demonstrates, lie in our imaginative responses. Like opera, pop texts are contingent upon image and recorded sound. Nicholas Cook (1998) considers how music transfers its own sets of attributes to audio-visual narratives. Cook's concept of musical multimedia discloses some of the assumptions and ideologies that spell out musical autonomy in audio-visual texts. Through conjoining pictures to sounds, music creates a seamless form that allows for new meanings to emerge. Cook, like Koestenbaum, perceives music as a reinforcement of inner thoughts and feelings that functions as a filter for more than what we see: what we desire. In multimedia settings, then, music mediates desire by instructing us to imagine what we see.

Let us say that by imagining what we see, we are taught to see, especially in the absence of visual codes. Throughout this book the recorded song constitutes the score, where the prescription of its musical form is framed within numerous contexts. Shedding light on the intricacies of musical details, I seek to verify some of the connotations that we hear narratively. For hearing music is about taking in the overall musical image, which conjures up chains of representational meanings that are organized socially and culturally. Tagg (1982) points out that this is what makes listening to music compelling; listening inscribes references to a genre and determines whether or not we gain something from a performance. Obviously there is a lot more to this.

How does a musical moment work performatively, for instance? By addressing this question from many angles,[12] and accounting for specific moments in a performance, it is possible to open up the musical material for analysis. In earlier studies (Hawkins 2001, 2003, 2007c) I have argued that a recurring problem is one of fixity, where the moment is frozen so formally that it annihilates the music's content. Identifying this through a theorization of 'moments', Berthold Hoeckner (2002) contemplates the rhetorical dimensions of music via the 'purple prose'. Primarily directed towards nineteenth-century absolute music, Hoeckner pinpoints the chasm between hermeneutics and analysis by drawing attention to close readings that are 'remote from the jargon used to bring music close to a non-professional audience' (Ibid., 2002, p. 4). Navigating a terrain that is intertextually cumulative, Hoeckner reconstructs musical insights through an essayistic critique. Useful here is his idea of associative interpretation, which is applied in a rigorous reconstruction of style that addresses visual, cultural and musical images. Inspired by iconography and nostalgic moments of reflexivity, Hoeckner advocates a model that illuminates the multifarious properties of musical performance.

---

[12]   Hoeckner (2002) argues for a thorough critique of the musicological anxieties that have bridged the gap between musical hermeneutics and music analysis, especially with reference to the ideology of absolute music as serious music. Hoeckner's discourse probes at the moments of transcendence and liberation that furnish nineteenth-century music with its ideals.

Which returns us to the audio-visual text. This cannot be separated from performance, its aesthetics or its linguistic voice.[13]

In the main, my readings of pop texts are informed by similar approaches to those of Hoeckner. Although I would hesitate to claim the popular song as *non*-standardized (in terms of its formulaic diversity), there are innumerable elements that make one song unique from another: instrumentation, style, production, mix and voice, and, extramusically, gender, class, ethnicity, character, mood and culture. Once more, in a Taggian vein, the particularity of music structure and form exposes the complexities of transferred meaning. Often decentred, the detail is elusive and even mislaid, its conceptualization disguised by ambivalence. By this I mean the ambivalence in one text to the next generates a great deal of curiosity and appeal, and, as I have argued already (Hawkins 2001), the musical detail is looped through systems of repetition, where its embellishment, its fantasy, is ultimately at the beck and call of the performer's – in our case the dandy's – interpretation.

The pop dandy's role has everything to do with interpretation on the part of the fan; every uttered melodic interval, harmonic voicing, off–on beat, vocal inflection expressed corresponds to something culturally definable. Conceived in terms of its physical properties, as much as its emotional effect, music not only provides narratives, but also ignites the interpretive process; a phenomenon we cannot bypass as analysts. Historically, narratives of style in songs say why musical decisions are made and what their extramusical consequences are. After all, every musical decision has its own history and set of contradictions. On this matter Allan F. Moore asks: 'Is the singer-songwriter of the new century the same beast as the countercultural singer-songwriter?' (Moore 2006, p. 332). Turning to punk rock, Moore questions the historical differences between punk of the mid-1970s and punk of the late 1990s and present. Genres that undergo 'analogous patterns of change' include both aspects of demise and rebirth, which, as Moore insists, is 'attested by the recent revival of (often acoustic) blues as a contemporary, vital form of expression' (ibid., p. 333) rather than an old, preserved relic.

Music thus functions as a historical mediator of musicians and their entourages. By identifying the phenomenon of pop dandyism, I build on a social historiography that locates the strategies of a group of male artists. Fascinatingly, they reinforce a long tradition of performative display that can be read as institutionally transgressive. An overarching question in this book therefore deals with how each

---

[13] Fred Maus (2004), in addressing the aspect of identification and domination, responds to Allen Forte's and Edward Cone's separate studies, which, in some way, sidestep issues of listening. Engaged with gendered representation, Maus positions normative types of listening alongside that of masochistic submission, within a framework of contemporary music analysis. Moving beyond structural listening, his approach kindles a broader understanding of musical composition, without relying on the totalizing models and systems connected to traditional music theory; for interpreting music is an ethical and political act that calls for strategies of listening and criticism that expand the potential of musical perception.

artist or band moulds this into their own signature. We might say that by eliciting reactions through 'hype', the pop act takes as its subject the success and originality of individuals who work according to market imperatives. Pop songs are, after all, recurring patterns of musical material whose historical precedents are wrapped up in notions of individuality.[14]

As already mentioned, dandyism has been integral to pop expression since the 1950s. The interpretive implications of this are a profusion of styles that relate directly to gestures, mannerisms and staging of memorable performances. For the musical practices inherent in a song or piece of music are about processes of imaginative listening that depend on the listener's knowledge (or blissful ignorance) of conventions in a specific social context.[15] Responding to music through the portals of aesthetic value, we, as listeners, cognize sounds as a direct result of human agency. In this respect, the preference for a social given has as much musicological as sociological mileage, hence my concern for interpreting visual performances and musical style rather than overemphasizing the technical details of musical structure.

Pop music, I argue throughout, prompts physical responses through the profound moments of pleasure that provide a means for entertaining and invoking powerful emotional response. In all his guises, the pop dandy offers up a form of entertainment that is a potent force, working as a mechanism for registering a range of social and cultural values. The reality is that the pop artist is not just a recorded entity, but also a person who lives out his individuality. A series of songs, albums, live concerts, videos and interviews over a period of time – say, by older artists, tried and tested, such as David Bowie, Ray Davies, Bryan Ferry, Mick Jagger, Rod Stewart – suggest that behind all the changes in musical style, fashion or gender representations over time, there is a core element that defines temperament. Of all the artists I have chosen, different degrees of genderplay define their subjectivity in a mobile temporal space.

At the onset of the early twenty-first century, there can be little doubt that pop music has emerged triumphant. As Jon Savage puts it:

> It's become integrated with the major media industries. It is one of the major planks of Western consumer culture. Pop has won, and there is a good side and a bad side to that. The good side is we can tell the stories of our youth. The bad side is it can become this ghastly mush.[16]

That which can easily be perceived as 'mushy' is the effect of a conglomerate of recordings and the repetition of musical codes that produce social ideals. Pop

---

[14]   See Small (1977) for an important debate on the implications of progress and originality in the arts.

[15]   See Hennion (1983), Tagg (1982), Middleton (1990, 2000, 2006) and Moore (2001, 2003) for discussions of this aspect that underpins the music analysis of popular music.

[16]   In 'Roll Up for a Magical Mystery Tour' in *The Times*, 5 May 2007.

is made special by us recognizing our own aspirations through the gestures, mannerisms, and structures of others performing, while dandyism is about the scrambling of subjectivities and the fantasy that results from new structures of autonomy. Thus, performing is about putting oneself on display, and turning one's identity into a theatricalized event. Pop dandies generally rely on performance strategies that are uniquely their own, aesthetically ritualizing their personal identity, often putting themselves at risk by being in the public eye.

During the ensuing chapters, many of these issues are attended to through musical events, texts, anecdotes, and performance phenomena. This is what inspires my readings of the dandy, and, moreover, fuels my curiosity for the continuous role of self-invention. I attempt to weave into my arguments a thematic thread that constantly returns us to the question of definition: what makes the dandy? Notwithstanding its nebulous quality, the term 'dandy' is productive and malleable when applied to a breed of pop artists who are located at a historical junction; for pop dandies, as I choose to read them, are embodiments of the categories that contextualize and historicize them. This assertion alone is revealed in the performing musician I turn to who exists as a formulation of instability and paradoxical elaboration.

Organizing the chapters in a way that addresses a hermeneutics of intertextuality forms a major objective of this study. The dialogues that ensue between text, author and artist, intertextually, are conceived to expose the junction of style and genre.[17] As a temporal event, music is a mediator of other texts. Conceptually, this opens up new pathways for understanding the potential of self-referentiality in audio-visual texts. Although I have historicized the origins of the dandy, and situated him in a culturally buoyant space (mainly in Chapter 1), this book is intended as a survey of pop identities at work through an interdisciplinary approach to music research. My selection of dandified subjectivities in Chapters 2 and 3 aims to profile the spectacularity of the pop performance within a media-saturated context, while considering belonging-ness as something grounded in the traditions and norms that control nostalgia and sentimentality. An idealization of the Baudelairean dandy through temperament and naivety is, therefore, a suitable template for situating boy idols in a British cultural space. I also maintain that the impact of French dandyism on British culture has much to say about the development of the star persona within pop music. The star, however, is not just a pop phenomenon, but also a 'real' person, a necessary ingredient for generating a sense of the person as more vivid than the role they adopt. What is more, the star shores up the elaboration of

---

[17] In the introduction to *Essays on Sound and Vision*, John Richardson and I have advocated a methodological approach to intertextuality that identifies strategies for encoding and decoding a text. We argue that all texts have the potential to impact on one another, and that intertextual references therefore 'operate as hooks for substituting and differentiating meaning' (Richardson and Hawkins 2007, p. 17). By way of problematizing the boundaries of the text, our position builds on the Bakhtinian notion that style should not be separated from genre.

roles, temperament and the situational contexts within the kind of society we live in (as I discuss from different vantage points in Chapter 3, Chapter 4 and Chapter 5).

Chapter 2 shifts the focus onto matters of style and subversion, by which various aspects of performance are inspected through the iconographic trends in British fashion and their function as precedents for the contemporary pop figure. Fashioning Britishness and staging the metropolis, London, during the latter half of the twentieth century frames the transient scenes of pop history. This links to some of the main debates in Chapter 4, where the topic of pop queering is visited, in a critique that centres upon representation and heteronormative categorization. If attached to queering (in many of its guises), dandyism lets slip the undulating contours of gendered performances which are loaded with connotations. This I set out to examine in the songs of Pete Doherty, Marc Almond and David Sylvian. In all three cases, institutionalized masculinity promotes the historical and social conditions that form the narratives of pop texts, and the queering antics of these artists offer an opportunity for reconfiguring masculinity. In particular, 'signifying queerness' magnifies the constrictions of a special type of performativity informed by the values of body politics and homosociality. Emerging from this part of the study, queerness, I discover, is elusive; it is always a matter of circumstance and degree. Accordingly, all the singers I consider possess qualities that bespeak theatricality, camp and irony. With this, their authenticity surfaces as an outcome of performing gender through the phantasmatic play on sexuality.

The main musicological focus of this study occurs in Chapter 5, where I address vocality and how it is delineated through different modes of performances. The recorded voice, a construction that idealizes self-representation, has an uncanny way of disclosing aesthetics at work. In this respect, camp address is taken up in conjunction with a discussion of intimacy, a chief strategy of the performer. In a range of songs selected for music analysis, the uniqueness of the voice lies in its transgressive quality, often 'put-on' and vulnerable; the rhetorical quality of singing is the most powerful marker of peculiarity in the dandy.

Flashy in terms of production, British pop connotes high camp. Extravagant performances epitomize the techniques that draw together the emotional and aesthetic entities of entertainment. How the pop artist shapes a fantasy around his own construction is to do with the way the self is relentlessly produced and 'mannered'. Richard Dyer goes as far as claiming that stars 'bring to the fore manners, the stuff of public life' (Dyer 2004, p. 12), demonstrating the ideology of the individual within contemporary society. Consequently, the discussion of performance mannerisms, especially through camp, leads on to the main topic of Chapter 6, namely that of strategies of masking. Foregrounding the motives behind masking, I contemplate the various tropes of behaviour found in the rehearsed narratives of pop texts. Moreover, the dramatization of desires in pop takes place through the imagined body, prompting specific forms of identification in the listening process. In this sense, responses to music are formative in that they relate to the comprehension of stylistic codes that surround our pop idols. Masking as a creative process, then, is productive for understanding the structuring of a performance through strategies of seduction that seek to draw fans into submission.

Space hardly permits a comprehensive overview of the major albums, videos and songs belonging to the artists referred to in the course of this book. This is not my purpose either, a point that should be made clear at the outset. Rather the music examples selected are the result of aesthetic, musicological and sociological phenomena deemed appropriate for arguing my points. Subsequently, my readings are organized more according to aesthetic criteria than chronology. Opting for the 'musical moment' in the material I choose warrants close attention to detail rather than to the full breadth of the text in question. Included in my readings are references to some of the collaborators behind the artists I discuss – the producers, directors, engineers and managers. Once again, time does not allow me to dwell on the entire teams of people who work to construct the *auteur*. Gathered from song recordings, film footage, live performances, documentaries, television appearances and music videos, my source material is employed as a backdrop for the pop performance in its spectacularized form. Indeed, the advantage of writing at this point in history comes from the resourceful outlet of the internet, which makes available a wealth of data accumulated in online magazines and journals, to artists' websites, to blog sites belonging to fans. Opinions and value judgements in open discussion forums have been invaluable in my evaluation of pop artists and their music. Of all the texts I am engaged with, it is music videos that mostly stake out the pop dandy's territory. Embodying the peculiarities of performance, music videos offer insights into the interrelationship between popular song and cultural identity in a way that aids the understanding of individual style.

Stage-managing his public aura through sonic images, the pop dandy presents us with a construction, and this is done complexly. Dandyism is a condition and result of intended responses. So, as long as the audio-visual image is manufactured, the dandy remains an affirmation of a process that appears in the form of scripting, acting and editing. During the ensuing chapters I might well risk over-generalization when it comes to dandy-spotting. At the same time, I am aware that each individual I consider is different; they are all subjects of fascinating rapport.[18] For expressing what it is to be human is to articulate the intangible qualities of music by moving flamboyantly in and out of cultural spaces. Ultimately, this is what it takes to be a pop dandy!

---

[18]    Connoting numerous things at the same time, polysemy is the capacity for one or more signs to possess multiple meanings. This term is used in music semiotics, in cases where each text generates an infinite number of meanings (for example, see Tagg 1982; Middleton 1990).

# Chapter 1
# Oh So Dandy! The Force of Peculiarity

Dandyism is a sunset; like the declining daystar, it is glorious, without heat and full of melancholy.

Charles Baudelaire[1]

'Dandyism is almost as difficult a thing to describe as it is to define', proclaimed Jules-Amédée Barbey D'Aurevilly at the end of the nineteenth century.[2] 'Those who see things only from a narrow point of view have imagined it to be especially the art of dress, a bold and felicitous dictatorship in the matter of clothes and exterior elegance. That it most certainly is, but much more besides' (D'Aurevilly 1988, p. 31). Intrigued by George Brummell, D'Aurevilly's fascination was not only for the person, but also for British society, of which the force of its originality defined for him a peculiarity. Only imagine how he would have viewed the cultural and social landscape one century later, or what he might have made of the unbridled eccentricity and frivolity of a small army of British rock and pop artists who took the world by storm. We shall see.

The dandy is a bewildering construction: a creature of alluring elegance, vanity and irony, who plays around with conventions to his own end. At the same time he is someone whose transient tastes never shirk from excess, protest or rebellion. Every age has possessed its own brand of dandies, and general characteristics distinguish one period from the other. From mannerisms to ways of posing and performing, the dandy revels in artifice simply for style's sake as a mischievous play with masks of calculated elegance. All the same, dandifying one's act is linked to self-thinking, sensibility and narcissism that exudes a put-on sense of social elevation. Now, despite their varying degrees of popularity, all the great dandies have been outsiders; they have been intellectual figures, artists and disaffected young men, eager to make themselves publicly visible through a conceit that is deemed their birthright. Driven by a desire to draw on a personal style, the dandy unabashedly states who he is and what he wants without giving a damn for what anyone cares.

I want to suggest that British pop dandies are the new arrivals and products of a post-industrialized society, following closely in the footsteps of Beau

---

[1]   Baudelaire (1964, p. 29).

[2]   Throughout this book I have turned to a 1988 reprint of the 1897 edition of *Of Dandyism and of George Brummell* (see bibliography) published by J.M. Dent & Company, London. Barbey's book is considered to be the pivotal work of the history of the dandy tradition.

Brummell, Count D'Orsay, Lord Byron, Edward VIII, Noël Coward, Oscar Wilde, Max Beerbohm, Cecil Beaton, and many others. Adopting opulent roles, they have taken style to absurd extremes with blasé sensibility and formidable panache. In the course of this chapter I will set out to trace some of the trends that have affected these pop artists, by considering how behaviour patterns are linked to performance always in impassioned ways. Inevitably, fathoming out pop subjectivities directs us to the principles and processes of musical performance and its function as entertainment, where individual agency is mapped against the forces that drive the music industry. Underlying this premise are questions of nationality and belongingness that define one's social class. Let us say that the peculiarity of the pop persona is governed by rules of etiquette that are mediated by specific cultural practices. This is of sociomusicological relevance.

In the period following the Second World War, rock and roll spawned a host of new trends on both sides of the Atlantic. Perry Meisel, author of *The Cowboy and the Dandy*, traces the social and historic developments through the 'long historical relation between Britain and its former American colonies' (Meisel 1999, p. 116). He is in little doubt that the rock and roll of the British Invasion (1964 to 1966) privileged American styles as 'original and a once-original British culture as copy', where the affinity between British rock and American rhythm and blues was significant. Meisel also draws the reader's attention to Jimi Hendrix, a black American from Seattle, and later an adopted British dandy, whose success in Britain was secured 'when an American original shares in the invention of the heavy electric guitar' (ibid., p. 118). Hendrix's guitar playing was an 'English version' of Chuck Berry's, albeit 'from a safe and steady distance', to the extent that the marriage between look and sound would be subliminal for its time. Playing 'Purple Haze' in public for the first time, Hendrix had on a jacket of polychrome blue-green-red-striped wool twill, finished off by gold, glittering buttons. His spectacle encapsulated the differences and oppositions that configured the 'cowboy and dandy, black and white, English and American, electric and voice' (ibid., p. 118).[3]

Meisel's reading of Hendrix is interesting on a number of counts and is grounded in the 'presumable inevitability' of the canon, 'a discursive necessity' (ibid., p. 129), which not only perpetuates traditions, but also myths. 'Like the novel in the nineteenth century', Meisel insists, 'rock and roll has become a protocol of life in the late twentieth, both as pop myth and as a kind of newly canonical music taken for granted as world culture's dominant one' (ibid., p. 132). So, if the pop myth gave rise to all sorts of pop dandies in the latter half of the twentieth century, then it was based upon the mediation of a new set of politics that crystallized into a historical moment in time.

In popular music 'happenings' speak volumes about the social processes that organize performance around values and tastes linked to musical preference. Further, the musical event is a blend of cultural and social signifiers that rouse intended responses. In this sense, the peculiarity of human behaviour exhibited

---

[3]    Also see Doggett (2004) for a comprehensive survey of Hendrix's music.

through the popular song directs one's attention to a range of subject positions. Like Meisel, I am keen to classify the pop dandy as a person constructed by diverse representations and interests, although my aim is not one of devising a typology of texts or a chronology of events. Rather, I am more interested in the stylistic inflections and indicators that categorize the pop figure. To this end, my focus falls on the mechanics of aestheticization within a narrative context, where visual and sonic mannerisms are a key element. Pop dandies, after all, are constructions of a visual music culture, where repeated viewings of them not only form a spectacle of entertainment, but also a sense of familiarity that perpetuates their myth.

Down the ages dandyism has been assigned characteristics that display the performativity of individuals. In itself a fascinating phenomenon, British popular music is distinguishable through attitude, imagination and style as much as language, the particularity of which draws on a long line of writers, musicians, composers and poets. Extending the aesthete of dandyism into pop culture, musical events have steadily led to a faddishness that signifies glamour and depth simultaneously. Moreover, pop's preoccupation with difference through genderplay (androgyny, transvestism, drag, queering) has over time radicalized male behaviour, and, in the context of this study, it is not just a coincidence that the subject is white and supposedly heterosexual.[4]

---

[4] Black involvement in the dandified process, albeit not a main focus of this book, is of crucial importance when understanding dandyism's role in popular culture during the early nineteenth century. Approximately fifty years after the cancellation of *The Disappointment*, as slavery was coming to an end in the North, Philadelphian African Americans would stage their own balls, which did not sit comfortably with the local white community. Satirical articles and illustrations from local newspapers bear this out. The *Pennsylvania Gazette* ran a report on a fancy dress ball in 1828 held for African Americans in Mr August's rooms, where an unruly white mob had gathered on the street outside, insulting the ladies as they came and went, tearing their dresses and frightening the horses (White and White 1998, p. 98). Soon another paper, the *Democratic Press*, would comment on the dress codes of the blacks, in particular the 'superb uniforms' that adorned the males. Subsequently, a four-page article in the *Philadelphia Monthly Magazine* would pay considerable attention to the ball itself and the African American Philadelphians who attended the event. The balls, as well as street parades, offered an ideal opportunity to parody the white locals, while, conversely, a voyeuristic fascination had 'reached its most heightened form in the scrutiny of what were termed "dandies", the well-dressed black males and females' (ibid., p. 91) who graced the streets of Northern cities. To be sure, the sauntering of black dandies and dandizettes along the sidewalks of Philadelphia, Boston and New York in the early decades of the nineteenth century provoked undisguised curiosity among locals as much as foreigners. There are many accounts of European travellers who were struck by the spectacle. A Swede, Carl Arfwedson, on arriving in New York in 1832 and sighting black New Yorkers, would write: '(T)he women wear bonnets decorated with ribbons, plumes, and flowers, of a thousand different colours', while the men's coats were so open that 'the shirt sticks out under the arm-pits; the waistcoats are of all colours of the rainbow; the hat is carelessly put on one side; the gloves are yellow, and every sable dandy carries a smart cane' (see White and White (1998)). Caricatures of this sort, in recounting the 'difference'

Consider Bowie's flirt with a range of unconventional sexual codes in the 1970s, which paved the way forward for an entire movement still in rage over the indictment of Oscar Wilde in Victoria's England. As one of the first pop performers to flaunt the constructedness of his celebrity status, Bowie, at the beginning of his career, challenged gender norms to the point that he turned 'barrow boys into screaming queens', setting up a 'sociological template' that reached its 'apotheosis with wedge haircuts and eyeshadow for a generation of teenage boys' (Bracewell 1998, p. 194). Resurrecting androgyny and transvestism through intellectual stylishness, Bowie not only rejected heteronormative constraints, but also heaped scorn on the machismo that typified the rock music of the day. Following in Wilde's footsteps, he ridiculed gender norms by rejecting the stultifying image of masculinity through an adventurous form of representation that set out to shock and amuse. London of the swinging Sixties, with all its happenings, was Bowie's playground. His expression was a revolt against conventions. Tapping into a Warholian world, where displays of transgression were conjoined to the atomic age of astronauts and aliens from other planets, his theatricality provided a stimulus for the punk rock aesthetic that followed. Effectively, Bowie slipped into the role of dandy to create an 'outsider figure for the modern age, the queer messiah from space' (Bracewell 1998, p. 194), which gave rise to an entire cult of imitators who became committed followers. Playing out narcissism and alienation from everyday life to extremes, Bowie's many impersonators channelled the glamour of pop representation (in the form of henna hair dye, dark eyeshadow, lip gloss and satin-sequin catsuits) onto the high streets of Britain. Most of all, the celebration of androgyny would call into question patriarchy and conservative attitudes.

Collisions of styles in the 1960s and 1970s gelled into some extraordinary performances. Take the band Roxy Music, a counterpart to Bowie, who turned nostalgic romance into a central reference point. Styled on the 1930s and 1940s inter-World War period, their performances marketed the glamour of dandyism. It was as if everything that Roxy Music stood for was contra the serious-mindedness of American rock, as they altered the pop scene into a domain of soft velvet and swooning boys and girls intent on romance and fancy dress. Like Bowie, Ferry's art education had a strong bearing on his music, where the fad for identifying art in everyday life became a new concept for its time (Frith and Horne 1987). Also inspired by Warhol, Ferry took on the task of packaging his glamour into music and glossy photo shots that redefined Romantic notions of creativity. Together with sound guru Brian Eno, Ferry aided the Roxy Music project in breaking away from traditional rock. Crafting a new stylistic direction, with their roots in the art-school tradition, Ferry, as with Bowie, placed as much emphasis on look and mannerism as on musical expression. As David Buckley puts it: 'Both Bowie and

---

of African American dandies, would reduce their representation to something of a 'joke', a condition of failed comedy and self-parody. For a related discussion on working class issues and blackface minstrelsy see Lhamon (1998), and on black dandyism and the extraordinary George Walker, see Webb (2001).

Ferry saw stage performances as drama and milked theatricality for all it was worth' (Buckley 2000, p. 143). Unlike Bowie, however, Roxy Music did not consider themselves part of the glam-rock movement on any count. Rather, their aim was to celebrate the ordinary and mundane through a fascination for objects of mass production. Essentially, this was pre-Warholian. Such tendencies can be traced back to the early 1950s when a small group of British intellectuals, the Independent Group, opened a shop at the ICA in Dover Street, London. Their enthralment with paraphernalia, in the form of billboards, pinups and posters, turned them into subcultural objects that confronted notions of 'good taste', while at the same time upholding the American Dream. Roxy Music's theatrical ability to turn pop culture into art, and vice versa, led to scorn and condemnation, for, as Buckley explains, they were not convincing enough as 'proper rockers', for their music and disposition was 'too arty and therefore fake' (ibid., p. 145). Further, Brian Eno's androgyny made Roxy the 'ultimate in heterosexual gender-bending' (ibid., p. 146), whose constructedness was for many too contrived. Notwithstanding such scepticism, Roxy Music's third album, *Stranded*, must have appealed to a wide audience as it reached number one in the UK charts in 1973, further riling those who cringed at the glamour and artifice in popular music.

Seen in a historical light, what directly preceded the explosion of punk 'turned the fans of David Bowie and Roxy Music into the stars of post-punk' (ibid., p. 202). Meanwhile, Bowie, in a stroke of genius, would shift his identity once again, this time in reference to Nicolas Roeg's *The Man Who Fell To Earth*. Just in time for the punk movement and the wave of robo-groups who suddenly swept through pop music, he reconfigured himself. The year was 1976 when punk destabilized pop masculinities by repudiating heavy rock and reviving early rock 'n' roll styles.[5]

Two years later, The Great British Music Festival at Wembley marked the Mod revival with The Jam, who made their appearance through a revival style that was underpinned by the sound of 1960s Mod bands. Their lead singer, Paul Weller, who would be affectionately referred to as the Modfather by the media in the 1990s, seemed the epitome of the dandy in look, attitude and sound. Weller's most

---

[5]   Kraftwerk made a huge impact on British popular culture in the form of a wry celebration of post-war industrialization. I would suggest that the four earnest German youths who formed Kraftwerk were dandified in a decisively European manner. With tongue-in-cheek clichés dealing with 'man and machine', Kraftwerk, West Germany's answer to the pop dandy, underscored everything they did with an ironic detachment; this would prove to have a major impact on the next generation of British pop artists. Woven into their image construction was a performance style that was born out of their machine-oriented aesthetics. Most of all their performance drew on a Warholian demeanour that was restrained yet ardent. A sulky-type of moodiness and a no-nonsense-approach to producing synthetic music was captured in a dehumanized attitude that would greatly influence British bands, such as Depeche Mode, the Pet Shop Boys, Human League and New Order. Socio-politically, these robo-romantics effected a generation of fans who were tuned into the repercussions of the Cold War and the emerging New Right governments throughout Europe (also see Lindvig 2008).

dandified moments are captured during the early part of his career with The Jam, a period when Mod revivalists signalled a nostalgic return to 1960s suits, and clothing items such as Fred Perry tennis shirts, fishtail parkas and jeans. Musically, The Jam's origins were in the 1960s Mod and beat bands, The Who, The Kinks, the Beatles and the Small Faces, with a curious blend of 1970s New Wave, punk rock and pub rock styles. The Mod revival also aroused interest in R&B and soul music, traceable in bands such as The Chords, The Merton Parkas, The Lambrettas, The Jolt, 007, The Mods, The Scene, Purple Hearts and Secret Affair.[6] Unashamedly nostalgic, these bands would articulate a British sensibility to a point of parody in a bid to emphasize their working-class roots, often turning to symbols of nationality, such as the RAF roundel and the Union Jack.

Happenings in Britain during the 1980s were also matched by a schizophrenic response to Thatcherism, with a move towards style culture (Hawkins 2002). In fact, the gendered ambiguity of the New Romantics and the Mod revival provided a critique of Thatcher's vision of Britain, as well as pandering to elitism and materialistic gain. A rush for new forms of pop expression were headed by the New Romantics – Spandau Ballet, Culture Club, Japan, Visage, Ultravox, Duran Duran and Human League. To be sure, MTV's dawn in 1981 saw a febrile production of pop videos by this new generation of pop celebrities who turned to an ironic sensibility that was distinctly British. Once again, London was the epicentre of design, fashion and video culture, as young men and women reinvented notions of Englishness in a context that was multicultural and media-fixated. Bracewell insists that the New Romantics 'took the machine aesthetic as its foundation, celebrating the triumph of cosmetics and computers over convictions' (Bracewell 1998, p. 212). And, with the dandies of the MTV era, skilfully commodified concepts and styles would amalgamate 1960s and 1970s popular styles into something new. The social, political and cultural implications of this would be far-reaching as we will see later on, but for the meantime I want to rewind to perhaps the most legendary British dandy of all time, Brummell, and a Frenchman, D'Aurevilly, who 'could not get him out of his head'.

## Britain, Brummell and Barbey

Prime exhibit A: George Bryan Brummell, born in London, 7 June 1778. Ever since his rise and fall, this arbiter of Regency fashion has been a great source of

---

[6]   All through the 1980s the Mod revival scene exhibited strong links with 1960s soul, Mod revival bands and Northern Soul, all of which would lead to the acid jazz movement of the late 1980s. Furthermore, this style crossed with the 2 Tone ska revival in the late 1970s and early 1980s in bands such as Madness, The Beat and The Selecter. Britpop, in the 1990s, was also influenced by the Mod revival, and by the twenty-first century indie rock groups such as Kaiser Chiefs, Rinaldi Sings and The Ordinary Boys embraced the legacy of the Mod style.

fascination for the French as much as the British. The younger Barbey D'Aurevilly (from now on Barbey), born in 1808, would turn his notes on the Englishman's life into a study of attitude and lifestyle.[7] Entitled *Du Dandysme et de Georges Brummell* (1845), Barbey's book superbly captured the charismatic George Bryan Brummell (from now on Beau Brummell), as everything the dandy should be. Much emphasis would be placed on Beau Brummell's moral revolt against the ideas and conventions of the day, and his self-elevation in relation to his world.[8]

It was while studying in the Normandy town of Caen in the 1830s that Barbey first caught sight of Beau Brummell, where the sheer spectacle of him was enough to prompt Barbey to write a most compelling documentation of the age of the dandy. This was a time when social advance in the preoccupation with style and elegance and colourful affectation gave rise to new attitudes and trends among men. Impertinent and sartorial in its elegance, the Regency period dawned in England, a country where mundane conventions had prevailed, and where an acute sensitivity for any nuance, variation, deviation and difference in mannerism would be immediately detected.

Perhaps most revealing in Barbey's treatise on dandyism is his genuine curiosity in the nationality of his subject. Although it must be said France has had more than its fair share of dandies. Sarah Niblock asserts: 'Dandyism arose in France and later in England as a protest against the rule of kings over fashion, just as democracy rose against the rule of kings in politics' (Niblock 2005, p. 309). In France, where there has never been a lack of fashion and elegance, the dandy figure in Britain might have seemed something of an anachronism. Well, at least on first glance. With Beau Brummell, though, things would be different. An obsession with detail distinguished him from anything seen before. A product of the cold, Northern, pale race, his identity was manifested in a stifling, puritanical devotion to style. Indeed, the emergence of such an eccentric figure in a British landscape, as Barbey noted, could only highlight the constraints placed upon individuals in a country over-regulated by laws and rules. Yet, Barbey would marvel at a culture

---

[7]  Somewhat paradoxically, Barbey's treatise on Brummell reveals a wealth of knowledge on himself as we get to learn about his own sartorial taste and laconic style which became renowned. The splendour of his attire, in stark contrast to Brummell's, attracted much attention; wide-brimmed hats, long frock coats, laced shirts with frills, black satin slacks, and wine red gloves were the order of the day. And with his appearance came a sharp wit and charm that soon made him a major focal point of the Parisian boulevards.

[8]  Barbey's literary skills in identifying the dandy would finally receive recognition through his appointment as critic for *Le Constitutionnel* in 1868. It is also worth pointing out that two of Barbey's most important and critically acclaimed works deal with the French Revolution: *Le Chevalier des Touches* (1864) and *Un Pretre marié* (1865). Ruthless in his writings, and highly critical of his contemporaries, it did not take long before Barbey was detested by those of the Naturalist school, including Emile Zola. Yet, certain authors, such as Baudelaire and Balzac, dandies in their own way, would sing his praises. As a result, in 1863 Baudelaire's *Le Peintre de la Vie Moderne* was published and was indebted to Barbey's studies into dandyism.

that excelled in role-playing; a culture that instantly could caricature anything that was abstract, sublime or just different.

A flair for frivolity, coupled with a talent for reaching heights of impertinence, revealed Beau Brummell's propensity for social climbing, which, for its day, must have been exceptional; a rare feat for one whose career started in the army. In 1798 at the age of 21, having reached the rank of captain, he decided to leave, for fortune would have it that he inherited the princely sum of 30,000 pounds, enabling him to set up a bachelor establishment in fashionable Mayfair. Soon he would become the *arbiter elegantiarum*, throwing lavish dinner parties for celebrities such as the Prince Regent. Added to this, his membership in the most exclusive of all gentlemen's clubs, Whites, led him to while away his hours socializing with select groups. Picture him reclining in the opulent surrounds of this club, in the famous bow window, observing, with acerbic wit, all and sundry walk by. Possessing a remarkable talent for converting the most ordinary circumstances into the most amusing anecdotes, Beau Brummell's every utterance soon resonated in all aristocratic circles: 'A word from George Brummell, whether of praise or blame, was at that time final. He was the autocrat of opinion' (D'Aurevilly 1988, p. 48). In fact, so intoxicated was he by his own elevated social standing that Beau Brummell eventually abandoned dancing, deeming it to be beneath his dignity. Barbey recounts:

> He used to stand for a few minutes at the door of the ballroom, glance round, criticize it in a sentence, and disappear, applying the famous maxim of Dandyism:–'In society, stop until you have made your impression, then go.' He knew his own overpowering prestige, and that with him to remain was unnecessary (ibid., pp. 48–9).

Quite aware of his own prestige, his impudence of manner, ambition and impeccable attire eventually turned Beau Brummell into an authority on any matter of fashion. Mark Booth provides the following detailed description:

> Brummell was the originator of that exclusive wit and provocative frivolity which we tend to think of today as inimitably Wildean, but which was really (all too imitably) Brummellian. He was also a collector of snuff-boxes, china plate and bibelots, and he wrote society verses including the famous *Butterfly Funeral* (Booth 1999, p. 71).

Years later, upon observing Beau Brummell in real life, Barbey would note his continued avoidance of exaggeration in dress. Never sighted in garish colours and ostentatious jewellery, his appearance was characterized by a scrupulous eye for tailoring, especially with regard to the jacket cut and height of the cape. Distinct from the average man on the street, Beau Brummell's morning dress consisted of beige buckskins with a blue coat and brass buttons. Extended to knee level, with lapels ending up at the ears, his coat tails exposed a coloured waistcoat, tightly buttoned at the waist, opening at the breast to exhibit a frilly shirt and cravat. Reputedly polished with champagne, his black shiny boots revealed equally shiny soles. Unlike most men of his era, Beau Brummell was a fanatic when it came to cleanliness and attire, as Robins accounts:

> He didn't usually emerge from his dressing room until mid-afternoon and spent at least two hours a day on his appearance. His regime was endowed with the precision of ritual. He brushed his teeth, shaved with extreme care, washed and scrubbed with hot water, and exfoliated with a stiff pigskin-bristle brush. He was proud of his personal hygiene, and avoided perfumes not because he disliked them but because he didn't need them (Robins 2001, pp. 72–3).

Not unexpectedly, his fastidious care for appearance became a trademark of dandyism as much as snide retort. Quentin Crisp has pointed out that it is difficult to imagine 'the coarseness and general nastiness that prevailed a hundred and fifty years ago among the rich – or, rather, among the rich men. It was then a cause for amazement that Mr Brummell changed his clothes and washed every day' (Crisp in D'Aurevilly 1988, pp. 8–9). But this did not necessarily make him an 'agreeable' character: 'By twentieth-century criteria, he was appallingly snobbish' (ibid., p. 9), and furthermore, he was a womanizer, which Barbey is keen to account for:

> There is no doubt, that, with his brilliancy, his power over opinion, his extreme youth, which adds to fame, and that charming and cruel wit, abused and adored by women, Brummell inspired many inverted passions – deep loves, inexorable hates (D'Aurevilly 1988, p. 49).

Given that Brummell was more 'house-trained' than most women's husbands, it is difficult to imagine that he never 'incurred the hostility of men', and, as Crisp insists, by modern standards he would definitely have been considered homosexual (Crisp in D'Aurevilly 1988, p. 11).

Once having acquired the highest social status as a pioneer of fashion in London circles, Beau Brummell soon faced his downfall; an acrimonious wit and caustic sarcasm would get him into big trouble. Dandyism is, after all, 'the product of a bored society' (D'Aurevilly 1998, p. 55), and being bored is seldom conducive to being kind or wishing to remain popular. Eventually, he would fall out with the Prince Regent and the Duke of Bedford, and rumour has it that on one occasion he caused the Prince to weep by criticizing the cut of his coat. Such incidents, while seemingly trivial, would have serious repercussions. Indeed, such grave miscalculations, and a reckless gambling habit, resulted in the loss of all his inheritance and inevitable alienation from society. Finally, due to large, recurring debts, he would be forced to flee to France in 1816, where he spent the rest of his life.

Abandoning the luxuries of London took its toll and he went into steady decline. Admittedly, only in the last years of his life would the young Barbey first set eyes on Beau Brummell, now almost unrecognizable through poverty and insanity. Not only were his clothes tattered and filthy, Barbey observed, but also he had become obese, displaying repulsive personal habits. What then was left of the great dandy we might ask? Uncannily, as Barbey purports, an element of self-respect was still detectable through the hint of a bygone splendour that was carried with stiff-necked pride. Furthermore, as Barbey would observe, his threadbare clothes were got up in a way that no provincial Frenchman would ever have imagined.

Intriguingly, Barbey paints a social narrative based on Puritanism and political resistance that contravened norms of behaviour. Putting dandyism down to eccentricity, Barbey would claim: 'It is the revolt of the individual against the established order, sometimes against nature: here we approach mania' (D'Aurevilly 1988, p. 33). Indeed, the Brummellian 'mania' that ensued would provide a social and cultural model for generations to come, from Oscar Wilde to Noël Coward to the pop dandies of the twentieth century.

Compared to Beau Brummell, Barbey's own dandyism was more in the tradition of another Frenchman, Charles Baudelaire, an *écrivain* dandy, who I will turn to in Chapter 2. Based upon ephemerality, Barbey's own personal philosophy was discernible in his unique appearance, as much as his literary skills. Preferences in attire, however, were different from Baudelaire, as he went for 'favoured flaming colours, flared coats, a red cape, a Spanish nobleman's hat, and a dagger'. Walden points out that this was despite 'the insistence in his essay that true dandyism, like true originality, was an English monopoly' (Walden 2002, p. 21). Even with relative poverty, Barbey managed to establish himself through his sartorial splendour as a leading French dandy of the day.

In *Du Dandysme*, Barbey would insist that after Brummell England had 'passed its zenith' (D'Aurevilly 1988, p. 23), with Queen Victoria now on the throne, and Britain far less attractive. It is worth bearing in mind that Barbey's treatise was published when a dominant bourgeoisie and new proletariat was emerging in France. Socialism brought with it something distasteful for Barbey, a fad that eradicated originality in people. After all, the dandy was a free spirit who manipulated society with political intent, and this was characterized by Beau Brummell's ironic detachment and aloof mannerisms – accounts of this are rife in the detailed footnotes of *Du Dandysme* that extol his style. Furthermore, Barbey would also make the claim that while dandyism (post-Brummellian) might have become dormant, one day it would awake again. How right he was, as we will see!

Like Brummell, Barbey was a *flâneur*, who used the boulevards of Paris as his catwalk. Insecure and ambiguous, a hero of modernity, he was attracted to the idea of the anti-hero/symbolic hero dichotomy as depicted by Brummell. Crucial to the *flâneur* is the perception of an urban landscape, where the longing for the world we have lost is prevalent. Such Arcadian qualities resound in the writings of Walter Benjamin, Max Weber and Karl Marx, which set out to tackle the utopian desire for something other than the urban phantasmagoria. Mostly, the *flâneur* is a spectacle of autoeroticism. Thriving on an outward appearance, he ambles down his favourite arcades and fashionable avenues in the metropolis, stopping at outdoor cafés to watch the world go by. As a consequence, the dandy during

Barbey's time would be the recipient of unkind remarks and jeering. If anything, Barbey modelled a type of masculinity where imagination was freed from all social constraints to wander at will. This is apparent in his account of Beau Brummell, which underlined his own disillusionment with the modernist models of urban space. Thus, by identifying intimately with Brummell, and, indeed, reviving him, Barbey engaged performatively through a politics of dislocation that was permeated by its antithesis. In due course, as we will see, his definition of the dandy would be manifested in his own reconciliation of the term's very own marginality and flamboyancy, a fitting precursor for us working out who would come next.

### Wildean Camp, Cowardian Satire and Warholian Glamour

Brummellian dandyism would spawn a new generation of dandies, such as playwright, poet and novelist Oscar Fingal O'Flahertie Wills Wilde, born in Dublin, 16 October 1854. The 'camp spirit'[9] that Wilde resurrected in *The Picture of Dorian Gray* was directly influenced by Beau Brummell's eponymous identity. Gratuitously promoting himself as immoral, Wilde's aestheticism fed off the pleasure of provocation, by route of many of the attributes associated with camp at the time of writing. Based upon a good-humoured allegiance to that which was decidedly 'precious', Wilde's intellect was full of quips about British class, his genius being to record the social conditions of the Victorian era. Showing how politics and culture are inextricably linked to individualism, he exposed the flaws in Victorian social ideology. Mostly, Wilde revealed the political structures of power in society by calling for the individual's role through the rhetoric of camp retort.

One of the leading forefathers of British camp, Wilde would not have conceived the term in the way it is now used. Historically, Sontag (1966) traces this term's first usage to Isherwood's *The World in the Evening* from 1954, while Booth goes even further back to Ware's *Passing English of the Victorian Era* from 1909, where a reference to camp actions and gestures is described as 'exaggerated' in relation to persons of 'exceptional want of character' (Booth 1999, p. 75). Even earlier than this, though, the French author Théophile Gautier, a dandy in his own right,

---

[9]   As a fashionable sub-genre in the late 1820s and 1830s, the Silver Fork novel critiques the frivolity and superficiality of the Regency and the morals of aristocratic society. Although the Silver Fork movement reached its peak between 1825 and 1837, it would continue to influence Victorian novels up to the 1860s. The term 'silver fork' was derisive and coined by William Hazlitt in his article from 1827, 'The Dandy School', and he is credited for generating the realism of social responsibility and awareness of social justice that would be found in the next generation of writers, such as Wilde. The first Silver Fork novel was Plumer Ward's *Tremaine* (1825), followed by *Vivian Grey* (1826) by Benjamin Disraeli, *Granby* (1826) by Thomas Lister, and *Pelham: the Adventures of a Gentleman* (1828) by George Bulwer-Lytton.

would describe *se camper* in his 1863 novel *Capitaine Fracasse*. Gautier's *se camper* stands as an important precursor to camp's associations with theatricality, dressiness and provocation within seventeenth century France; the period of Louis XIV and Versailles that has been so idealized and satirized.[10]

Most certainly camp was Noël Peirce Coward, born in Middlesex, 16 December 1899, whose direct lineage to Gautier through Wilde and others would influence numerous pop artists. In particular, his musical performance style – spoken dialogue with music – would also have a profound effect on American musicals.[11] Coward's songs and cabaret performances are imbued with a brilliance of wit that set out to satirize the mannerisms of upper-class English society. As playwright and songwriter his work formed part of the Edwardian tradition of light operas and drawing-room comedies that were brilliantly witty. Occupying a special place in British culture, Coward's contribution to popular song (in the form of revues and musical theatre) won over generations of admirers. Standards such as 'Twentieth-Century Blues' (1931), 'Mad about the Boy' (1932), 'A Marvellous Party' (1939) and 'Sail Away' (1950), path-breaking songs in their own right, were predicated upon wry observation and sardonic humour. Mostly, Coward's lyrics vividly caricatured social plots and situations with high doses of *double entendre*, denoting a style that can be best described as a blend of pathos and satire that expresses a bitter-sweet yearning and loss (Summers 2004). As in the case of Wilde, much of Coward's output features the hopelessness of the moment and the infatuation with the unattainable. In particular, his cabaret performances, depicting him as the British sophisticate, shaped the uniqueness of a dandy character. Unashamedly camp, he would perform his songs with a cigarette in a long holder, hand raised, reminiscing over things while delighting audiences that consisted mainly of ordinary, everyday people. Coward's impact on British pop cannot be overstated, and was borne out by Neil Tennant's tribute album in 1998, *Twentieth-Century Blues: The Songs of Noel Coward*, featuring artists such as Paul McCartney, Pet Shop Boys, Bryan Ferry, Sting, Suede, Damon Albarn, Elton John, Marianne Faithfull, Robbie Williams and Vic Reeves. In an interview with *NME* in 1997, Tennant said:

> We decided we would concentrate on having British artists because Noel Coward was such an important British figure, and we could make a statement about pop music through the whole thing by bringing together artists who seemed to have some link, albeit vague, with what Noel Coward represents today.[12]

---

[10]    Louis XIV's Versailles was a 'paradigm of high camp society' (Booth 1999, p. 76) and instrumental in moving the nobility into the margins of French life.

[11]    During the 1950s and 1960s Coward's appearances on American television were popular, especially in the show from 1955, *Together with Music: Noël and Mary Martin*.

[12]    *NME*, April 1997.

Interestingly, Coward's time in the USA would serve to introduce into British popular music jazz and African American influences that were not there before, transforming both British theatre and music. Moreover, his legacy would shape British camp in popular culture.[13]

However one might choose to recount the historical developments of Wildean and Cowardian camp and its relation to the British pop dandy, it is near impossible to overlook the effect of another dandy's impact on British pop culture, this time an American. The contribution of Andrew Warhola (better known as Andy Warhol, born in Pennsylvania, 6 August 1928) to pop art forms part of one of the most powerful critiques of post-war US and European society. Turning motifs of camp and glamour into a critical response towards industrialization, as much as the avant-garde art of the day, Warhol prised open questions relating to the role of dissident sexualities as forces of labour in opposition to bourgeois culture. Challenging the disavowal of gay culture and Otherness by the avant-garde, one of Warhol's main strategies was to demonstrate how white patriarchy was a controlling force over popular culture. In his critique of the Hollywood film industry, Warhol appropriated elements from this culture in order to critique it. And rather than rejecting Hollywood per se, Warhol would demystify it by introducing the ambiguous and risky workings of camp; in the main, his political mission was to carry this out through deconstructing glamour.

For Warhol the glamorous images that infiltrated Hollywood culture provided much more than a means for escape. Considerably enhanced by music, lighting, make-up, camera shots and costumes, film stars, when magnified on gigantic screens, were exaggerated constructions. Warhol recognized this as an effect of hyperrealism and mystification. Acutely aware of Hollywood's control over audiences, he would set out to display passivity as a controlling force. Taunting the voyeuristic gaze, Warhol highlighted the binary divisions of female passivity and male passivity, demonstrating how the Hollywood spectacle disseminated glamour. Matthew Tinkcom claims that he extended the capacity of film by a 'camp re-visioning of the world' (Tinkcom 1999, p. 352) exploring the margins of spectatorship and Otherness. Tinkcom's reading of Warhol's 1964 silent film *Haircut* exposes the issue of disengagement and modulated distancing that has to do with the 'pose'. The intention behind *Haircut*, as Tinkcom argues, was to drive the viewer 'back into the realm of the mundane' (ibid.), highlighting the efforts the individual makes to gain acceptance in their own world. The three men in this film fix the viewer's gaze: 'Cool and remote, like Harlow or Crawford, the stars of *Haircut* share with us the pleasures of being seen and *knowing* that one is being seen' (ibid. – original emphasis). Conventions and norms are also problematized in Warhol's *Lonesome Cowboys* (1968), an assault on heteronormativity in the

---

[13]    In the same interview (op. cit.), Tennant states that Coward would have been 'horrified' to be considered as camp, for 'he went out of his way not to be thought of as in any way effeminate'. Straight-acting, Coward was also attracted to the same kind of men. Tennant insists that his bisexuality 'was more the norm in those days'.

form of a spoof on the good old Western.[14] Defying stereotypes, the Warholian cowboys, mildly put, are a weird assortment. Moreover, their interaction with one another provides satirical statements on 'brotherly love', androgyny and sexual artifice through a nonsensical plot. Including scenes of a cowboy working at his ballet exercises or the irritating instruction on the wrong use of mascara, *Lonesome Cowboys* is camp, goofy and awkward in the way it parodies masculinity. Mostly, the performative dimension of the narcissist in the form of the cowboy provides a clue as to how Warhol's aesthetic could influence popular music. Infatuated with stardom and glamour, Warhol's films are characterized by the psychological aspect of self-alienation, where his voyeurism demands just this. The advantage of such an approach was that 'it allowed the artist to work through personae' (Bannister 2006, p. 150) that avoided the strains of a personalized biography. On this issue, Matthew Bannister makes the point that in rock discourse the suspicion of a 'too obvious self-aestheticisation' has smacked of gayness, hence in the case of Curt Cobain, where his private life and work were virtually inseparable. For Warhol the celebrity was his public counterpart, who existed through market forces of popular culture that created the work of art through the spectatorial gaze.

Up to 1968 Warhol's films consistently critiqued Hollywood's role in popular imagination and the notions of marginal viewership. His creative use of the media, together with a subversive approach, created a tension in the avant-garde by uncovering the dynamics of mass-cultural production. Above all, his inimitable style of contestation made a profound impact on all facets of pop culture from film, literature to pop art. Disengaging passivity through camp would challenge gender stereotypes and satirize the relationship between performer and audience. Because of Warhol, pop expression would come to illuminate the strategies of avant-garde posturing, as well as paving the way forward for new generations of aspiring pop artists.

## Emergence of British Pop Dandies

Warhol's strategy was primarily that of the voyeur. Enticing an audience without ever looking back at them was grounded in the liberation of the artist through a packaging of life-style and fashion (Koch 1974). In this sense, the emphasis on 'culture-as-advertising' foresaw the advent of commerce-as-art. Fuelled by the distinction between 'fine' artists and 'designers' in the art school context, this movement gave rise to the pop dandy. In Frith and Horne's words, Warhol's parody of the advertisement 'got the point [as] (e)veryone, for a market moment, [could] be an artist' (Frith and Horne 1987, p. 69). Art would be turned on its head, as Warhol opposed the Romantic conception of the artist as tortured subject out to redeem the world. Concerned that 'capitalist culture recuperates everything' (ibid., p. 111), Warhol's intention was not so much to oppose (or expose) the idea of the

---

[14]    My thanks to Sarah Niblock for reminding me of this path-breaking film.

avant-garde artist as to exploit it. Hence, it was pop culture that would drive the main cogs in Warhol's machinery.

Particularly, his involvement with The Velvet Underground led him to consider a career as pop musician, as well as extending the pop event into 'a total environment' concept with lights and effects. The Velvets, somewhat paradoxically, ended up less commercially successful than one might have expected, giving 'shape to a recognizable art school music scene' (ibid., p. 112) in the USA.[15] Despite their limited commercial success, no band had a greater influence on the emergence of alternative or art rock musicians and audiences during this period. Initially scorned as a band of fags, the Velvets turned camp into a stylistic marker, integrating Warhol's' 'blankness' into their rock aesthetic. Bannister sums this up:

> [M]any Velvet songs are visions of decadence and excess, but rather than celebrate excess (as in hippy culture), the Velvets' approach was to stare blankly at it – responding to mass cultural critique by confirming it – implying that, yes, they were disconnected and numbed by mass media, and, no, they really didn't care. Like punks, the Velvets proclaimed their unshockability – their supreme indifference to the human spectacle unravelling before them, which is in turn to some degree incited by their very presence and gaze (Bannister 2006, pp. 45–6).

Thus, an entire generation of British musicians and artists would absorb The Velvets' type of presentation, fully aware of 'presence and gaze'.

Modern and democratic, Warhol possessed a quality that 'consisted of glorifying the ordinary, of making celebrities of the people, of dandifying the mass' (Walden 2002, p. 47). Pop music, for him, could create a myth around ideas of individuation. In this way, the affectations of performance would place more emphasis on presence than words and music. Now although Brummell and Warhol were one century apart, their tendencies and attitudes were strikingly similar. Especially in terms of appearance and attitude, they both sniggered at social, cultural and economic conventions. Walden puts it succinctly: 'Brummell had his pantaloons distressed, [while] Warhol made a fetish of worn jeans' (ibid., p. 48). And, as the latter marketed mass-produced prints of film stars to millions, the former supplied dandy-oriented style and fashion for the Prince Regent and other aristocrats in London. But the main commonality between the British and American dandy lay in a playfulness and passion for social happenings, where

---

[15]   They had a direct bearing on the Mercer Arts Center in New York, which brought together art school pop graduates with experimental artists, such as Laurie Anderson. This venue consisted of separate rooms for theatrical, video, and cabaret productions. By the mid-1970s, art activities in New York and other American cities consisted of integrating media-oriented forms of fashion, advertisement, TV, and pop with traditional artistic expression. Notably, groups such as the New York Dolls were unable to reach large audiences as they did not accept or understand popular taste.

'one glamorised the individual, the other the multitude' (ibid., p. 48), all for the sake of hedonistic engagement. Warhol's campness ultimately ushered in a ratified, intellectual approach to musical performance, as well as a new breed of masculinity that denied traditional roles. This is discernible in The Velvets' songs and performances, which are enshrined in a desexualized numbness and 'echoed in the characteristic narratives of Reed's writing', who maintains a 'cool, almost clinical distance, as if he is handling laboratory specimens' (Bannister 2006, p. 47).

Warholian aesthetics undoubtedly paved the way forward for the modern British celebrity culture. Since the 1960s an entire generation of camp 'loveys' include chat show hosts Jonathan Ross, Cilla Black, Julian Clary and Graham Norton, game show hosts Lionel Blair, Matthew Kelly, Dale Winton, Bruce Forsyth, Bob Monkhouse and Des O' Connor, and magazine, food and breakfast show hosts Lorraine Kelly, Jamie Oliver, Ainsley Harriott, Nigella Lawson, Gloria Hunniford, Richard Madeley, and others. In keeping with these celebrities, style journalists have benefited in every conceivable way, from the gastronomical expert, the hair-stylist to the furniture designer, all of whom glamorize the trends of the day. The best art scene proponents of the 1980s and 1990s were Gilbert and George. They would blatantly extend Warhol's style into everything they did in the name of art. Daring perpetrators of nonchalance and enigma, Gilbert and George's disengagement has involved a blankness, a disengaged white male gaze, that stares back at us through images of them in their art. Similarly, these types of images of a voyeuristic nature are ubiquitous in the sports world. One of its most prize dandies, David Beckham, displays a construction predicated upon the characteristics of the pop star. That Beckham might be more talented as a footballer than many others seems less relevant than the details that are laundered from his private life, not least his relationship with former Spice Girl, Posh. According to Graeme Turner, the discourse of expertise/talent that surrounds Beckham does not exempt him from the same critique encountered by all other celebrities who have achieved their prominence through establishing a public persona that can seem more important than their professional one (such as Paris Hilton). Turner's insight into celebrity culture is situated in a discursive framework of the local, national and global:

> Frequently representing the nation formally (in the national team, for example), their professional careers depend upon how successfully they perform. In most cases this will mean the quality of their sporting performances, but there are other areas of performance that matter too (sportsmanship on the field, their behaviour when celebrating in the bar after the game, their conduct while sharing an airliner with public and so on) (Turner 2004, p. 105).

Turner goes on to suggest that the legacy of the ideals latent in sport achievement stems from the late nineteenth century, where the establishment of sporting competitions took off and became the breeding ground for male heroism. To a greater extent than film and pop stars, sports celebrities are reminded constantly of their duties as role models for their fans:

> As 'ambassadors' for their country or for the game they play, standards of appropriate behaviour will apply far more stringently for the high profile member of the English soccer team, say, then for the star of Hollywood movies (ibid.).

If we follow Turner's reasoning, in Beckham's case there is more pressure on him to conform than for film stars, such as Brad Pitt, Jude Law or Tom Cruise, and for that matter pop stars. As Turner suggests, the greatest pressure comes from the media, whose censorious position is even more pronounced than that of the fans.

Perfectly groomed, Beckham is fully aware of the pressure from the media and his unprecedented role as a 'British ambassador'. Image-wise, he befits a fashion model, whose 'natural good looks' and manner of speaking can be read as a faking of naivety that props up a metrosexual spectacle. Public appearances with 'Queen Victoria' on his arm places Beckham high on the list of British loveys at the time of writing this book. And, as a relic of Blair's Cool Britannia, Beckham's image is recognizable in the capriciousness of the gaze, the head angle and entire gamut of dress codes that form the canvas for his *faux naif* masquerade.[16] Undoubtedly, his status is achieved on the basis of his pop construction, and like pop stars, Beckham, has profited from the media spotlight. Turner insists that showbiz culture is a serious business that rests on the ambition of a successful career, and it is this phenomenon that also underpins the construction of the dandy. Notwithstanding style, talent and appearance, temperament marks and masks the celebrity dandy, which I will address in Chapter 2 when I turn to the work of Baudelaire. Robins insists that 'whatever lies behind this sense of difference, dandyism has been the method used to gatecrash the visible world. Dandyism is both a pedestal on which to stand and a mask behind which to hide' (Robins 2001, p. 4). For in an age of off-the-peg design labels, the dandy in pop culture looms larger than life as an icon of irresistible, commercial allure. The issue of address and the transgressive forces of gender-bending are therefore part and parcel of understanding this phenomenon.

## Questions of Bending and Display

Throughout the 1960s into the 1970s masculinity was packaged with mixed codes of sexuality. Indeed, glam-rock was modelled on a Warholian aesthetic that had a profound effect on how young people started exploring sexuality. Subsequently, this paved the way forward for future generations of male artists. The hype that surrounded Bowie's sexual ambiguity provided 'a breathing space both for queers and for those who weren't sure about their sexuality or their feelings about the

---

[16] See Pountain and Robins (2000) for a historical and social account of the term 'cool' within a Western and exoticized Other context.

sexuality of others' (Gill 1995, p. 110). At any rate, these decades signified a major breakthrough in male representation, where 'young men sometimes willingly risked homophobic assault by dressing in the manner of their pop idol, even if they themselves weren't homosexual' (ibid., p. 112). As such, by the early 1970s a sea of changes in sexual attitude were visible in 'a busy cross-traffic between gay fashions (in music, in dress, in drugs, in other cultural apparel; films, books, design, nightlife, travel) and rock fashions' (ibid.). So profound was Warhol's impact that Bowie wrote a song called 'Andy Warhol' (on the album *Hunky Dory* (1971)), which Warhol allegedly hated. Significantly, though, Bowie's look and sound from this period would emulate a queer sensibility that acknowledged a fascination for Warhol's work, not least in terms of his theatrical productions. A memorable attendance of the London performances of *Pork*, based on taped conversations made by Warhol, impressed Bowie greatly and rubbed off on his later songs (Auslander 2006, pp. 121–2).

In the same year that Bowie released his track 'Andy Warhol', he made a television appearance, wearing a frock while playing the acoustic guitar. Designed by fashion designer Michael Fish, this dress was not unlike the one worn by Mick Jagger at the Stones' free concert in Hyde Park in 1969. In these early years Bowie's appeal rested in his much-flaunted artificiality and ridicule of sexual stereotypes. A refusal to play into the rules of convention, especially when it came to appearance and behaviour, was borne out by his countless experimental performances during the 1970s. Flamboyantly, Bowie emasculated the manliness of the rock icon through a strategy of queering that blatantly displayed the constructedness of his subjectivity.[17] Yet, Bowie moved fast, outgrowing glam and reaching out into other less glamorous domains. Effectively, such image shifts provided him with a shield that had numerous advantages (Savage 1996, pp. 112–16).

Wide ranges of political positions emerge from the shared experiences of certain social groups. But rather than emphasizing ideology or group affiliation, my focus will fall on the liberation of a specific constituency marginalized within a broad context. When linked to performance practices, representational politics provide ways of understanding personal and group distinctiveness. What I want to suggest by this is that performances provide a road into identifying the differences that are reified by dandyism. As masculinity belongs to no single gender, sexuality, race or discipline, there are valid reasons for considering why bonds and desires operate and structure all aspects of culture.[18]

---

[17]   In earlier studies, I have emphasised the socially constructed status of male identity in the context of pop culture (Hawkins 1997, 2002, 2004, 2006, 2007a, 2007b, 2007c). I intend to build on this in a way that addresses the implications of drag, cross-dressing and imitation, all of which form the pop spectacle, where gender is seen and heard as theatrical display.

[18]   Sedgwick (1986) implies that through relations of social and economic exchange, varying degrees of homosociality exist in all men. When it comes to the homosocial bonds

At first glance, the act of challenging norms and conventional roles seems to be part of the dandy's main mission in a context where the unmistakable images of Otherness are ubiquitous, and where the display of difference can quickly evaporate into the norm. As discussed earlier, pop music's links with art-based institutions shaped the marketplace as advertising corporations steadily embraced images that purposefully inscribed identity as ambivalent. And by paving the way for a strong alliance between pop and commercial enterprise, the art school tradition would contribute to the aestheticization of masculinity. So much so that by the 1980s the male pop artist would be contextualized by representations of a more sensitive, less macho type; it was as if mainstream culture had shifted the focus onto a type who unabashedly saw himself as an object of desire. Subsequently, images of the male through the 1980s and into the 1990s signified a subtle blend of the soft and hard; a chiselled muscularity framed by beautiful clothes, make-up and flawless complexion.

Research studies into the re-ordering of consumption trends in British society have addressed the effect of this through the spectrum of identities available to young men. Frank Mort describes how the cultural landscape of Britain in the 1980s and 1990s was shaped by the competitive dynamics of the market in ways never experienced before. Thatcherite market politics would mirror the new rituals of shopping and personal goods during a time when the 'commercial address to men provided a way into posing a number of broader questions about contemporary changes to masculinity' (Mort 1997, p. 10). While the relationship of young men to traditionally feminine roles of shopping, taking care of appearances and style journalism had its origins in earlier decades, there was an intensification of this. An escalation in the plurality of masculinities meant that by the late 1980s the fashion palette for male consumers had become extensive, as evident in men's magazines, tabloids and music videos from this period. And, contrary to the po-faced expressions of American fashion models of the time, their British counterparts were feeding off dandification as a prime selling point, spawning a diversity of styles.

All of this had a strong bearing on the homosociality found in pop happenings. Glaringly visible in the last decades of the twentieth century, a mixed bag of male representations, from androgynous boys to New Romantics, boy bands to indie groups, rock stars to soul singers, were branded through their unique displays of masculinity. Above all, the emphasis would fall on a narcissistic display that challenged and upheld traditional norms of virility and toughness. Amongst the bands that stood out were the Pet Shop Boys, Communards, Bronski Beat, Depeche Mode, Frankie Goes to Hollywood and Soft Cell who, to their advantage, set out to articulate a more ambiguous masculinity.

The line-up of pop dandies selected for this study consist of Marc Almond, Adam Ant, Marc Bolan, David Bowie, Jarvis Cocker, Ray Davies, Pete Doherty,

---

that operate between and within women, Sedgwick emphasises that social and economic control gives way to an identification of being on the 'other side' of the gender divide.

Paul Draper, Stephen Duffy, Bryan Ferry, Neil Hannon, Justin Hawkins, Mick Jagger, Jay Kay, Steven Patrick Morrissey, Robert Palmer, David Sylvian, Neil Tennant, Robert Smith, Rod Stewart, Sid Vicious, Paul Weller and Robbie Williams. Albeit in vastly different ways, these artists symbolize some of the main developments in popular music during the past decades through the unique coding of their spectacle. In all the examples I refer to, the body is displayed through the antics of self-promotion and self-aestheticization. As such, the dandified subject is a historical and cultural construct that has evolved through the evolution of new gender roles and masculinity. Historicizing this, Alice Cicolini identifies:

> [T]he 1780s crisis of Regency aristocracy, the 1890s scandal surrounding Wilde's homosexuality, the 1950s postwar wave of immigration and rise of the teenager and the 1970s era of women's liberation and Stonewall. Since 1980, Britain has witnessed the character of the male change with whirlwind speed – the New Man, followed swiftly by the *Loaded* Lad and most recently, in the early twenty-first century, the Metrosexual (Cicolini 2005, p. 13).

That the metrosexual male has had more to do with consumables is reflected in pop over a span of fifty years, offering up a spectacle of masculinity never imagined in Brummell's day. Cicolini makes the argument that the overlap between art and luxury that Brummell was part of 'has been driven by twenty-first-century dandies' (ibid., p. 13). Pop dandyism is about the fashioning of dress codes and glamour that is channelled through musical expression. Moreover, the British pop dandy is a cultural construction, whose musical performance is regulated by behaviour patterns and established gender codes – the patriarchal masculine, the maternal feminine, the impassive straight white male, and so on.

In the staging of his performance, the pop dandy displays his individuality through musical identification. And, in this sense, his subjectivity is shaped by musical codes that draw on the spectacle of the body. Because pop is underpinned by glamour, the artist is free to flirt openly with any aspect of his representation. This is how pop showmanship works. This is how it provides an idealized model for the reactionary and the rebellious in one go. From this, then, the pop dandy's mission is not only to express individuality, but also to use musical performance as a model for self-expression and something unique. In a bid to explain this phenomenon, a substantial amount of attention has been paid to subjectivity and musical production. As I argue, ideas about performance are based upon the differences in sound recording that distinguish one artist from the next. In effect, then, the conglomeration of technical, artistic and physical forms of expression are what determine whether or not someone is dandified. The pop dandy utilizes music for triggering off emotions that validate his identity, and to succeed requires varying degrees of symbolic representation that are predicated upon mimesis. As such, the dandified performer invests in representations that normalize his subject position, highlighting his agency at the expense of others.

Signifying difference through musical practice, then, confirms the aesthetic status of the artist. And, the individual's tendency towards gestural elaboration makes a convincing case for reading performances within a mediated cultural space, where gendered display provides a clue to how pleasure is mediated musically. What I am advocating, then, is the idea that pop dandyism accommodates the performative aspect of the performer with all the trappings of self-aestheticization. Dandified performativity is about recorded musical expression, and, again, this says much about who I have included or excluded from my list. Definitions of a pop dandy, as I have discovered during the years of writing this book, can easily become a personal battleground. If one artist is classified as dandified, what makes another not? Elton John, Antony Hegarty, Boy George, Freddie Mercury, Mick Hucknall, Ozzy Osbourne, George Michael, Sting and the Oasis brothers are not included on my list. Why not?

## Conclusion

On first impression, the dandy might appear coy, if not camp and contrived. Take Morrissey and Doherty, who exhibit a put-on vulnerability, or David Bowie, Robert Smith and Mick Jagger, who parody maleness through a heightened degree of affectation. And then there is the funky, whitened-up act of Jay Kay, the cheeky, chirpy Robbie Williams, or the pantomime-like buffoonery of Adam Ant and Neil Tennant, who tend to overdo their spectacularized display. Without doubt, all these spectacles are set to music in the form of songs in ways that complement their look, where the characteristics of their act lie in the subtleties of staging themselves. Working out how this functions requires the location of the points of mediation that define subject positioning and constitute agency. Because the dandy is a paradoxical creature, bent on entertaining and charged by a super-ego, by default he exposes the potential of his own fragility. Seen in this light, pop dandyism is about continual renegotiation of the link between gender display and musical expressivity, where the shaking-up of conventional codes can be captivating.

So with this definition, I arrive at a general premise: that the disciplining of dandified display encountered in British pop informs an ongoing narrative of individual agency. What stands for the British male dandy is not only a construction that distinguishes him from being female, but also a fabricated figuration that marks out the terrain of dissident masculinity. Pop dandyism is about recognizing something intrinsic in the articulation of gender that is adumbrated by nonverbal aural and visual signifiers. That is to say, dandified performativity is resolutely manifested in the playing-out of identity, and the pleasure derived from viewing the staging of another's persona. In terms of such a construction, the politics of representation are tenuous and intensified within the realm of the spectacularized performance. For the fragments of a performance have countless sources where the manifold possibilities affecting the staging of an audio-visual recording are matched by the complexities of individual agency. What then does this have to say about the task of working the effects of dandyism through the recorded performance, and how do we go about interpreting this?

Throughout the ensuing chapters I will address pop dandyism as a facet of identity politics that converges on popular musicology in ways that shape this hypothesis of individual agency. Dandies, so my argument goes, are defined by the ways they perform songs, and a great deal more. As their subjectivity is mainly mediated in recorded form, it designates notions of style and belonging that have their origins in a studio environment. In the next chapters, I will take up this issue alongside a discussion of a range of performances that are mediated by strategies of seduction, all the time keeping in mind Barbey's cautionary note that dandyism is as difficult a thing to describe as it is to define.

# Chapter 2
# Pop Subjectivities: Poise and Spectacle

> Dandies can be highly dislikeable people, whose affectations we love to hate, and who for that reason are in perennial demand.
>
> George Walden[1]

Searchlights dotted over London's Earls Court arena on a freezing February night as we the fans were warmed up for the glam and razzmatazz of the Brit Awards 2002. For one delicious moment all the baggage of being a musicologist dissipated into the darkness of the auditorium. Opening with an avalanche of booming sound, Gorillaz, silhouetted against giant screens in brilliant animation, were joined on stage by rappers, a fraction of their size, for a unique performance of their hit 'Clint Eastwood'. One had the sense that Damon Albarn's spirit was musically brought to life.[2] A few acts later, Kylie Minogue made one of her most memorable entrances attached to a giant-size CD, lowered hydraulically onto the stage. How could we get her out of our heads? Clad scantily and wearing thigh-high boots, she lit up the stadium with her pop classic 'Can't Get Blue Monday Out Of My Head', in a futuristic dance routine with an army of troupers spoofing the robotic sensibility of the mash-up arrangement. Flamboyant Jay Kay, Britain's funkster dandy, followed a few numbers later in a double act with Anastacia in the song 'Bad Girl', entering the stage with a spectacular long slide on his knees. The Brit Awards 2002 was yet another big year for pop dandy Robbie Williams, who picked up an award for British Male Solo Artist, thanking his fans on a screen relayed from the US. Little did he (or we) know then that three years later at the Brit Awards he would scoop his fifteenth BRITs trophy in a special award, the BRITs25 – Best Song Award for his song 'Angels'. Remarkably, at only 30, Williams had been on a winning streak for 10 years.[3]

The focus of this chapter falls on the many facets of spectacularity within a media-saturated arena. How is British pop dandyism framed by traditions that raise

---

[1]  Walden (2002, p. 41).

[2]  This event I attended with John Richardson, and I am grateful for his comments and conversations on the spectacularity of the show. Also see Richardson (2005) for an article on this event that focuses upon Gorillaz's performance of 'Clint Eastwood'.

[3]  All the razzmatazz of this big media event was brought home by the BRITs25 opening act with Scissor Sisters, whose camp performance of 'Take Your Mama' involved a set that consisted of an enormous pink bird, a choir of watermelons, a singing shed and a troupe of dancing eggs. That same night Scissor Sisters received awards in the categories International Album, International Group and International Breakthrough.

questions of subjectivity and spectacularity? Of relevance to this are the politics of
male representation that inform the discourses of pleasure that are promulgated by
the music industry. Middleton (2006) has argued[4] that the music industry makes it
virtually impossible to think outside the problematics of structures of authenticity;
we simply have to. For the complex junctures of narrative, music, words, gestures
and performance in popular music all concern issues of what is felt as the 'real
thing'. Recorded audio-visual texts shape spectacular performances, from live
concerts, video promos, TV shows to club nights, holding clues as to how pop
identities are constructed. From this we might say that the recorded performance
is an ongoing process of *transformation* that shapes the act in various ways. This
idea ushers in a main objective of this chapter: to discover how performances
inscribe patterns of relationships that articulate subjectivity in pop.

Consider that the pop dandy brings into alignment a host of characteristics
that depend on the interpellation of musical style. Contours of musical genre,
style, and idiom invariably pull together all that we make sense of in a pop
performance. This is a creative process that entails the listener making something
of the subjectivity of the artist or group through visual and aural elements. In this
respect, the performance space – the material basis for pop's evaluation found in
concert venues, on cinema screens, MP3 players, radios, home systems and in the
press (magazines, internet pages, newspapers) – frames an audience's listening
competence. In practice, what subjectifies the artist is based on the listener's
techniques of making sense of a musical performance, where distinguishing one
style from the next becomes a salient point for interpretation.

Another discussion that enters this debate is that of the conflation of British
pride, often at the exclusion of others, within or without national boundaries
(Biddle and Knights 2007); for pop stars choose a range of criteria that highlight
their cultural and national exclusivity. Let us say that elements of nationality are
mythologized in numerous ways, and traceable through the idiosyncrasies of
performance practices in all forms of musical traditions, such as opera, dance,
pantomime and music hall. Showbiz conventions of music hall and cinema, for
instance, are historically grounded in sentimental ballads with light-hearted and
ironic storylines. Take Gracie Fields, who in the height of her career during the
Second World War, travelled to France to entertain the troops. Primarily, her
singing style defined her role and nationality. Frith explains: 'By spoofing her
voice (rather than her looks), by displaying her vocal range (in terms of style
as well as pitch) as a bit of a joke, Fields became endearing, beloved – "Our
Gracie" – as a kind of favorite aunt or big sister' (Frith 1996, p. 213). Not only
was it Fields's sensibility towards *playing herself* through moving between comic
routine and sentimental ballad, but also the nation's identification with her in
doing this (mainly via the radio). One of Britain's greatest stars during the Second

---

[4]   By music industry institutional practices, Middleton refers specifically to the
distinctions between musical styles and genres, record labels, radio stations and channels,
sales charts, journalism and A&R departments (Middleton 2006, pp. 199–246).

World War, Fields's impression of a 'real' self became a central component of a subjectivity, a logical precursor of the British pop star. Indeed, the vulnerability-on-display that Fields mastered when communicating with crowds not only raises the question of stardom, but also naivety as a critical aspect of twentieth-century pop performance practice. For the pop persona is projected in an exaggerated guise of self-deprecation, 'sincerity', self send-up, intense emotional outpourings, and so on. Indeed, the drive behind dandyism is to turn oneself into an 'original' by masking things. And by arousing curiosity and appealing to the masses, this character draws on the empathic responses of fans in situational contexts of national importance.

In addition to the lead singer/songwriter, the intentions of the producer and the rest of the team of collaborators in a recording is to construct identities that sell. One empirical angle in working out the pop dandy's avowed motives might be measured by the relationship between musical performance, the song and the production team. By this, I am keen to argue the concept of performance as an outcome of collaborative effort, while still focusing primarily on the artist in the role of the lead singer. And in attempting to trace some of the trends in musical performance, I will position the dandy as a tenuous cultural construction, a product of the most trenchant articulations of subjectivity, a personality who waits, poised, to fashion his identity. After all, poise tells us how social identities are spectacularized musically, and why transformation occurs along a continuum that is differentiated by behavioural displays.

Also crucial to the pop performance is the high visibility of bodies on display. In tandem with music, the body obeys the operative rules of physical movement and mannerism; hand gestures, shoulder shrugs, facial contortions, head nods all relay sets of emotional responses from one social setting to the next. In this chapter we will see how the pop performance owes its uniqueness to the body and its *temperament*, which is partly addressed through the writings of Baudelaire. Any employment of subjectivity as a concept needs to be carefully measured. In theories of subjectivity the individual is an actual person, while the 'subject' is constituted by a set of roles constructed by cultural, ideological and aesthetic values. Linguist Emile Benveniste (1971) asserts that the subject only exists within the confines of the 'discursive moment', and therefore is continuously redefined by discourse. Critiquing the subject, then, following this line of thought, challenges notions of individuality per se and that the subject might only possess one meaning. So, on to the subject-positioning of the pop dandy.

Baudelaire's theory of dandyism, which I will now turn to, was not only part of a myth of spiritual self-sufficiency, but also the locus of modernity. In keeping with both Baudelaire and for that matter Barbey, the dandy in pop music might be conceived as a symbol of universal passion, a relative cultural phenomenon; the recorded document of a history of events. Moreover, the subjects we idolize, see and hear are often blatantly aware of the contradictions they represent, ridiculing themselves while exploiting their originality.

## Baudelairian Temperament and Audio-visual Agency

Prime exhibit B: Charles Pierre Baudelaire, born in Paris, 9 April 1821. Denouncing the utilitarian aspirations of the bourgeoisie, he treated the topic of temperament with the utmost earnestness. His philosophy of dandyism and idealization of the British Romantic would be analysed through a decadent aestheticism that claimed temperament emanated from the most banal of biological positionings. Suggesting that it was the psychosomatic intentions of the individual that shaped aesthetic response, Baudelaire articulated a terse discourse that helped pin down the particularities of individualism. According to Baudelaire, when artistic originality is rooted in temperament, its aesthetic appeal always stands in relation to a wider historical relativity.[5] Addressing aspects of temperament, Baudelaire concentrated on the sensory surfaces of performance, considering how they magnetized the gaze of the onlooker. How this works, he claimed, involved locating the temperamental proclivities of identity while processing the sensory entities of the body. A central facet of temperament uncovered in this process, he would argue, is *naïveté*,[6] a quality that Baudelaire used to proclaim the virtues of the 'true dandy' (Howells 1996).

A beguiling characteristic found in many people, naivety suggests something excessively simple – a trusting view of one's environment – and often the result of youthful expression and inexperience. Accordingly, this definition can be construed as romantic, charmingly straightforward and refreshingly unaffected. Naivety's charge, if we concur with Baudelaire, also lies in its peculiarity, which is underlined by moral conventions and cultural expectations. Bridging notions of nature, birth, nationality and all the determinants of context, naivety appeals to the ideals of individualism. Understood in this sense, it arbitrates the 'natural' as much as the cultural, and, in contributing to the criteria for dandyism, designates an aesthetic positioning.[7]

With naivety high on the agenda for theorizing dandyism in pop, I want to turn to the theatricalized social space of a post-war British context, where performance practices have steadily altered and developed over time. Alone, the role of music television in charting the rise of the pop musician is a tumultuous phenomenon of audio-visual representation. Its role in the second half of the twentieth century would change the reception of music, especially when one considers how rapidly signals beam pop music from one corner of the globe to the next. In plain terms, television has shaped the norms and dominant tendencies we now associate with

---

[5]    See Baudelaire, *Oeuvres complètes*, 2 vols. (Bibliothéque de la Pléiade 1975–76).

[6]    Other terms that Baudelaire closely links to *naïveté* are *défaut, exclusif, point de vue* and partial, all of which refer to the nature of perception itself.

[7]    Baudelaire attributes the accolade of dandy to those with whom he empathizes in terms of an 'in-depth understanding'. However, as Bernard Howells has insisted, Baudelaire's conception of intellectual heroism in his later years 'does not allow a cult of personalities' (Howells 1996, p. 173).

pop identification (Middleton 1990; Frith 1996; Warner 2003). In this regard, I want to suggest three aspects of representation that exhibit the performer through audio-visual display: biography, text and the recording.

First, the profiling of biography is crucial for promoting and marketing musical performance, where more often than not the artist is taken to be the songwriter and/or protagonist of audio-visual texts.[8] Contesting the political status quo is often narrated through the artist's temperament, which, as Cicolini has stated, happened through 'the veneration of style and beauty', bringing together a 'radical, bohemian and flamboyant dandyism from Wilde, through the Sitwells' intellectual elitism and the media manipulation of Andy Warhol, to the star theatrics of Mick Jagger and Jimi Hendrix, the glam-rock of David Bowie and the performance art of Leigh Bowery' (Cicolini 2005, p. 11).

Second, the audio-visual text, a conveyor of conventions and practices, is the product of representation, positioning both the performer and spectator in disparate ways. Acts of listening and viewing are generally directed to what is represented in a text as well as the underlying processes of representation involved. The polysemic text, in this respect, is useful for conceiving the interrelationships that exist by implication (Barthes 1977). Throughout this study I employ the term 'text' broadly to refer to any part of the recording that can be *read* for meaning. My claim is that nobody can experience a music video without being aware of the context to which the text alludes, and, as such, the text constitutes a primary frame for interpreting the temperament of the artist.

Third, the recordings themselves assist the star on the way to heights of profound vanity, laying emphasis on the nuances of temperament that beset the spectacle of the body. In terms of their social significance, audio-visual recordings are self-referential in that they reveal, in close-up, the intricacies of self-aestheticization. Recordings, therefore, offer a material site for the positioning of the artist's temperament, whereby the spectator is obliged to adopt a subject position that is predetermined through the structure and codes of the text. Furthermore, recording technology induces repeated listening (and viewing) that is conditional on familiarity and memory. What seems at issue here is the dialogic relationship of visual and sonic material as established by the viewer as much as by the performer. This implies that the recording not only contributes to the visual construction of identities, but also reconfigures them as part of the process of pleasure.

Because recorded performances hit us in milliseconds, they reinscribe bodies across vast spatiotemporalities, enabling us to imagine what is the 'real' thing. Taking this one step further, temperament becomes a chief component of sonic reality by proxy. Such a notion is central to understanding how a simulated

---

[8]  Notably, there are also non-representational music videos where the artist is not depicted at all. Since music videos are intended to profile the artist, such videos are rare; two early 1980s examples, however, are Springsteen's 'Atlantic City', and Prince's 'Sign O' the Times'.

performance filters the original event in a space where just the hyperreal remains.[9] Indeed, in the heavily contested area of cyberspace, music is contingent on a heterogeneity of subjectivities; for virtual representations are replete with the co-existence of countless subjects that have a major impact on the construction of our own personae.

How then is subjectivity linked to genre, and what accounts for someone being dandified? At this point I want to turn to Baudelaire's essay *Le Peintre de la vie moderne* [The Painter of Modern Life], from 1863, which is largely devoted to idealizing the male persona (in the form of the draftsman, Constantin Guys). For Baudelaire the personal style of the Romantic cult figure implied a new originality. Rejecting Rousseauism, his critique of the rising tide of mass culture was prophetic, while his fascination with the cult of images emerged as one of his greatest passions. Elegance, he would insist, was the dandy's cornerstone, signifying the distinction of being painted by one's imperious self. Such an idea belonged to the aesthete's spurious intellect in late Romanticism, which combined elegance with power.[10] Divorcing art from its social context, Baudelaire's dandy would import a cool, narcissistic sensibility into modern life. Possessing a cold exterior that came from an unshakeable determination to remain unmoved, the dandy was in revolt and strictly bound up in the satisfaction of never revealing himself. On this matter, Baudelaire would argue in *The Painter of Modern Life* that vice is something natural (in that it is selfish), while virtue is artificial because it causes us to restrain our impulses in order to be orderly and well behaved. Further, the dandy, as aesthete, symbolized the leading example of a totally purposeless existence; a gentleman whose cool smile and demeanour never made him vulgar. Yet, rather than accepting the principles of aesthetics and abstract notions of the beautiful, the Baudelairian dandy would centre upon the 'lived experience'.

By 1846 Baudelaire had gone as far as condemning philosophical poetry as a false genre, arguing that art's value could only be constituted in itself. Baudelaire's association of the modern with artifice and decadence would also prove that dandified characteristics were more than attitudes of nonchalance and originality in dress. Instead they were the vital traits of personality and temperament. For Baudelaire it was Beau Brummell's stroke of genius, as arbiter of elegant masculinity, to impress others. And, it was not surprising for Baudelaire that this would be imitated and reproduced by generations to come, so much so that by the

---

[9]    Jean Baudrillard has insisted that *hyperreality* is the result of a technologically advanced postmodern society, where the inability to distinguish between fantasy and reality is omnipresent. Baudrillard's cynical position on simulacra and simulation owes much to phenomenology and semiotics. See Baudrillard (1981a; 2005).

[10]    As Camille Paglia has insisted, Late Romanticism was 'arrogantly elitist', and there is no getting away from it that Oscar Wilde was a part of this, despite his sentimentalization by 'modern admirers' (Paglia 1990, p. 428).

mid-nineteenth century *la mode* signified the imitation of a model that was driven by a need for social freedom as well as individuality.[11]

Down the ages the dandy has emerged as a figure of desire who sets out to please and entertain, although this has not necessarily always been a pleasant affair or entirely intentional, as exemplified by Beau Brummell and others like Marcel Duchamp. In recent times pop music and its proponents have definitely had their fair share. Consider rebel Sid Vicious, who went as far as insulting and violating his fans and audience, leading to physical injuries (Marcus 1989, p. 84). Playing on a Baudelairean sensibility, The Sex Pistols were in combat against all that was trivial and glam. Vehemently, they would denounce the stereotypes of the 'culture industry' by setting themselves up in opposition to the dominant paradigm (albeit, paradoxically, ending up as prized commercial artists), and unmasking the norms and performance practices of their time. This was done through fashion and clothing that challenged class identity (Barnard 1996). In musical terms, their brand of punk opposed the boring, safe styles of the early 1970s and the bourgeois culture that produced them. Malcolm Barnard describes how their look reflected the music: 'hair was cut in a variety of bizarre styles; dyed in such colours as "hay yellow, jet black or bright orange", it was teased and gelled into "Mohican", spiked and tufted styles. Make-up, like the clothing, displayed the signs of its own construction' (Barnard 1996, p. 131). Through a youthful indifference, Vicious ridiculed all those around him who took themselves seriously, especially the kind of musicians who played 'well'. Probably the nastiest of all punk dandies, he idealized the individual by offering a site for contestation that forced back the limits of social convention. Begging for 'the ritual devouring of the star by his followers', he became a 'representation of a representation, even streaked with his own gore' (ibid.).

Crass and repulsive, vibrant and appealing, punk, albeit for a short moment, chucked out the love song by producing songs about 'masturbation, jobs, class, cigarettes, traffic lights, fascist dictators, race, the subway' as this weird breed of artists 'played with Adorno's negative dialectics, where every "yes" turns into a "no"' (ibid., p. 77). Such exhilarating, anti-art acts were illustrative of the anarchic gestures of public offence, where decadence in behaviour belied an acute understanding of the futility of human existence. One might say the type of dandyism that characterized Vicious was discernible in the 'cult of the self', where, in Baudelaire's own words, 'the joy of astonishing others, and the proud satisfaction of never oneself being astonished' (Baudelaire 1964, p. 27–8) was the punk dandy's strength and eventual downfall by way of overdose.

---

[11]   Significantly, the lack of freedom for most women during this period resulted in them taking charge of *la mode* in order to instate their membership in social groups and identify their individuality. It was this that the male dandy would pick up on and appropriate for his own ends. Thus, by turning the cause of fashion into a masculine model, the dandy took from the diva a strategy that would blur traditions and upset the divisions of gender.

## *La Mode* – **Fashion and Desire**

If fashion is 'some kind of approximation to an ideal for which the restless human feels a constant, titillating hunger' (Baudelaire 1964, p. 33), then it should never be considered as dead things. More to the point, fashion should be seen as 'vitalized and animated', as beautiful as the people who wear it. Had Baudelaire been around one century later, he might have marvelled at what would greet him on the British high street of the 1960s, where people adorned the sidewalks with attitudes of pride and indifference (see Décharné 2006). In the wake of Presley's outrageous play on codes of 'feminized' masculinity (Jarman-Ivens 2007), a new androgyny constructed pop fashion in Britain. This involved a merging of continental European 'exotica' through the artifice of institutions, such as pantomime and music hall; the British pop dandy would look back with nostalgia at the same time as experimenting with the future. Again, technology helped stylize British pop music and fashion, furnishing it with an aesthetic that was reflexive and ironic. And the backdrop to this was a political ambiguity, a form of satire and comic retort, that grounded countless pop acts in an array of styles derived from rock 'n' roll.

During the course of the 1960s, technological advances in recording afforded artists greater control over their music and persona.[12] Hence, by the mid-1970s punk had emerged as the antidote for altering the course of pop only to create a stampede in the opposite direction, towards the New Romantics. With an increase in ambivalence towards Britishness, the New Romantic pop performer symbolized the gloss of a postmodern collision of styles situated in a virile political context where Thatcherite economic strategies could not fail to gain momentum. A booming consumerism became encoded in a sensibility that masqueraded through a British cultural landscape heavily under deconstruction. Michael Bracewell has claimed it was as if the age of the metaphysical pop trickster had dawned, whose style 'seemed to flirt with self-consciousness at a time (the Me Decade) when self-consciousness was precariously balanced on the edge of self-obsession' (Bracewell 1998, p. 215). However ironic, the post-punk style of the New Romantics was, at least on the surface, about reinvention and reconstruction (Rimmer 2003). And then with Britpop's birth a decade later, London would enter another renaissance, rising out of the doldrums of Thatcherism, becoming the world capital for pop, fashion and contemporary art. Swinging once more, London, a metaphor for cool Britishness, would be flanked yet again by the abrasive regional urban centres of Birmingham, Manchester, Cardiff, Edinburgh and Belfast, all of which produced their share of pop dandies.

---

[12]   Barthes (1967), in *The Fashion System*, explores the signifying nature of fashion clothing, focusing on the language used in fashion magazines. In this study Barthes concentrates on the word implied by 'fashion', and the distinction between *le vêtement-image* (image clothing) and *le vêtement écrit* (written clothing).

Many elements of the 1990s are traceable back to the 1950s when post-war fashion trends mirrored the processes of national reconstruction that were underway, and the dialectical directions of cultural production. Urban Britain during this decade, vividly frozen in the photo shots of the ISLFD (Incorporated Society of London Fashion Designers), shows the haughtiness in demeanour of female models, which 'hinted at an Albion unbowed by years of bombs and rationing' (Breward 2002, p. 561). Images of lean women in corsets and petticoats, signalling the end of the hard years of the Second World War through an astonishing display of lurid female dandyism, stood in comic relief to the patrician facades of London's Trafalgar Square, St James and Horse Guards Parade. In his ruminations on this period, Christopher Breward points out the distinctive flair behind the male look (whose topography prompted even more of a revolution than female fashion), underpinned by a growing concern over the arrival of a US mass consumer culture into the UK. The problem was its association with 'feminine interests and desires'. Part of this reaction appeared in the form of a neo-Edwardian revivalist style, and an opting for an early twentieth-century sartorial style:

> Bowler hats, polished shoes and rolled umbrellas hint at the glamour of the regimental parade ground, a space which had always provided important inspiration for the London dandy, white velvet collars, embellished waistcoats, ticket pockets, covered buttons and turned-back cuffs recall the ostentation of the Edwardian race track and music hall (Breward 2002, p. 562).

The sartorial stereotypes described by Breward would undergo significant transformation in the 1950s, highlighting the double-edgedness of dandyism. Flair and innovation thrived on the one side, conservatism on the other. Such populism was visible in the changes in men's clothing, epitomized by the unlikely juxtaposition of aristocratic style and youth culture. Moreover, the intensified effect of a masculine revival was inspired by post-war London's changing landscape of new architectural tower blocks, steel structures and glass plates. Describing the parallel fashion revival by young males, Harry Hopkins points out that this was manifested in the Teddy outfit, which emerged as the 'badge of a half-formed, inarticulate radicalism' (Hopkins 1964, p. 427). Above all, the features of this suit were English and class-based, symbolizing social resistance; hence, its instant appeal and consumption by a growing teenager sector.

A central icon of British post-war society, the Teddy boy's advent was about dismantling working-class ideals and this was aided through the sheer impact of American culture.[13] Endemic in the attitude was a sense of territorial protectiveness and gang mentality. It is hardly surprising, then, that writers and artists such as

---

[13]   Dick Hebdige's seminal study into British subculture traces this decisive trajectory through music and fashion. See Hebdige 1979. Also see Gelder and Thornton (eds) (1997) for a wide range of essays dealing with subculture in music, media and fashion, and Wilson (2007) on the construction of glamour in fashion.

Minton, MacInnes, Welch and Orton would become obsessed with documenting this new metropolitan icon, setting him against the backdrop of newly bombed London. As Hopkins argues, the Teddy's shifting features were constructed around both 'imaginative and spatial specificities' that ensured the proletarian dandy's status as romantic hero in the form of an urban folk legend (ibid., 1964, p. 566). The Teddy's demeanour fed off the iconography of American gangster films, an important source of entertainment for British adolescents long before the Second World War. In particular, this was complemented by a wardrobe consisting of loose flannels, belted jackets, garish ties and elaborate hats, all of which helped to set off a swaggering and slouching type of posturing.

A precedent for the Teddy was the 'spiv', who also nurtured a distinctive look by turning to 'the sleek glamour of the Latin crooner in front of his bathroom mirror (good looks aiding his professorial role as a swindler)' (ibid., 1964, p. 571). At about the same time the Savile Row suit, a major icon of British masculinity, continued its course, undeterred by the Second World War. Conservative in its understatement, the suit was adaptable to the subtle emergence of a neo-Edwardian style. In the main, it paid homage to Brummellian dandyism, articulating an aversion to modern-day life. In contrast to the neo-Edwardian look, caricatured by the Teddy in the 1960s, the suit also epitomized middle-class fashion during a period when there were more dance halls and cabaret shows springing up in London than even in Paris. For a moment, the Savile suit collided with Edwardian outfits and quiff hairstyles in a response to the leisure and entertainment scene of the day. Certainly, it was on display in London's West End in the 1960s, where the transitory display of neo-Edwardian fashion became a structuring tool of social, political and cultural life.

Meanwhile, emanating from this urban context, countless new subcultures were created and paved the way for the next decade. The early Mod style that began in 1958, with teenagers from London and the south east of England, was distinguishable by tight Levi's, the parka, Fred Perry tennis shirts, and later slim-cut Italian suits. Adhering to the latest in fashion, the first wave of Mods, stemming from the Teddys, pursued a different sound, adopting African American modern jazz, blues, soul, rhythm and blues, and then moving on to Jamaican bluebeat and ska.[14] The Mods, up to the mid-1960s, had portrayed an image of being stuck up, snobbish and full of attitude. Dressed in suits, the boys wore neat narrow trousers and pointed shoes, while the girls displayed a boyish image, darkening their eyes and cutting their hair short. The accessories of a Lambretta GT 200 or a Vespa GS 160 scooter, the ultimate symbol of being a true Mod, completed a unisex appearance. In the meantime their rivals, the Rockers, who had also originated from the Teddy boys, inheriting the attire of black leather, grease and motorbikes, invaded the countryside in their hoards. Rivalry between these two groups is captured by Nik Cohn:

---

[14]   During this period the Rolling Stones, the Yardbirds, The Pretty Things, The Kinks, the Downliners Sect and The Small Faces were the most in vogue bands.

Mods thought that Rockers were yobs, Rockers thought that Mods were ponces. They hated each other deeply. Both of them, they were fanatic sects and their fights became holy wars, each truly believing that right was might, that the gods were on their sides (Cohn 1969, p. 194).

Bank holidays in 1964 were crossed off as special occasions for rivalry between Mods and Rockers as they descended upon southern seaside resorts (Brighton, Hastings or Margate), smashing and pillaging everything in sight. Besides a few arrests, the police could do little. Interestingly, following these incidents, the Rockers remained resolute while the Mods retreated, just becoming more beautiful and bored. As a Mod, Cohn recounts the fun he had in 1964 and 1965 when he did little more than buy clothes, over-eat and 'gab' under the illusion that he would never have to work in his life again: 'It was futile, of course, pop has always been futile but it seemed elegant, it was easy living, and English pop was better than it's ever been, than it's ever likely to be again' (ibid.). Nostalgic recollections of this kind highlight the alliance between youth culture, temperament and fashion, which forged a stylized revolution in male fashion that cut across class barriers, transforming many of the traditions of style.[15] In this way, British pop emerged as a symbol of change and hope for millions, and, thanks to media coverage, would thrive on incidents of moral panic for decades to come.

**Fashioning Britishness: The Kinks**

An important question facing the Mod would have been: Who am I? And how should I come across? Forging masculinity through a Mod sensibility in the 1960s symbolized a quest for an identity that could be institutionalized culturally. Often this was mediated by heavily coded satire and social observation. Probably one of the most satirical voices in pop was that of Ray Davies of The Kinks, whose Mod style and social critique can be read as politically nostalgic and dandified. With his younger brother Dave Davies, bassist Pete Quaife and drummer and percussionist Mick Avory, he formed The Kinks, a rock group which is still ranked among the most influential British bands, and is part of the Big Four – the legendary British Invasion bands of the 1960s, including The Who, the Beatles and the Rolling Stones. Less commercially successful than the others (largely due to a four-year ban from the US in the mid-1960s), The Kinks' influence on British popular music has been just as profound.

Musically, they represent something quintessentially British, and their trademark has been inherited by a host of bands such as Supergrass, Oasis and Blur, the New Wave bands the Pretenders, The Jam and The Knack, and the

---

[15]   I am grateful to Simon Frith for his views on this, pointing out that both Mods and Rockers represented, at least initially, different sectors of the working class: urban/suburban, old/new. On the matter of youth culture and musical expression, also see McClary 1994.

*fin de millennium* bands Franz Ferdinand, Babyshambles and The Killers, whose wide-eyed worship is undisguised. After their first major hit, 'You Really Got Me', Ray Davies wrote most of The Kinks' songs. With his art-student background (Hornsey College of Art, London), his experimental style from 1966 to 1976 paid off as the band enjoyed great success. Songs from this period paint a diverse and original picture, opening up new stylistic directions for rock and protopunk, as well as embracing the time-honoured tradition of British music hall. Davies's songwriting discloses the dandy at work, whose transition from Mod culture to psychedelia is marked by his versatility as singer and songwriter. Tempestuous probably best describes the relationship between the Davies brothers, which became a crucial part of the narrativity concerning boys misbehaving;[16] a strong undertow in their musical expression and display of masculinity.

Relics of Mod culture, The Kinks' songs charter the cultural and social terrain of swinging London. As commentaries on British culture in the 1960s they helped fashion a pop style. Originating from the word 'kinky', the band lived up to their name in the early years – stylish boots and sweeping leather capes were often worn on-stage. Attempting to be as un-American as possible, The Kinks managed to turn everyday quips into satirical wit by mining the culture around them of everything quintessentially English: class distinction, social problems, political commentary and, most of all, a sense of humour that could only be British. Emblematic of The Kinks' identity were their album covers, iconography and film footage, as well as the tailoring of their clothes: drainpipe trousers, frock coats and side-zip elastic ankle boots. But, ultimately, it was Ray Davies, the epitome of the Mod, who encapsulated what the band stood for.[17]

Davies's homage to music hall defines The Kinks' style. The song 'Dandy', from the *Face to Face* album (1966), incorporates music-hall features that turn it into a perfect vignette of British pop.[18] Sneeringly, Davies ridicules the swinger, playboy-type character of the day in this song. Opening with the lines 'Dandy, dandy, where you gonna go now? Who you gonna run to?', the song is a jibe at the

---

[16]   The Kinks' history is littered with countless tales of strife, with new members entering and exiting in rapid succession. In 1969, following Quaife's departure, the band was reduced to the original three members, who continuously changed their bassist and keyboardist. By 1984 problems had arisen between Dave Davies and drummer Mick Avory, which resulted in the latter leaving. At this point it was only the two brothers left as the original members. In the mid-1990s the relationship between them degenerated to the point that they split to pursue solo careers. Liam and Noel Gallagher's scraps might have fuelled media hype in the 1990s, but they do not match those of the Davies brothers. The strife between Ray and Dave Davies led to Kinks' songs such as 'Two Sisters' from 1966, in which sibling squabbles are turned into a narrative about a married woman's envy of her sister's freedom.

[17]   I am grateful to Sarah Niblock for verifying this point, and, moreover, for providing such an apt description of The Kinks' effect on British popular music in the mid-1960s.

[18]   Somewhat paradoxically, 'Dandy' became a hit through a jaunty cover song by the group Herman's Hermits in the same year as The Kinks' original, 1966.

pretentiousness of Mod culture. Eschewing the lyrics, Davies manages to pull off a critical, bemused commentary on the dandy fops of the day. All through the song satire is encoded by the musical style and vocal performance, which transports earnest lyrics. Davies's temperament surfaces through the endearing quality of a simple tune, set to child-like phrases that are instantly memorable. Everything in this relatively short song (2:12), well under the standard formula of three minutes, leads to the climactic final refrain, 'And Dandy, you're all right', with the phrase 'you're all right' being repeated five times. During the song the lead vocal becomes edgier right up to the final two phrases, which are yelled out in a tormented manner, culminating on the word 'right', on the first beat of a short two-bar instrumental outro over the tonic chords, D – Dsus4 – D. Melodic treatment of 'you're all right', based upon the tonic, includes intervallic leaps up a third (F sharp) and a fifth (A), as an embellishment of the simple melody. Such simple devices work effectively as a mechanism for heightening the passion of the moment, as Davies heaps scorn on the character he is singing about. Mostly, it is an out-of-tuneness that distinguishes his handling of pitch, creating a tension that is underpinned by a disciplined sticking to the beat and the regularity of its subdivisions. His register, in this final refrain, becomes higher, increasing the emotive tension of the narrative (with a slide up to the mediant and then down from the dominant). Extending the register and volume results in a reduction of vocal resonance that creates a tautness in sound that is unleashed when he yells out the three words 'you're – all – right' on the strong down beats. Vocal straining of this kind is paramount in connoting effort and elation, where the refusal to temper pitches precisely and embellish tones in a 'trained' manner is an integral part of the aesthetic. Furthermore, gruffness in vocal timbre, which comes from a 'head tone' rather than chest and throat, affords all the connotations of 'everydayness'. All these aspects of singing highlight Davies's personalized approach to theatricalizing his songs. Released in the same year that Mod culture was in decline, 1966, 'Dandy' says a lot about the dandification of Mod culture. For there is something in Davies's compassionate delivery that undermines the superficial status of his subject, at the same time as it appropriates the frivolity of British music-hall tradition: with its rousing melody and bland and regular rhythmic accompaniment, the song brilliantly satirizes the pleasantries of a culture so rooted in entertainment.

With its origins in the London saloon bars of public houses dating back to the 1830s, the music-hall song gradually became associated with a certain kind of singer.[19] Paving the way forward for British popular songs, it addressed the everydayness of social life through humorous retort and comedy (Scott 1989). The *Lions comiques*, some of whom were known as swells (or the foppish macaronis who I refer to elsewhere in this book), were comedian-type entertainers within the music-hall tradition. Parodying aristocratic airs and graces, the swell would pick up on the social pastimes of going to the races, drinking champagne, gambling

---

[19]   This was mainly from the 1870s onwards when artists attached to the genre of music hall emerged as stars.

and womanizing. Performances of this ilk were loaded with wisecracks and executed through songs that were a good laugh. Probably the most renowned *Lion comique* was the veritable George Leybourne, whose song 'Champagne Charlie' became a roaring success (!), elevating him, paradoxically enough, to the class he was parodying.[20] In fact, so successful was his promotion of champagne that the prestigious French company Moët et Chandon sponsored him with crates of their product; proof enough that commercial sponsorship of popular artists is nothing new.

Born one century before Ray Davies, Leybourne was the Victorian equivalent of the 1960s pop dandy. His 'Champagne Charlie', from 1867, gave him the wherewithal to flaunt his celebrity status as he rode around London in a carriage drawn by four horses and surrounded himself with beautiful women. His dress code included a fur-collared coat and shiny top hat, set off by 'Piccadilly Weepers', huge, cultivated whiskers, while the songs he performed drew their subject matter from daily life: mothers-in-law, infidelity, hen-pecked husbands, drink and debt. Blatantly patriotic and nostalgic, his lyrics pandered to idealistic concepts of Arcadia.

With no recordings or television around, the venues for music hall were where fans would have to go to hear the same song (and patter) more than once. It should be stressed that Leybourne's singing technique was quite different from the slovenly style of Davies, which, in a 1960s context, worked effectively as a technique for narrating tales in the most ordinary way. Released in 1968, the album *The Kinks Are The Village Green Preservation Society* provided Davies with an opportunity to sketch out aspects of Britain in the 1960s. Now viewed from the twenty-first century, some 40 years on, this album is a remarkable snapshot of post-war Britain, depicting a nostalgic yearning for the values of a bygone age. With more than a touch of self-parody, the songs from *The Village Green Preservation Society* conjure up humorous images of Arcadia with a longing for things to remain just how they always were. Musically, the idiosyncrasies of Britishness are performed out in an unpretentious sing-along style. For Davies believed he could foresee the destiny of British culture, especially under the threat from the US.

Davies has acknowledged the inspiration taken from Dylan Thomas's *Under Milk Wood* for the songs off *The Village Green Preservation Society*, with the title track of the album, 'Village Green', thematizing all the songs as a plea to conserve a litany of national objects, from little corner shops, custard pies and draught beer to china cups. Conceptually, the songs come across as flowery, tranquil and dreamy (as in green and pleasant England), portrayed through a musical sensibility that is shaped by music hall as much as by touches of US rock 'n' roll. Moore, in

---

[20]    Derek Scott (1989) notes that 'Champagne Charlie' would not have been deemed appropriate for music lessons in schools during this period, while contemporary minstrel songs were. In the 1870s it was important that children attending schools in Britain were taught the differences between good and bad music, and, hence, minstrel songs of the 'improving variety' were used (Scott 1989, p. 196; also see Middleton 1990).

his reading of this album, claims however that '(e)ven in the English village, the presence of safe American cultural heroes is accepted' (Moore 2001, p. 101).

One of The Kinks' most persuasive references to music hall is found in the track 'All of My Friends Were There', a nifty number delivered in a quirky, quasi-Gilbert and Sullivan style with a quick tempo. During this song we are reminded that there are hardly any rock artists who epitomize the British bourgeois popular music tradition more than Davies, who turns to stylistic codes as 'the surest way to break with American influences' (ibid., p. 102). Nonchalantly rebellious, these recordings are balanced, and, yet, convoluted as the protagonist sings: 'Came the day, helped with a few large glasses of gin, I nervously mounted the stage once again'. All about friends who turn up when they are least desired, this eccentric narrative is executed eloquently in terms of wry observation. Mockingly, he laments the trivial dilemma that besets him: 'Say what they may, all of my friends were there, not just my friends, but their best friends too', concluding, somewhat petulantly, with the stubborn repetition of 'I don't care!' Choosing to end on a dominant seventh chord makes the song resolve awkwardly, leaving the listener (his so-called friend?) in a position for deep reflection.

Over a lunch with *NME* journalist Keith Altham, Davies would concede, 'I suppose I tend to be rather cruel to my friends', hastily adding, 'but I'm really getting at myself as well.'[21] Musically, such self-referentiality is evident. Harmonically inventive, the textural and melodic material is kept simple, especially in terms of the rhythmic structuration, which consists of a regular 4/4 sequence in the verses and an oompah-pah waltz pattern in the chorus. The strategy of turning to uncomplicated rhythmic gestures and a no-nonsense instrumental backing helps reinforce the passion of the lyrics. Oscillating between quadruple and triple metre – a common device in music hall – helps to steer the melodic phrasing, cushioning the chord progressions while driving home the lyrics. Lyrically, there is little doubt that Davies possessed the gift of the gab as he sold his stories with great panache and poetic precision. Indeed, something arbitrary and affected in the performance style thrived on coinages that are emblematic of subtle English word play, where the cut and thrust of their meaning brings to life his character. In the end, Davies's self send-up in 'All of My Friends Were There' and 'Dandy' is a satirical sketch of the sort of people Mods were. British social snobbery, after all, is as old as the culture itself, and linked to a Shakespearian ability to lampoon the vain and affected qualities of the absolute gentleman (for example, in *Hamlet* the courtier Osric speaks in flattering terms about Laertes). Profoundly, Davies's incisive critique of the 1960s, borne out by these two songs, aligns the British class system and stiff upper lip with his personal fascination for foible and etiquette.

Preservation of the countryside and dreams of Arcadia did not prevent The Kinks venturing into more risqué areas. Living up to their name, they would address unconventional aspects of sexuality and gender through a number of songs that tapped into the world of outsiderdom, distancing the band from the machismo

---

[21]    In *NME* 4 November 1967.

of rock. The single 'Lola', from the 1970 album *Lola versus Powerman and the Moneygoround, Part One*, groundbreaking in its narrative content, deals with the romantic relationship between two men who meet up in London's Soho. Inspired by an incident where The Kinks' manager, Robert Wace, spent a night dancing with a black transvestite, Davies decided to turn this into a song. Reaching number two in the UK charts and number nine in the US, it signalled a much needed comeback for The Kinks. Becoming their main sing-along song at live concerts, 'Lola' was not only controversial for its sexual narrative, but also for the reference to Coca-Cola, which led to the BBC refusing to play it because of commercial branding, an uncanny recurrence of what had happened to the Beatles one year earlier when they used Coca-Cola in their song 'Come Together' from the *Abbey Road* album. Subsequently, 'Lola' was re-recorded with the term substituted by 'cherry cola'. Speculation surrounds the meaning of this phrase, one suggestion being that it referred to cocaine.

Acerbic yet tender, Davies's delivery of the final line 'Well I'm not the world's most masculine man, but I know what I am and that I'm a man' is a *tour de force* display of a persona that is gender conscious. Other songs that address issues of gender difference are 'I'm Not Like Everybody Else' (an ode to the social outcast), 'David Watts' (a golden schoolboy who was gay but couldn't tell the girls who were after him), and 'Dedicated Follower of Fashion' (a pointed jab at the Carnabetian dandies). Years later The Kinks would be resurrected in the form of a spate of very British bands which consisted of angry, determined lads.

## Britpop, Anglomania and Boy Icons

Britpop stormed in with a victorious and sartorial style and attitude. Again, history was repeating itself, now in the form of a strong resistance to US band Nirvana's success in Britain, which in 1992 seemed to rule the rock world.[22] In contrast to Seattle, Manchester and the Madchester scene was best epitomized by bands like The Stone Roses and Happy Mondays. Against the grey backdrop of Britain in the late 1980s, the ascension of Britpop in the 1990s seemed predestined. In every way nostalgic, Britpop's stance was not only against grunge, but also the outside world. Suede, whose debut single 'The Drowners' came out while Blur were on tour in the US, strongly celebrated their British roots while opposing any US influence. And while Pulp was gaining popularity for a bunch of wry songs about everyday life, there was Oasis with their narratives of class-consciousness. In no uncertain terms, the Britpop period was all about style, poise and a coolness not witnessed since the late 1960s. Authenticating a national style is as much about creating bonds and boundaries as cultural capital, and Britpop emerged as a statement against the

---

[22]   It seemed, at least from a British perspective, as if Nirvana had become spokesmen for a restless generation, best exemplified in their protest album *Nevermind*, and their single 'Smells Like Teen Spirit'. For its time, grunge seemed cool, with Seattle its rock capital.

downcast bands of the early 1990s, the anonymous producers of electronic dance music, as well as the US grunge movement. Images of exuberance, youthfulness and new laddishness became a phenomenon for media celebration. The inspiration and recognizable sources of Britpop would emanate from the most British of all, the Mod movement (The Who, The Kinks, the Small Faces), 1970s glam (David Bowie, T. Rex, Roxy Music), punk and the New Wave (The Jam, the Buzzcocks, Wire, Madness, Squeeze, Elvis Costello), The Smiths and, of course, Morrissey.

How then did Britpop draw on nationalistic sentiments and why was this so short-lived? Writer and broadcaster John Harris comments: 'When someone came round the corner singing about dingy suburban England, losing your money on fruit machines and greasy spoon cafes, I thought "aha, yes, I understand".' It reminded people both of their own lives, and also of the music that had soundtracked those lives 10 or 12 years before Britpop surfaced during a time when Britart, British films and British designers were doing very well. Songs like 'Some Might Say', 'Country House', 'Common People' and 'Stay Together' (in order, Oasis, Blur, Pulp and Suede) were so appealing because they mirrored British identity in the mid-1990s. In sum, the Britpop movement was a British media construction that orchestrated a society still reeling from Thatcherism, and through the revision of BBC Radio 1, the UK's most popular radio station, middle-aged hosts were replaced by younger ones. This is how Britpop happened.

Britpop enabled the British music industry to celebrate homespun success more conspicuously than at any time since the late 1960s, as home-grown bands enjoyed spectacular success in the UK without bothering with the rest of the world. Transporting British alternative rock into the mainstream, Britpop bands contributed to the cultural phenomenon of 'Cool Britannia' through tuneful, guitar-based pop. At the same time this brand of pop was fixated on being commercial, with flashy hooks and refrains framing an over-glamorization of stardom. By targeting British youth, who could revel in their own culture, their own heritage, their own lives in Europe, it did not matter if Britpop lost popularity overseas. The result, quite expectedly, was that Britpop rapidly faded out by the end of the decade.

On the subject of social class and musical performativity from this period, a new political ideology was rearing its head in the disguise of a glib 'Goldilocks'. Tony Blair's accession to New Labour's throne in 1994, and then election as prime minister in 1997, following his party's landslide victory, meant that he would be the youngest British prime minister since Lord Liverpool in 1812; all of which eased the way forward for 'Cool Britannia'.[23] Would Blair have known that this term was first used in a song title by the group Bonzo Dog Doo Dah Band in 1967, and that 'Cool Britannia' has little to do with the modern coinage of the

---

[23]  Similar terms for Wales and Scotland, 'Cool Cymru' and 'Cool Caledonia' respectively, were coined but had next to no currency whatsoever, and to this day most people have never heard of them.

term? Resurfacing in the mid-1990s as a registered trade mark for one of Ben & Jerry's ice creams (vanilla with strawberries and chocolate-covered shortbread), the brand name 'Cool Britannia' was intended to presage the era of New Labour in May 1997. Quickly adopted by the media in advertising, it surfed in on a wave of modernization, with a youthful new prime minister who played rock guitar and gave the country a breath of fresh air. Well, so it seemed.

Embracing the transient fashionable London scene – the Young British Artists (YBAs) such as Damien Hirst, Stephen Adamson and Sarah Lucas, and a whole batch of trendy magazines – Cool Britannia exhibited outpourings of national pride, crudely manifested in displays of the Union Jack: Noel Gallagher's guitar, Geri Halliwell's skimpy dress, Madonna's t-shirts and Bowie's Union Jack jacket worn on his 1996–97 *Earthling* tour (designed in collaboration with Alexander McQueen). This movement also marked the popularity of Austin Powers alongside a resurgence of Bond films. Finally, things peaked in March 1997, when the US magazine of fashion, culture and politics, *Vanity Fair*, chose to publish a special edition devoted to 'Cool Britannia', with abrasive Liam Gallagher and Patsy Kensit posing on the cover to the caption 'London Swings! Again!' The issue also featured Alexander McQueen, Damien Hirst, Graham Coxon and the editorial staff of *Loaded*. Cracks further appeared as the Spice Girls' *Spiceworld* album hit the top of the charts, and by 1998 *The Economist* had proclaimed Cool Britannia's death, declaring that people had become sick of a phrase that was now derogatory.

Many unexpected things happened in British pop in the 1990s. As well as Oasis, Manchester was home to the hugely successful British pop boy band Take That. This was the year that Robbie Williams rebelled and split from the band and started partying with Oasis at Glastonbury. Creating a huge media stir, Williams's role was grounded in a stroppy, 'badly behaved' character whom the British would love and hate. Fuelled by gossip, virulent anti-Gary Barlow stories, wild parties, brawls and clinical detoxification, his characterization by the media seemed perfect for a pop career. Seldom have critics been so mistaken in predicting Williams's downfall after splitting from Take That. By 1998 the Stoke-on-Trent boy was at the helm of towing the UK into the next century with his song 'Millennium'[24] (analysed in Chapter 5).[25] Williams is a prime example of how the star is located within some inner, private core when it comes to perceptions of personae. Let us ponder over this a while. Richard Dyer explains the star phenomenon as something that

---

[24]    This song entered the UK singles chart at the top in September 1998, while 'I've Been Expecting You' made it to the top of the album charts two months later.

[25]    Williams failed to win over American audiences when he toured in support of *The Ego Has Landed*, a compilation of the best tracks from earlier albums for the US market. By and large this point in itself is most significant when considering Britishness as a construct that collides or aligns itself with a US market. Notwithstanding his relatively low popularity in the US, though, Williams nevertheless owes much to the US for his authenticity, which is the subject for another debate.

'reproduces the overriding ideology of the person in contemporary society' (Dyer 2004, p. 12), and that the magic of the star is that he can appear to be his private self within the public sphere. For the private/public dichotomy is what makes the star possible, with the suggestion that 'there is a sense of "really" in play' (ibid., p. 13). That the star is 'really' himself in the public eye, and in play, is one of the 'ironies of the whole star phenomenon' (ibid.). Expertly, Williams grasped this from the outset, coming across mischievous through his alluring banter, quirky grimaces, Northern accent and jokey mannered voice. Instinctively it was as if he knew how to work the pop star with just the right dose of humility.

The video of 'Rock DJ', released in 2000, a curious take on vulnerability, depicted Williams stripping naked, and then tearing off his body parts. Encircled by a troupe of lightly clad female adorers, Williams is positioned in the centre of a roller blade rink. As the video progresses he strips to nothing, exhibiting his muscular physique, in order to catch the attention of the girl DJ. All this seems in vain until he pushes into an outrageous sequence that threatens to turn the video into a horror film. Peeling off his skin, tearing away his muscle tissue, Williams starts hurling his organs at the hungry onlookers. Set to a throbbing groove, the music is raucous, carnivalesque, catchy and egged on by the chant-like chorus hook 'I don't wanna rock, DJ, But you're making me feel so nice'. Williams's attention is divided between the fan (through the camera's lens) and the female DJ, the clichéd object of *his* desire, who, symbolically, ends up being the recipient of his heart as the organ is thrust into her face. Only after full surrender, so the narrative goes, is he able to win her. The video culminates with her dancing with his remains in the form of a skeleton. 'No Robbies were harmed during the making of this video' is the somewhat ironic, obligatory warning that rolls up in the titles at the end of the video.[26]

Rich in symbolism, the video 'Rock DJ' can be interpreted on many fronts: as a statement on mainstream pop culture and materialism; a commentary on the plight of the male pop star; or a cynical critique of narcissistic display. Claiming that the video was the ultimate striptease experience, when preparing for the shots (ok, right!), Williams would concede to have gone to great lengths to 'buff up' for this act. Quite literally this paid off. Much in the staging of the worked-out male body in music videos displays a vanity that can be read as a send-up of traditional masculinity. The sight of Williams singing, dancing and stupidly flaunting his over-sexed body in time to the groove of 'Rock DJ' is indeed suggestive of an assertive style that is taken to extremes in terms of self-empowerment. In effect, the wilful stripping away of the male body that leaves the voice solitary can be read as the only remnant to hang on as the body is finally subjected to female control. But there is more to this than meets the eye.

---

[26] MTV, VIVA, MCM and numerous music channels in Europe edited the video at the part where Williams starts peeling off his skin. Not unexpectedly, this video received, among many awards, the MTV Video Music Award for Special Effects in 2001.

Centrally operative, Williams's masochistic act signifies a type of roguishness by virtue of a raw virility that is bold and narcissistic. Self-annihilation through the complete obliteration of the flesh is a daring act by any standards, and certainly a source of self-fascination in the age of the Game Boy.[27] Incessantly, the music authorizes his disembodiment, as he, the protagonist, follows its every detail. Cartoon-like, psycho and sick in a laddish way, Williams comes across as on the edge of a very put-on nervous breakdown. This is why the narrativity in 'Rock DJ', I would suggest, functions not only as a form of masking, but also a convincing indicator of how masculinity is signified in different ways in pop. Let me explain.

As a master of reinvention, Williams takes on new roles with every new album released. Following his *Sing When You're Winning*, the album *Swing When You're Winning*, released in 2001, depicted Williams on the album sleeve conservatively dressed in black tie and tuxedo. Suave, handsome and comfortably conventional, he would now turn to sealing his status through a wider audience. The Frank Sinatra-tribute album *Swing When You're Winning* contained an original of ole blue-eyes himself mixed into 'It Was A Very Good Year', as well as a sexy collaboration with Nicole Kidman on the aptly titled track 'Somethin' Stupid'. How could Williams fail to seduce millions of new fans? All of which led to his one-man show at London's Royal Albert Hall on a night when this dowdy old hall would be converted into a glitzy venue.

Framing a massive video screen were his initials, R W, lit up large, looming over an orchestra that was divided by a Vegas-type staircase, with a grand piano gracing a lower stage surrounded by wine and dine tables occupied by distinguished guests. Sheryl Garratt, for *The Observer*, wrote: 'What a swell party it was. Not being an opera fan, I don't often see 3,500 people in black tie and evening gowns.' Over Williams's charisma Garratt would enthuse: 'Cheeky, witty, good-looking with a talent for self-deprecating humour and plenty of flaws to make him human, he can charm your granny on chat shows, make your little sister scream, and make all but the most cynical of us smile.'[28] Clearly there was little new in this act. The combination of personal style, affectation and flawless production in *Swing When You're Winning* followed remarkably closely in the footsteps of other suave dandies, one of which is a legendary icon.

Old enough to be Williams's father, with a background in fine arts (from Newcastle University), Bryan Ferry had an avid interest in American pop art of the 1950s and 1960s. Over the years he would cultivate an elegance that is polished with a verve and intensity that drew on a mix of Sinatra, the French chanson crooning of Gainsbourg and the passion of Johnnie Ray. Ferry's change of style in the late 1970s and early 1980s capitalized on the New Romantics' melancholic

---

[27]   Developed by Nintendo the Game Boy is a handheld game console used to control top-selling computer games, such as the killer game *Tetris*, which sold around 30 million copies in the US.

[28]   'Robbie Williams: Royal Albert Hall, London', *The Observer*, 14 October 2001.

lustre and glamour: tailored suits, white single-breasted jackets, windswept jet black hair, perfectly chiselled face and a slim physique would complement the velvet voice that has dominated decades of British pop music. In an interview with *Melody Maker* from 1975 Ferry described his approach:

> I try to throw in some witticism or a twist, just to relieve the tension. I like to interlace, not so much humour, but wit whenever possible because it can all seem as though it's getting too heavy. There's something very English about that.[29]

Equally revealing in this above extract is the interviewer, Caroline Coon's response to Ferry, whose subjective adulations highlight his dandification: 'He's something of a masochist, living on the knife-edge of an identity crisis. He strains himself to the limit, turning his dilemma and struggle into great music.' Then shifting the focus of her critique from Ferry's songs and artistic production to aspects of his persona – dress code, attitude, temperament, class and sexual orientation – Coon enthuses:

> He aspires to a cultural style which is the antithesis of Newcastle's bleak Victorian back streets. But so far his attempts at finesse and refinement have been as rustic as Rousseau's attempts to paint realistically were primitive. Which is not to say they have lacked charm. His conquering strength, through this attempted metamorphosis, has been his *total lack of self-indulgence*. He pares the fantasies and desires down to the bone. His despair, dragged across the stage, could so easily become cheap melodrama. But it never does.[30]

A spate of promo videos from the mid-1980s to late 1980s fit neatly into the characterization described by Coon above: 'Slave To Love', 'Don't Stop The Dance', 'Windswept', 'Help Me', 'Kiss and Tell', 'Limbo', 'Let's Stick Together' and 'Is Your Love Strong Enough?'

Now aside from the astute promotional trickery that met the demands of MTV in its early years, the effect of these videos is located in the schmaltz of their seductive messages, conveyed through the poise of a self-centred persona. Vanity and *ennui* are mastered in a way that wins over the viewer through a sultry, enchanting charm. Image-wise, Ferry owes much to the London fashion designer Antony Price, whose chic clothes designs have been highly acclaimed.[31] And as part of the wider discourse on hegemonic masculinity, Ferry's romantic narrative formula is one of the male seeking love and attention of females, as his videos serve to illustrate.

---

[29]   'Bryan Ferry: Putting On The Style', *Melody Maker*, 12 July 1975.

[30]   Ibid. (my emphasis).

[31]   Antony Price has also designed clothes for artists such as the Rolling Stones, Duran Duran and Bowie.

'Slave To Love' tells us how Ferry is a 'slave to love' and that 'to need a woman, you've got to know how the strong get weak, and the rich get poor'. Excessively stylish, even for its time, this romantic ballad is visually staged through dark colours; an abundance of shadows and night scenes prevails, with an ever so obvious touch of *film noir* to create a soft mood. All the way through, beautiful, slender women glide around, flirtatious in their address.[32] Voyeuristically, Ferry is positioned as onlooker at the beginning, toying with the art of seduction at the same time as somehow conveying his vulnerability. Gradually, absorbing more of the camera's gaze, he entices the viewer into the inner world of his web.[33]

Only half way through the video for 'Slave To Love' is Ferry seen singing (or rather miming) the song's hook. Up to this point it is the females who mouth his words. Seamless in its flow, this video accentuates the seductive skills of the romantic balladeer. Brimming with emotion, Ferry's voice is distinctive as he tells the girl he can't escape being a slave to her love. Most of all, his timbral resonance mirrors his masculine, debonair appearance as a clear instance of 'vocal costuming'. Something mysterious emerges in the sleekness of Ferry's look or rather 'gaze' as he moves with effortless grace through the scenes of this video, always diverting his gaze from the camera to the women.[34] Disseminated by a blatant strategy of seduction, Ferry's performance in this video places vanity high on the list of priorities for the male performer. Marketing his own desirability, his degree of self-aestheticization evokes an impression of coolness, which attempts to be laid-back and non-elaborate.[35] In this sense, there can be little doubt that Ferry's elegance and nonchalance falls under the rubric of dandyism *á la Brummell*.

---

[32] Beautiful women regularly feature in his videos and as cover models on his and Roxy Music albums. Take singer and disco queen of the 1970s, Amanda Lear, who Ferry dated and who was photographed with a black jaguar for the cover of the Roxy Music album *For Your Pleasure*. She later went on to have a relationship with Bowie. Ferry's relationship with Jerry Hall broke up following a simultaneous affair with Jagger. Speculation suggests that his song 'Kiss and Tell' from the *Bête Noire* album was a response to Hall's tell-all book about their relationship.

[33] That Ferry's videos from the 1980s were stylized in this way speaks volumes about the cultural and social temperature of this period in British history. Also see Buckley (2004b).

[34] The construction of the decentred spectator is a result of the artist not meeting the camera's gaze for anything more than a short moment. A requirement of MTV has been to entice the young viewer in ways that would keep them watching. As E. Ann Kaplan puts it: 'The overall commercial framework of MTV (as of all television) requires (...) locking the spectator into the hypnotized state of *impending* satisfaction; "centering" must take place for short periods if the requisite consumption mechanism is to work' (Kaplan 1987, p. 47, author's emphasis). In Ferry's videos the 'centring' effect is created by shots of him lip-synching for short periods that are usually juxtaposed with shots of beautiful women who, in the case of 'Slave To Love', also lip-synch his voice.

[35] On the matter of flamboyancy in pop, I am in agreement with George Walden that Elton John's extravagance in dress codes excludes him from classification as dandy (Walden 2002, p. 53).

Let us turn to the music. The tempo of 'Slave To Love', a main element in maintaining tension throughout, controls the erotic, languid groove. Textures are porous, accommodating contrasting timbres in the form of guitar fills and synth swirls, while Ferry's voice is highly reverbed and dominating. Slinky melodic phrasing, steady and assured, affords Ferry recourse to smoothing out phrases leisurely, elasticizing certain tones to heighten the narrative. The studio mix of this song is set for Ferry's outpouring of sentiments dealing with falling in or out of love. His biography stages subjectivity, which is accessed by every musical code, while his vocal mannerisms emerge in alliance with his relationship to the narrative and the persona he takes on. An amalgamation of musical features (crooning, soft vocal tones, gentle synth sweeps, tidy guitar fills, pleasant studio effects, and so on) is the result that fetishizes the dandy character; a character that has not been without its controversies in the public sphere.[36] Reading his masculinity in this way, a whole range of strategies come to the fore that symbolize the New Man of the 1980s. Now to a very different type of performance that has also evoked responses of Anglomania.

### Ashes to Ashes: 'The Music is the Mask ...'

Bowie's iconic 'Ashes to Ashes' video is a fascinating relic of what was happening in the run up to 'Slave to Love' and the New Romantic scene. Directed by David Mallet, this original video helped shoot the single to number one in the UK charts in 1980. As a sequel to Bowie's first big hit and video 'Space Oddity' from 1969, 'Ashes to Ashes' is even by today's standards one of the most lavish videos ever produced. Featuring Bowie in the famous silver metallic net Pierrot costume

---

[36] In 2006 another big hit from the 1980s, 'Don't Stop the Dance', became the music used for a TV commercial to market clothes for Scandinavia's huge men's clothes chain Dressmann. In the same year Ferry became the face of the clothing range *Autograph* for Marks and Spencer, which coincided with the release of his new album *Slave To Love: Best of the Ballads*. Personal biography and temperament plays a major role in establishing and perpetuating celebrity status, which, as we have seen, is not without its problems when indiscretions trip up the artist. An interview with the German newspaper *Welt am Sonntag* outraged readers in Germany and abroad when Ferry declared his admiration for the Nazis, claiming that he called his studio in west London his Führerbunker. This incident was brought to the British public's notice in an article run by *The Independent*, 'Bryan Ferry's Nazi gaffe', 15 April 2007, where they cited Ferry: "'My God, the Nazis knew how to put themselves in the limelight and present themselves", he said. "Leni Riefenstahl's movies and Albert Speer's buildings and the mass parades and the flags – just amazing. Really beautiful.'" Such tactless opinions are fodder for the media and stark reminders that controversy shapes the rhetoric of pop. Pop spectacles are also about cultural identity and convey narratives about the social and political spaces we occupy. The implication here is that patterns of behaviour comprise the rituals between artists, fans, journalists and musicians, which, in the end, reflect the credibility or realness of their currency.

designed by Natasha Kornilof, with the hat created by Gretchen Fenston, the video breaks new ground for its time by integrating solarized colour scenes in contrast to bold black and white ones, with the aid of the Quantel paintbox pioneering technique. The spectacle of Bowie's ornate Pierrot costume, a central marker for his *Scary Monsters* period, is made memorable by the appearance of British pop icon Steve Strange, lead singer of Visage, and other members of the London Blitz scene,[37] all forerunners of the New Romantics movement in Britain.

But from where did the idea for this Pierrot look derive? In 1967 Bowie had appeared in a Lindsay Kemp mime production, *Pierrot in Turquoise*. Kornilof also designed the costume for this production, an elaborate affair sporting a spotted blouse, knee breeches and Elizabethan ruff. With white clown make-up, Bowie's androgynous image had direct associations with the representations of the Pierrot figures found in *commedia dell'arte*. A French variant of the Italian Pedrolino, Pierrot was conceived by Jean-Gaspard Deburau, the protagonist of the famous folk song 'Au Clair de la Lune'. What is striking about Pierrot is his temperament; he is naive, the object of ridicule and pranks, yet always trusting. Frequently, Pierrot is depicted as moonstruck, vacant and far removed from reality. Notably, Bowie would perform his 'The Man Who Sold the World' with New York opera star Klaus Nomi, dressed in Pierrot costumes.

In a song all about spacemen turning into junkies, Bowie reintroduces Major Tom (from his hit 'Space Oddity'), who, no longer a hippy astronaut, is 'hitting an all-time low'. References to Major Tom are evidenced by Bowie's spacesuit, as he is depicted trapped within a padded room on a hospital life-support system. The music contributes significantly to the visual coagulation of a wide variety of frame shots and the image shifts by Bowie. Mallet's extravagant video, with solarized colour, is equally matched by Tony Visconti's spectacular production of Bowie's vocal performance. Positioned in a complex mix, his voice is staged alongside stark multitracked guitar synthesizers, a raw funk bass line and eerie strings. One might say his sonic conception lives up to the artifice of his Pierrot construction, as the playfulness of his persona is registered through vocal transformations from the high pitched nasal sound of his Ziggy Stardust character to the lower, raspier lines, with a wide use of effects.

Filming pop performances, such as 'Ashes to Ashes', has undoubtedly played a critical role in paving the way forward for marketing British identity. With the

---

[37]    The Blitz Kids were a group that frequented the Blitz nightclub in the early 1980s, including Boy George and his friend Marilyn, Steve Strange, Martin Degville, Phillip Sallon and others. As a reaction to the punk movement, the Blitz Kids, androgynous by all counts, sought a new direction by wearing garish home-made costumes and clothing and buckets full of make-up. The Australian performance artist Leigh Bowery was reportedly the weirdest of all. He would turn up to the club in an outrageous outfit each night and one of his most memorable attires was several rivulets of melted candle wax that ran down his head across his candelabra. Boy George paid tribute to the Blitz Kids in his musical *Taboo*, in which he played the role of Bowery.

launch of MTV, Bowie and Ferry, already in their mid-thirties, cast themselves amongst the next generation of pop superstars. The packaging of pop artists now occurred on a scale never witnessed before. Both these men were ideally suited for the MTV era and stadium rock venues. In Bowie's case, as Buckley puts it: 'The 1980s had finally caught up with what Bowie had been doing since around 1968 – mixing media' (Buckley 2000, p. 386). Accordingly, his videos became more polished, while his image was toned down to become less confrontational. One of the most iconic videos of the 1980s, 'Ashes to Ashes' attests to the mutability of Bowie's masculinity and his propensity for reinvention. And while the fantasy at work in a long line of songs might have hinged on multiple roles, his Pierrot character was embedded in much of his earlier material. In an article for *Rolling Stone* from 1972 he would link this to musical expression:

> What the music says may be serious, but as a medium it should not be questioned, analysed, or taken too seriously. I think it should be tarted up, made into a prostitute, a parody of itself. It should be the clown, the Pierrot medium. The music is the mask the message wears – the music is the Pierrot and I, the performer, am the message.

Intriguingly, Bowie's enactment of different types of masculinity, both regressive and progressive, has maintained his immense popularity. Imitation, a prime ingredient of Bowie's act, is something that typifies the dandified performance, as artists cross-reference one another in a variety of ways.

Another song and video that exemplifies this is from an earlier period, 1967. 'We Love You', written by Jagger and Richards for the Rolling Stones, sets out to disrupt stereotypical codes of gender and social inequality. Parodying the Beatles' 'All You Need Is Love', it consists of phrases, such as 'we don't care if you hound we' and 'you will never win we'. Powerfully political for its time, the song stands as a commentary on the sentences dished out to two members of the band who were caught in the possession of drugs. So draconian were these sentences that the editor of the conservative newspaper *The Times* published a harsh, damning lead commentary that became legendary.[38] Quite ingeniously, the video references the infamous court trial of Oscar Wilde in 1895 by featuring Jagger, Richards, Marianne Faithfull and Brian Jones in theatricalized roles not unlike Bowie in 'Ashes to Ashes'. Jones, heavily under the influence of drugs while filming, spoofs the social hypocrisies of Wilde's historic trial through his own personal journey into psychedelia. Experimental musical devices, such as the mixing of Watts's drum parts at the fore, an overdose of phasing, tape effects and distortion, all contribute to the small sample phrase implanted from the flipside

---

[38]    As editor of *The Times*, William Rees-Mogg was critical of the court's decision in an editorial. This is thought to have contributed to the success of the Stones' appeal against the sentences. He concluded that tolerance and equity were necessary and that Mr Jagger had the right to be treated exactly the same as anyone else.

song as a tag. 'We Love You' brings to the fore the traditions that govern etiquette through the repetition of conventions and British style, parodying them from start to finish. Certainly, the crafting of flamboyancy in 'We Love You' and 'Ashes to Ashes' helped lay down the foundations for musical trends in the next decades, reminding us that in pop stylistic regurgitation is one of the richest sources of innovation, dependent on large doses of nostalgia and insanity. With such over-the-topness it is impossible not be impressed by the sheer flamboyancy of such pop acts from the 1960s and 1970s. For in the creative flair of Bowie, Jagger, Ferry and the others we have considered, that personal quality which Barbey referred to as *esprit* is omnipresent. Always among the attributes of musical performance are comedical mannerisms, physical features and vocal sounds that stand out and give weight to wit, humour and fun – 'the three-sided *esprit* of England' (D'Aurevilly 1988, p. 57). Barbey would insist that the *esprit* of the British dandy was so unique that it could not be transferred from one place to the next: 'Like certain wines, which will not bear a voyage, it must be drunk at home' (ibid., p. 58). On top of this, in his adulation of Britishness, he would add that 'the *esprit* of a country is of the same nature as the most beautiful roses, which are the first to fade' (ibid.). With regard to pop trends in Britain Barbey's claim certainly seems to have rung true.

## Conclusion

One of the most irresistible aspects of pop is its idealization of subjectivity. As we have seen in this chapter, performance spaces provide the material basis for understanding why genres evolve and how listening competence is shaped. Working out the subjectivity of an artist opens up a range of categories for considering further the exclusivity of male performance. Not coincidentally, performance practices are linked to the way we pigeonhole national characteristics.

Which brings us back to playing out one's identity. Musical performances are about sustaining an emotional reality that prioritizes fidelity and solidarity, hence giving audiences a sense of the 'real self'. In his mission the pop dandy feeds off empathic responses in order to achieve his goals. Mastering one's act within situational contexts is a central imperative. There is a reason Baudelaire identified temperament as a main part of the dandy in relation to his historical and cultural surrounds. The one bothersome constituent of temperament is naivety. Depending on one's own interpretation, this offers a way forward for understanding subjectivity, and as Baudelaire insists, its charge lies in the arbitration of the 'natural' as much as the aesthetic qualities of representation.

Audio-visual texts, as we have seen, highlight aspects of dandyism, conveying the conventions and practices that profile the subject according to nationality, class, gender, sexuality and race. With the recording, then, the magnification of the star, aurally and visually, reveals in close-up the body as much as its temperament. Self-aestheticization through the body on display is an intricate matter in pop analysis, and contingent on technology's role in creating the image and enabling its every repetition. For video performances are simulated events, reinscribing the body in ways that only appear 'real', but in actual fact are idealized. This is why temperament is a problematic facet of dandyism, a metaphor for 'painting oneself' and using this as a strategic tool. Baudelaire theorizes vice through the individual's motives for painting himself as a 'natural entity', which qualifies the aesthete's existence. By 1846, though, Baudelaire's vision of the dandy had altered as he began to argue that art could only be constituted in itself (rather than the individual). This would support his argument that the modern characteristics of decadence and superficiality proved that the dandy's temperament was unique.

In popular music punk illustrated a pop style in revolt as Vicious provided a mocking critique of not only the fashion of the day, but also the music and how pretentious performing music had become. Dispelling the images associated with prog- and glam-rock, Vicious gave a biting commentary on British culture by way of musical anarchy. Earlier than this, the Mod movement of the 1960s had had similar intentions, as reflected in The Kinks' songs one decade earlier. The Mod look and sound, shaped by this group's unique performance style, would motivate a new generation of dandies, an aspect I will explore at the start of Chapter 6. To what extent musical traditions have defined pop music has as much to do with nationality and ethnicity as gender. Given the resurgence of countless styles following The Kinks, there is a good argument for tracing the influence of the Mods and their special variant of Britishness. Pop artists are fitting examples of this, as they preserve structures and features that are historically grounded in notions of belonging.

A key aspect of the pop performance centres around spectacularity, and pop dandyism is framed by the changing attributes of representation and poise. Spectacularly, pop artists aestheticize themselves through an acute awareness of their personal assets. Constructing oneself for the entertainment of others, though, throws up countless contradictions. For music complicates our making sense of a performer and working out what is for 'real'. This is the subject of the next chapter, where I propose other ways for understanding the antics of the pop dandy.

# Chapter 3

# Virtual Insanity or the 'Real Thing'?

It's the difference between being hip and being straight, between Mick Jagger and Paul McCartney. I think dandyism comes in non-conformity, and I've always been drawn to the rebel.

Nick Hart, British fashion designer[1]

Resurrecting the topic of authenticity, my debate in this chapter relates to musical materialization, vocality, and interpretation. What makes a performance or performer convince an audience? And how does the articulation of voices in pop illustrate the self-referential qualities of music? In a process where structures of identification are animated through musical positions and 'afforded corporeal form', the pop fantasy depends on what Middleton has described as 'a variability only enhanced when structures of video or film gazes intersect with the network of voice positions' (Middleton 2006, p. 237). Middleton's application of the concept 'voice positions' concerns the rituals of address that convey subjectivity. At the core of this is the experience of 'authenticity-markers' and their incorporation into narratives. Implicated in this is the 'popular voice', which operates in specific ways. Generically, all audio-visual indicators in pop cannot be divorced from assumptions of personal taste. And, like their fans, pop artists draw on notions of style and genre to cross-reference one another. In this way, musical citation frames and legitimates one stylistic preference over another.

Pop videos exemplify this brilliantly by their spectacularization of subjective desire. The disciplining of the body during musical performance is demonstrative of the type of bond that exists between performer and audience. When a singer's intimacy is structured through their high visibility (often larger than life if one considers the technological ramifications of mediation), it is always made appealing through bodily display (Kassabian 2001). As a result, the performativity of the singer is self-referential, and has to do with artists being conscious of themselves as objects of desire. Varying in their ways of showing off, artists will go to great pains to make themselves desirable. Casting oneself in the role of entertainer inevitably suggests something vain, yet at the same time deeply personal. In this light, then, I want to examine closely how the body functions with music and what kind of interrelationships exist between personal style and spectacle.

In the case of the late Robert Palmer, he turned to countless popular styles during the span of a relatively long career, where his style of performance says much about his construction of masculinity. His representation, as we will see, is

---

[1]    In Cicolini (2005, p. 48).

chauvinistic; it normalizes masculinity at work, albeit elegantly and superficially. Much the same applies to Ferry (post-Roxy Music), whose smooth, crooning vocal style is seductive through a range of love songs. Conversely, Robert Smith of The Cure reveals a tactic of distancing and withdrawal. Displaying a Gothic-type masculinity that is about disengagement, Smith's persona slots into the escapist ideology of the New Wave romantics of the day. Impassivity, in his case, works as a strategy for distancing the male performer from the confines of normative masculinity (Biddle and Jarman-Ivens 2007).

During the course of this chapter the performance strategies of Williams, as well as Kay, Morrissey, the Pet Shop Boys, Palmer and Smith, will shape the argument that the gendered body forms a major part of understanding how musical style functions. In fact, to understand any type of pop subjectivity, we need to talk about the body. In her discussion of music's impact on the body, Susan Fast critiques Middleton's notions (1990) of the prelinguistic level of musical understanding by considering the kinetic qualities of riffs. That sound 'touches us' physically and creates intimate forms of human contact has, according to Fast, important implications for studying sexuality and music, especially through the homosociality of boys performing. Musical sounds are special because they are 'out of the ordinary', and, as Fast ascertains, they are usually 'louder than everyday sounds for a sustained period of time' (Fast 2001, p. 131). Consequently, sound steers our attention in a physical and emotional direction as its impact is *felt* directly through the body. But it is not only the 'tactile nature' of sound that is relevant here. It is also the 'suspension of everyday time' (ibid., p. 132) through sound that secures us and permits us to reconnect with the orders outside our daily lives. Temporally, then, gestures and movements respond to music in ways that always 'tell a story'.

My intention in this chapter is to reveal the close connection between music and visual imagery and the signifiers of play that operate on multiple levels. Identifying selected moments of audio-visual spectacle are therefore intended to further expose the temperamental traits of the artist, which, in turn, give rise to readings of representation. Building on Middleton's discourse of the 'real thing' and Fast's idea of 'out-of-ordinariness', this part of my study takes on a critical reading of conventions and norms in popular music. Pop performances, after all, are an affirmation of subjectivity that becomes an orthodoxy for evaluating musical practice.

## Let Me Entertain You! Spectacular Robbie Williams and Jay Kay

The pop identity is imitative of its historical, political and social grounding, where musical genres are constantly negotiable. 'Let me entertain you', Williams belted out for the most part of 1997 as he parodied the tongue-wagging, glam singer Gene Simmons of the rock band Kiss. Cavorting around in a tight latex catsuit, with clips of him off-stage making out with his groupies, the video of 'Let Me Entertain

You' is a striking example of stylistic appropriation. In an over-spectacularized manner, Williams's performance is not only pure spoof of 1970s rock, but also an example of camp, excess and self-parody: 'Hell is gone and heaven's here, there's nothing left for you to fear, Shake your arse come over here, now scream.'

In the make-up room prior to the big event, Williams prepares to go on stage to face a packed stadium. The soundtrack is an expansive, glossy production, energised through overlaid swells of instrumental backing that build to the anthemic chorus hook. Both sound and imagery magnify Williams's larger-than-life persona as his musical style pays tribute to a legacy of artists – David Bowie, Freddie Mercury, Marc Bolan, Gary Glitter, Elton John and the New York Dolls, to mention a few. Williams has no qualms in slapping on the make-up and sidestepping the conventions of masculinity. Unashamedly pretentious, his performance pays homage to the rock and metal artist.

Performativity in 'Let Me Entertain You', however, is of a different kind from that in the 'Rock DJ' video (see Chapter 2). Playing around with rock conventions in a send-up that involves a bizarre set of mannerisms, Williams turns to a wide array of props. Garish costumes, lighting and make-up make Williams's hedonistic act a vibrant spectacle. Conditional on all sorts of physical responses, his temperament is shaped by nuances of musical expression rich in connotation. Mostly, it is his vocal delivery that tells us where he comes from and where he belongs. Frith has stressed the importance of 'national characteristics' through which a 'nodded head can be "yes" or "no", eye contact a mark of respect or contempt' (Frith 1996, pp. 216–17), and so on. Williams's quasi-conversational style in 'Let Me Entertain You', his working-class accent, quirky mannerisms and speech are all cultural-specific examples of this. Unmistakeably British through all the innuendos of language, mannerism and humour, his act effortlessly turns into seduction.

While much of the success of British artists comes about through the popularization of American style and accent, especially in terms of language, Williams tries to orbit this by adhering to Northern Englishness.[2] Operating within established genres such as blues, R&B, rap and hip-hop, often results in a more Americanized accent, as a copy of the original. However, this practice is not seen so overtly in many British artists, where English accents are deliberately sustained to perpetuate notions of Britishness. Consciously, bands and artists authenticate a part of their identity, which, when placed in a broader context, constitutes a reaction against genres that are foreign and that quintessentialize North American music (Moy 2007, p. 59). For this reason many British bands and artists appropriate one another in order to hold on to their 'real selves'. Take 'All Around the World', from

---

[2]   Shara Rambarran has accurately pointed out that Williams's Northern-ness is not entirely without its problems (personal correspondence). Brought up in the Midlands, he has a local Stoke-on-Trent accent. But as this is an adjacent area to Greater Manchester (one hour away by car on the motorway), it is only subtleties that will disclose any difference. Rambarran has also suggested that when he joined Take That (a Manchester band), his accent was strikingly Mancunian.

Oasis's third album, *Be Here Now*.[3] This over-indulgent performance style harks back to the Beatles. Not only with the obvious reference to 'Yellow Submarine', the main refrain from the Beatles' 'Hey Jude' is more than a subtle referent in the backing vocals towards the end.[4] Oasis songs frequently demonstrate that nostalgia, a prime ingredient of pop style, is evident in the repetition of a subjectivity that projects values that are 'home-grown' and safe.

Which returns me to the question of subjectivity and how pop texts contribute to the construction of the staged persona. As I read it, the effect of dandifying is desire-inducing and contingent on bodily display. Granted, the body is turned into the pop star's greatest virtue. Far removed from Williams is dandy-boy Jay Kay, lead singer for Jamiroquai. Once described as Britain's only white funkster, he has been referred to as the 'cat in the hat' because of the elaborate headgear he dons.[5] Of all the artists discussed in this book, Kay stands out most for his quirky appropriation of African American style. In one of Jamiroquai's best-known videos,[6] 'Virtual Insanity', directed by Jonathan Glazer, the stage is set for performing out a fantasy in a memorable dance routine. Consisting of a brightly lit white room with a grey moving floor, the main performance space is simple enough to profile Kay's sport-like choreography. Facing the camera for most of the time, his agility is characterized by nifty footwork that enables him to glide over the moving floor. Interpolated with shots of the rest of the band being blown away through a corridor, is a magnified cockroach crawling around the floor and a crow flying in slow motion in and out of the picture. Stylistically, the abstract insertion of random objects visually mirrors Kay's musical hybridity, which is lifted from acid jazz and the dance scene into mainstream funk pop. Moving to the tightest groove, his slick choreography taps into a legacy of African American artists such as George Clinton, Michael Jackson, Prince, Little Richard and James Brown.

Kay's colourful performances match his biography off-stage. Fashioned around extravagance and excess, his temperament, 'as we know it' from the

---

[3]    This song peaked at number one in January 1998, 30 years on from the Stones' 'We Love You'.

[4]    Taking Valerie Faris and Jonathan Dayton six months to produce, the video of 'All Around the World' is as ostentatious as the song. Allegedly, a team of 24 computer animators were brought in to produce a video that resonates with references to the Beatles' film *Yellow Submarine*. Shot in a yellow spaceship, the band appears against a psychedelic backdrop of animated iconography, which in turn works to profile Noel Gallagher's affected and characteristically insolent performance style.

[5]    In 2005 he founded his own trendy label, Quai. See http://showbiz.sky.com/showbiz/article/0,50001-1186640,00.html.

[6]    This video won four awards at the 1997 MTV Video Music awards, and in 2006 was voted ninth on an MTV poll for the most path-breaking music videos of all time.

media press, is wild, reckless and hedonist.[7] Gossip surrounds his quick temper, love of fast cars, beautiful women and designer hats. Pop subjectivity, after all, is dependent on being seen in 'real life', a quality that is constituted within the expressive zone of stylization and foisted on the artist by the media. Ultimately, the oscillation between stage presence and the private sphere is a compelling indictment of the hyperrealism associated with the dandy persona, where pent-up feelings, judgements, slander and public condemnation impact our perceptions of a performer as we meet the camera's gaze. Always layered, stardom leads to the belief of experiencing the 'real person'. That the narrativity of Kay's playboy existence informs his screen and audio performances is part of the disciplined figuration of musical performance.

---

[7]    One case in point involves reports of a brawl with the paparazzi outside the trendy London club Kabaret Prophecy, which resulted in Kay launching a verbal and physical attack on the nearest reporter, Alan Chapman, leading to an arrest and a caution for common assault. Again, this is an example of how media hype narrates the conditions of the dandified subject, authenticating his star status. Ben Walsh's concert review verifies this point:

The majority of the 18,000 crowd appeared to appreciate the return of the diminutive eco-funkster in his obligatory silly (sorry, trendsetting 'the man's a style icon', according to GQ) hat. This evening, he sported some preposterous shiny, Native American-style headgear. [...] There was a great deal of this Prince-lite material that Kay bombarded us with. 'Sugar spice/ I'm on the phone/ It feels good I need a little sexfunk right now/ I want you, I wanna lick you up and down', he exclaimed on the single 'Feels Just Like It Should'. He duly explained to us that the song is about the 'sex', and quite frankly we could have done without Kay's 'comic' interludes. At various points, he warbled on about the local council (for not allowing the gig to go on later than 9 pm), his speeding offences (he was caught doing 111 mph in 1998), and his old drug habit. It's this sort of baloney that gives the band a bad press and inspires an exceptional degree of vitriol – one paper ran a gig review under the headline 'Prat in the Hat', and Blender magazine dubbed him 'the white, talentless Stevie Wonder' (*The Independent*, 5 July 2005).

Another article, also in *The Independent*, one month later, this time an interview with Jay Kay (by Dan Gennoe), includes the following account:

It's a very different Jay Kay waiting at the end of Horsenden Manor's winding gravel drive. Dressed head to toe in black, he looks business-like and purposeful; every inch the self-assured 35-year-old, whose single-minded determination has seen him sell 20 million albums and swap a squat in Ealing, west London, for a 72-acre Buckinghamshire estate, complete with meadow, trout lake, recording studio and race-track. The 300-year-old estate is the perfect retreat for an ecologically minded multi-millionaire with a serious car habit. Calm and serene, there's nature, green and lush, by the mile, and garage space to match. The gleaming black £500,000 Ferrari Enzo, the Aston Martin DB5 and Coco Chanel's stretch Mercedes, highlights of one of the world's most enviable private car collections, remind you that their owner is one of the last of a dying breed: the genuine rock star. Today though, the cars are staying in the garage. Kay has only just got his licence back after a six-month ban for speeding – his fourth – and he'd like to keep it a little while longer. In any case, it's clear that he's not in the mood for living up to his wild reputation (*The Independent*, 6 August 2005).

### 'You Have Killed Me!': Tropes of Hyperbole in Morrissey and the Pet Shop Boys

Another artist whose biographical material mobilizes signifiers of desire, appeal, control and ironic intent is Morrissey. Known for his ambivalence, he plays on notions of mystification by taunting the fan (Hawkins 2002). Middleton points out that a strategy of ambiguity 'leaves sexual identification blurred' (Middleton 2006, p. 127). Invariably, this disrupts norms. Sexual ambiguity in pop is 'extensively shaped by modes of performative display predisposed to the attractions of camp' (ibid.), a matter I pursue in Chapter 5 when discussing Morrissey's vocality.

The structuring of temperament in self-conscious aesthetes like Morrissey is positioned by a calculated stylization. Vanity makes a pop artist adorable. What's more, everybody who is a Moz fan knows that the melodrama of the miserable depressive unveils a true splendour. Cunningly, Morrissey's sentimentality is crafted by a rhetoric that is nonchalant and highly contrived; a prime characteristic of the dandy that Barbey proclaimed 'gives a man that sphinx-like air which interests as a mystery and troubles as a danger' (D'Aurevilly 1988, p. 55). As part of the contract with his fans, Morrissey passes 'from expression into action – attitude, gesture, and the inflexion of the voice' (ibid., p. 56). Let us consider this by means of a video example.

Characterized by mournfulness, his vocal tone promises an intimacy that entices the listener. 'You Have Killed Me', the first cut from Morrissey's album *Ringleader of the Tormentors*, released in 2006, vividly theatricalizes the storytelling tactic of his act. Much hype surrounded the launch of this song, which carries a cryptic reference to the film *Accattone*, from 1961, directed by the famous Italian film director, philosopher and writer Pier Paolo Pasolini.[8] The first two lines of the lyrics, 'Pasolini is me, *Accattone* you'll be', are a chilling reference to Pasolini, whose brutal murder on the beach of Ostia, near Rome, has never been cleared up.

---

[8] There is little doubt that Pasolini's murder was tied up to his political views. Intellectually, he could stoke up scandals and debates unheard of for their time. Unlike Morrissey, Pasolini was politically uncompromising on many issues. During the disorders of 1969, for example, when students went to the streets in Rome to demonstrate against the police, Pasolini declared himself on the side of the police, who he insisted were the real proletarians who were sent to fight against spoilt brats of the same generation, who had had the fortune of being able to study. Such a controversial statement by a communist did not prevent him from contributing to the Lotta continua movement. Undoubtedly, Pasolini was a fierce opponent of *consumismo* (consumerism), which he insisted had destroyed the fabric of Italian society during the 1960s and early 1970s. It is the subproletariat class that he portrays in his film *Acccattone*, to which he felt an affinity sexually and artistically. Pasolini reacted against the replacement of the *joie de vivre* of boys by the bourgeois, heteronormative pressures of house and family. In addition, he also protested against the general diminution of Italian dialects by writing some of his work in the dialect of Friulian, from the region where he grew up.

Melodramatic in its delivery, the video opens with an introduction in Italian by a compère introducing Morrissey to an audience that is decidedly bourgeois.

Throughout the video Morrissey performs to an audience of a bygone era (set in the 1960s, discernible by hairstyles, clothes, spectacles), as much attention is drawn to their responses. His performance strategy stands out on two counts. First, through the nostalgia of his own legacy (he was 47 when filming this), which strongly references his earlier videos from The Smiths period, 'This Charming man' and 'Panic'. Dressed in a light suit and an open black shirt, he is positioned on stage with his band in the background, silhouetted against a garish pink backlit wall. Exaggerated gestures extract the passion of his delivery. Swaying to the music, Morrissey jerks back his head defiantly on high notes, eyes rolling, with an expression that overemphasizes his earnestness. On the chorus hook 'You have killed me', his mannerisms become all the more expansive as he drives home the message relentlessly. By the time the last lines of the song are howled out, 'I forgive you', resolution is attained as he opens his arms up to the audience who burst into applause; this is camp at its best. Nearing its end, there is a sense of foreboding as to whether the audience is going to be shot, with more than a hint of a reference to Sid Vicious's legendary video 'My Way' from 1977 (see Chapter 6). Alas, Morrissey saves his audience from this indignity.

The second aspect relates to the perpetuation of Morrissey's own biography. Crucial to this performance is a sense of nostalgia, visible in his desire to mine his cultural environment and feign his vulnerability. Fuelled by the elegance of his prose, Morrissey's 'You Have Killed Me' is not dissimilar to Davies' song, 'All of My Friends Were There', where his propensity for wit and snide observation displays the strength of his self-reflexivity (Woods 2007). There is nothing more layered and contradictory than self-mockery. Always transitive, his songs are frank biographical referents that legitimize his celebrity status through an admission of his dramatized crises; the phrase 'you have killed me' can only be destined for sublime irony when performed by Morrissey. For what does it matter if the enemy (the media) has killed him when his longevity is assured by his star status? In many of Morrissey's songs there is evidence of whimsical conjectures of his own mortality, which, as I read them, are indicative of a narcissism that collides with the loathing of his body and disdain for sexual relations (see Chapter 5). Consummation for Morrissey can only be acquired by violence and self-annihilation in the form of a disavowal of his own corporeality. This would explain why Morrissey also assumes a 'masochistic relation' to his male fans by eroticizing men in terms of their 'powerful working-class masculinity' (Bannister 2006, p. 152). Bannister suggests that he flirts with his fans by intimating that he is 'saving himself' for 'that impossible moment' (ibid., p. 154) when he meets them person to person; this is the fantasy of his act that keeps the flame alive.

Biography involves a range of signifiers that are sourced on multiple levels. Seldom have I doubted that the spectacle of the body personalizes musical style. Indeed, the sequences of events the camera follows in the video 'You Have Killed Me' are carefully regulated coded references to a melancholia that is in protest against patriarchy. Such a performative aspect is contingent on intended responses (Tagg 1982). John Richardson makes the valid point that the 'various implications for reception' are based upon 'the attribution of a powerful sense of agency' (Richardson 2007, p. 423). This is borne out by Morrissey's agency in 'You Have Killed Me' and the way he is framed by the 'gaze'. That the backing band serves him also heightens his credibility. This aspect of musical performance is significant. Camera-work in this video captures his every emotion, especially through the use of close-up shots (head and shoulders). Above all, Morrissey's gendered representation raises the question of the gaze – who is this directed towards and why? Bannister's reading of Morrissey's gaze is that it 'forces us to recognise the homoerotic content of our own desire' (Bannister 2006, p. 154). But the reflexivity of such an alienated subject is what actually empowers him. For theatrical display in pop is embodied in various ways, where the emphasis falls on ordinariness and sincerity at one end of the scale, extending over to the superficial and out-of-ordinariness at the opposite end. The performance in 'You Have Killed Me' is one of countless examples of how pop maximizes hyperbole as an emotional crutch.

Two other British artists who turn to hyperbole and sentimentality are Neil Tennant and Chris Lowe. From the outset the Pet Shop Boys have grasped the value of artwork, photography and design in their video productions. Carefully calculated collaborations with scores of creative personalities have contributed to them establishing themselves as leading pop dandies. From 1984 to 1991 they enlisted the help of photographer Eric Watson, who had a major influence on their iconography.[9] They also owe much to graphic designer Mark Farrow (who created the cover for their first album release in 1986). Again, the link between design and musical style conflates masculinity. Hidden in the space between the theatricalized performance and subjectivity is a musical sensibility that fashions their male-ness. Fred Maus puts this down to musical expression:

> The Pet Shop Boys combine the insistent but unaggressive rhythms of dance music with a persistent opulence of timbre, texture and harmony. Rich string timbres, seventh chords and other lush harmonies, reverberation and other devices recreate the *unmanly*, luxurious sound of disco (Maus 2001, p. 385 – my emphasis).

Describing Tennant's voice as 'small, high, thin' and even 'unmanly' is not without its problems. That Maus reads such masculinity as 'full of longing' comes about through an indirectness he perceives in their lyrics and image. Ambivalence in their musical style, as Maus reads it, is intentional and a safeguard against homophobia.

---

[9]    In 2006 the Pet Shop Boys released a retrospective book, *Catalogue*, which impressively documents their achievements not only in electronic pop music, but also artwork and design; this was similar to the legendary collaborative relations of Depeche Mode to Anton Corbijn or New Order to Peter Saville.

This also raises the issue of 'evasion', which, when realized by double-voicedness, renders their style glamorous to a mainstream audience. For a certain audience codes of glamour such as these, as I have argued in earlier studies (Hawkins 1997, 2001), belie a structuring of banality in a manner that might not be perceived as 'unmanly' on any count.[10] On the point of aesthetic perception Maus and I differ, in that I interpret this as an intentional part of their performative display. I will attempt to clarify this by means of example.

Released on DVD in 2003, *Pet Shop Boys: Pop Art – The Videos*, an impressive collection of videos, document the duo's career over almost two decades, highlighting their fun in reinvention and transformation. Personal commentaries and quips accompany each video. Their own references to stylization and artifice underpin a camp sensibility that runs through all their performances. What is more, their esoteric approach to 'pop art' is Warholian in terms of a celebration of artifice and blankness.[11] Carved out by an iconography that depicts them detached and vulnerable, aloof and silly, bland and profound, they are *very* British and Cowardian in mannerism. With Tennant always positioned up front and Lowe lurking in the background, glued to his synthesizer, their flair for entertaining and being earnest emerges as a prime determinant of their queerness.

Their camp sensibility operates as a common denominator, motivating their continual image transformations. This allows them to register shifting emotions without the shamefulness of losing control. A case in point is their dramatic shift in image during 1993, which took place when they collaborated with director Howard Greenhalgh. Furnishing a new look as part of a promotional package for the *Very* album, they donned themselves in garishly coloured costumes with tall cone hats. Advanced computer technology was used to manipulate their looks and movements through a futuristic recasting of themselves. Brilliantly captured by the video 'Can You Forgive Her',[12] this look was matched by an over-the-top disco arrangement as Tennant satirized, with 'heartfelt sensitivity', the anguish of a young man unable to accept his own difference. Plagued by his girlfriend's awareness of his insecurities, the protagonist mockingly punishes himself

---

[10]   Maus argues that Tennant's ambivalence moves beyond the specific issue of closeted gay sexuality, and that the over-articulate style of Tennant, when mapped against Lowe's embodied presence, suggests an 'incompleteness' that establishes their pervasive effect (Maus 2001, p. 386).

[11]   Pop art spread to the USA in the 1960s and Andy Warhol's paintings of soup cans and movie stars intended to make art more meaningful for everyday people. Inevitably, pop art was scorned by high art critics who viewed its vulgarity and sensationalist qualities as absurd and vulgar. Two other prominent pop artists worth mentioning are Roy Lichtenstein and Claes Oldenburg.

[12]   Neil Tennant's use of the song title is taken from the famous Victorian novel *Can You Forgive Her?* by Anthony Trollope, which was first published in serial form in 1864 and 1865. As the first of six novels in the Palliser series, the book was ridiculed by *Punch* (a satirical British newspaper) which referred to it as 'Can You Stand Her?'

by meeting her demands. Throughout the track an element of pretence in the self-loathing aspect of the lyrics is dispelled by the festive and carnivalesque disco arrangement.

As the only pop group to have employed theatrical directors for every one of their live performances and videos, much weight is placed on the details of the spectacle. To take another example: for the promotion of their seventh studio album *Nightlife* in 1999, peroxide wigs, floor-length frocks and NHS glasses were used to present an out-of-the-ordinary image. Camp mannerisms once again accompanied a bizarre look, which, like their musical style on this album, was playful, witty and daring. All in all, the audio-visual codes of such spectacles disclose an idealized form of transgression that intellectualizes their music as oppositional to the norms of mainstream masculinity. In sum, Tennant dandifies his persona through the cultivation of an anti-macho image that is not necessarily unmanly.

From this, I would suggest that this duo's performativity contributes to the signification of masculinity in British pop, the result of a discourse that partakes in yielding up male vulnerability. This point is central to any interpretation of males performing and brings home the rituals of behavioural display among artists who seek the glare of the media spotlight. In the end, how the look conforms to musical expression tells us much about the entertainment space. For pop is ultimately about a set of relations that are meticulously fashioned from start to finish to entice the fan. In this light, the Pet Shop Boys' *esprit* hinges on various fabricated positions, and it is the negotiation of these positions that inscribes reflexive embodiment.

Thus, the spectacles offered up by Morrissey and the Pet Shop Boys affirm their pop identification as based on style, originality, individuality, embodiment and fashion. And, as we have seen, it is the star persona that reinforces codes of categorization in the pop video, with characterization taking place through the body in movement. In pop production the body draws on fashion to entertain, and this becomes the determinant per se for dandyism.

## Fashion and Differentiation in Prince Charming

Fashion, according to Jean Baudrillard (1981a, 1981b), is one of the most effective ways that capitalism restores social discrimination and cultural inequality. Cynically, Baudrillard saw fashion as masking the unchanging aspects of domination under capitalism. In order to become the subject of spectacle (as in the case of the pop dandies presented in this book), the individual has to be automized from various logics that indeed define it. This is the moment, Baudrillard argues, where the subject is recaptured by the formal logic of fashion. Referred to as the 'logic of differentiation', the formal logic of fashion needs to be disentangled from other 'logics which habitually get entangled with it' (Baudrillard 1981b, p. 66). The first is a functional logic of 'use value' (practical operations and utility), where the object is perceived as an instrument with which to do something. The second is an economic logic of 'exchange value' (logic of equivalence), which is linked to commercial exchange, while the third is a logic of 'symbolic exchange' (logic of ambivalence) that refers to the considerations involving relationships. In effect, all these logics can be rendered as possible sources of exchange value for the modernist object, its elements representative of the advertisement's modernity. Baudrillard would insist that an object is only an 'object of consumption' when it is 'released from its psychic determination' as a symbol, and when it is liberated as a 'sign to be recaptured by the formal logic of fashion' (Baudrillard 1981b, p. 67).

Baudrillard's idea of liberation was to argue that the sign is always determined by its differences – for meaning is the result of coded difference. Malcolm Barnard has argued in his study of fashion that the item of fashion (as a Baudrillardian sign) 'exists only within a network of differences' (Barnard 1996, p. 154). As soon as one item is replete, another is created in its place as part of a cycle of 'in-built or planned obsolescence' (ibid.). Consequently, the desire for the latest design is satisfied by this cycle, whereby the play on difference produces notions of 'beauty'. In a postmodern sense, beauty in fashion, like musical style, is a product of projected difference that is capable of presenting the most eccentric traits as eminently attractive. But only as long as they are 'sufficiently different from what went before' (Baudrillard 1981b, p. 79).

Baudrillard's account of fashion also introduces the idea of allegory, which is central to his thoughts on postmodernity. Baudrillard's conception of the object as a reflection of social and economic development is in danger of being reductionist, as he circumvents a need to consider fashion as a structure of intertextual relations. Barnard, in opposition to this, insists that fashion is the 'product of the context' in which it appears, and is an item that can function as fashion in one moment and as just clothing or anti-fashion in another (Barnard 1996, p. 171). Take the platform shoe of the glam-rock and disco period. This could be interpreted as a symbol that both enslaves and liberates, where meaning is produced and destroyed by its own relationships to other objects, symbols and discourses; the point being that fashion and music operate in conceptual spaces that challenge identities and social positionings. With this in mind, I now want to turn my attention to one of the most flamboyant pop dandies of all time.

Enter Adam Ant (his name a pun on adamant). Back in the early 1980s this pop artist self-stylized the role of the highwayman dandy with an avid commitment to fashion. Indebted to original punk groups and artists such as the Sex Pistols, Billy Idol, Chrissie Hynde and Siouxsie Sioux, Ant created a style that encroached on the terrain of glam-rock and masculine gender performance. As well as musical appropriation, he borrowed from the fashion world. Influencing his look and the band's sound was guitarist Marco Pirroni, who, having worked previously with Siouxsie and the Banshees, became lead guitarist and co-songwriter. While maintaining their punk roots, Adam and the Ants turned to a hard rock style that, coupled with a flamboyant look, defined them as one of the first New Romantic bands. Signing with CBS Records, their first break came with the album *Kings of the Wild Frontier*, which topped the UK charts in January 1981. During the same year *Prince Charming* was released, yielding the two single hits, 'Prince Charming' and 'Stand and Deliver'. The lavish videos that promoted these songs are symptomatic of the craze around the start of MTV in 1981.

The video of 'Prince Charming' profiles Ant in the role of a swashbuckling, glamorous dandy surrounded by his band, with an unconventional line-up including two drummers. Ant's dress code spectacularizes this video from start to finish. Remarkably, he dons the same elaborate costume worn by David Hemmings in *The Charge of the Light Brigade* (1969) – a satirical film that thematized the horrific cavalry charge of the British during the Battle of Balaclava in the Crimean War in 1854. 'Prince Charming' is set against a musical backdrop of New Wave, 1950s style guitar twang, African drumming and intensely rhythmic gestures. In contrast to this is the video of 'Stand and Deliver', depicting the protagonist, Ant, at the gallows with a noose around his neck. Finally saved by the other members of the group, he is filmed being cut free from the noose. Melodramatic scenes include Ant leaping through a window onto a banquet table, which was apparently not without its perils. Recalling the fun that went into making the video and dressing up, he recounts: 'I wore a black tricolour hat, black cape, mask and big white shirt over breeches' (Ant 2007, p. 174). He admits that from the outset he reckoned on slapstick and self-ridicule gaining a greater access to a public. Thematically, his spoof of highwaymen would easily appeal to a British audience, designating a romanticization of a bygone age when the phrase 'stand and deliver' was the command ordered during robberies. When rehearsing for this video, Ant had to prepare for the shoot by researching into the *commedia dell'arte*, the tradition from which British pantomime derives. Defending this choice, he would insist that while 'people might just think that "Prince Charming" was "panto", they should know that there's a lot more to the tradition than men dressing up as women and fake cows' (ibid., p. 178).

Rather than being labelled as punk or a New Romantic, Ant preferred to see himself as an entertainer and part of the show business world: 'The music press never got it. They could understand pop stardom, but the videos they were dismissive of because they weren't anti-establishment in the way they wanted' (ibid., p. 179). Turning to videos that were idealistically and romantically oriented, Ant aimed at promoting 'hope in the world', which is 'why 'Prince Charming' has the chorus 'Ridicule is nothing to be scared of'. It meant 'Go out and do what you want to do, believe and you'll succeed' (ibid.). In no uncertain terms, Ant's naivety displays an ego in overdrive. Underlying his glam-oriented post-punk persona, his musical idiom is brought about by a transfusion of styles and mannerisms that aid him in 'putting on' his style. In a video that used a cast of thousands and enlisted the great British actress from the 1960s, Diana Dors, Ant's style could be described as pop operatic and complicit with masquerade. It was as if everything in his performance eschewed the romanticization of the pop idol. Moreover, the high degree of fantasy in his spectacle would enable him to knowingly 'fake' his characterization, while permitting a glimpse of his 'real self' on his terms.

Ant's temperament stands as a reminder of how video representations function as a structuring device, operating differently from one artist to the next. One might say that in both these videos the hero, vulnerable yet in control, can be situated within a wider narrative of male hegemony. In actual point, Ant's excess in dressing up adds a curious dimension to his masculinity, especially in 'Stand And Deliver', where his flamboyancy and dashing good looks only just manage to sustain the modality of heterosexual desire. Moreover, the figuration of the masculine through elaborate pirate costumes, uncannily similar to Johnny Depp's look in *Pirates of the Caribbean*, is spectacularized through a camp quality that positions his act at centre stage. Thus, it is not hard to appreciate why vocality and image in 'Stand And Deliver' would mesmerise the viewer through the total effect of filming, editing, scripting, acting, lighting and, of course, music.

Dwelling on Ant's representation discloses the artist's desire to theatricalize. Somewhat paradoxically, while singing 'I'm the dandy highwayman so sick of easy fashion' in 'Stand And Deliver', he changes his tune in 'Prince Charming', bellowing out the lines, 'Don't you ever, don't you ever, stop being dandy, showing me you're handsome'. Passionate delivery of this kind, with somewhat mixed messages, can be read as charming and camp. This is how musical performance is passed down through the codes of his nationality, social class and gender. Understood in this sense, Ant's act is conditional on playing out the drama of his own construction, as the ground is cleared for his superego to emerge in the form of imaginary characters. The lyrics, as much as the look, are about the male heartthrob who, when falling outside the law and rule, is subjected only to the evaluation of taste. Confronting the camera – face made-up, hair styled, clothes bejewelled with accessories – he acquires his credibility through masquerade, implicating the viewer in his personal fantasy. Such powerful relics in the first generation of MTV stars meant sufficient confidence in one's staged configuration, which worked through musical performance. What then would Baudelaire have made of this?

Baudelaire's conviction was that art is about living, a richly sensuous experience and a vital entity for continually reinventing the imaginative space around us. For Baudelaire, artistic expression had to possess a real utility (not in the way that nineteenth-century utilitarians understood it as art for art's sake, but in the way it addressed the requirements of the human psyche in its practical application). The expressivity of the pop spectacle is traceable back to common human origins, which, as Baudelaire claims, shows up individual sensibility as a two-way process: it is about a relationship between the creative artist and the ambient cultural surround that both nourishes and inhibits him (Howells 1996, p. 62). The most poignant moment in 'Stand and Deliver' occurs not at the climactic point (when death at the gallows is narrowly averted by the protagonist being saved by his fellow band members), but rather in the last repetition of 'stand and deliver your money or your life'. In these few seconds something enchanting occurs, not by virtue of the artist's wilful vanity, but as a result of a vulnerability that turns reality and appearance into cause and effect. Barbey and Baudelaire would insist that the dandy is a symbol of the rejection of a history we are caught up in. With little doubt Ant's princely charm earns him this accolade.


## Judicious but not Capricious: Robert Palmer

Of quite another 'princely charm' was the late Robert Palmer, whose trademark, one might say, was more judicious than capricious. As one of the UK's central blue-eyed soul singers, Palmer was branded a contemporary Casanova-type character in the 1980s, following the release of his album *Riptide*. Soaring to first position in the US charts, the song 'Addicted to Love', from 1986, is closely associated with its legendary video, which not only underscored Palmer's persona, but also immortalized it.[13] The identically clad, pouting, beautiful girls who appear in the video not only taunt the male gaze, but also heighten the sense of visual hyperbole and irony. Directed by Terence Donovan, the video shots depict Palmer surrounded by heavily made-up sexy women, encapsulating one of the most iconic looks of 1980s pop. While on one level a reading of gender trouble in the video might seem pre-eminent – a band of identical-looking girls stare ahead vacantly while simulating the playing of their instruments (Kaplan 1987; McClary 1991) – I am keen to consider a number of other elements.

Roaming over the female bodies, tightly fitted into black mini-skirts, it is as if the camera panders to the 'male gaze' as the girls frame Palmer's performance. Relaxed in his singing style, he sets out to seduce, assisted by the upbeat groove: 'Gonna have to face it, you're addicted to love'. So successful was the video for its day that Palmer would draw on it thematically for many of his other videos: 'Change His Ways', 'Simply Irresistible' and 'I Didn't Mean to Turn You On'. Notably, the video also became the inspiration for a number of other artists, such as Beyoncé's 'Green Light', Shania Twain's 'Man! I Feel Like a Woman' (in which Palmer's women are substituted with men who move in the same way) and Tone Loc's 'Wild Thing'. Coincidental or not, the iconography in 'Addicted to Love' resembles the art deco style of American artist Patrick Nagel, whose style became famous for its attention to the female form. Nagel's representation of the female is discernible through a distinctive shaping of the eyes, black hair, full red-lipped mouths and snow-white skin. An intensity of stylization in Nagel's seductive women not only makes them highly sexualized, but also empowers them in an unobtrusive way. This might be because none of his illustrations involve relationships to men. As well as designing work for Intel, Lucky Strike, *Playboy* and Budweiser, Nagel's international acclaim in the pop world would be sealed by his artwork for Duran Duran, notably on the cover of their best-selling album *Rio*.

---

[13]    The first cut of 'Addicted to Love' was recorded with Chaka Khan, but following contractual problems with her record company, she was withdrawn from the final mix.

As a musical maverick, Palmer would shape his musical style around countless popular styles during the span of a relatively long career (up to his untimely death in 2003). Capitalizing on his natural good looks, a soulful voice and a compelling stage presence, he attracted a huge fan group. Shortly after its release, Palmer would insist that 'Addicted to Love' was not intended as chauvinistic, but rather as a testament to a performance style that captured an era in pop culture of youthful glamour and sexiness. His role in this video can be read as twofold, as 'turn-on' and 'send-up'. That the mechanisms Palmer employs are in part a mockery of the normative notion of love is not in doubt. In a video lacking special effects or fancy editing tricks (as in Ant's 'Prince Charming', Ferry's 'Don't Stop the Dance', Jamiroquai's 'Virtual Insanity' and the Pet Shop Boys' *Nightlife*), Palmer relies solely on his charm (reinforced by the females' charmless expression) to win over the viewer.

The issue of musical schmaltz, though, belies a subversive intention. It would be scarcely possible to imagine a dandy who is not seditious in some way; indeed, the very proposal of attitudes that counteract one another bear this out. Yet Palmer's qualities as performer are mediated as more fun-seeking than capricious. Crooning sonorously, with an ever so slight touch of vibrato and ornamentation, he executes his catchy melodies with a heartfelt sincerity that borders on exaggeration. His vocality involves drawing on a timbre that is rich, deep and male in a middle register; sonic codes like this are the hallmark of a flirtatiousness that can hardly fail. Mixed into the glossy production, his voice is closely miked at the fore of the mix with just enough reverb to harness an intimacy. In other words, the music production helps objectify him as a sex object. On top of this, this video demonstrates that the gendered codes are shaped more by a mainstream masculinity than some of the other artists I have already presented. And in terms of 'manliness', Palmer's construction is less challenging than Ant, the Pet Shop Boys, Jagger, Bowie, or Morrissey. Not only is this borne out by the iconography in 'Addicted To Love', but also by the relaxed, assured singing style that fashions a cool masculinity, a subversive, foppish expression of vanity, which is framed by the groomed body, fetishized and destined to be adored.

Contemplating the traits of Palmer's vanity and the depth of his influence over a generation growing up in Thatcher's Britain, I want to reflect on his aspirations as a pop performer in the 1980s. Historically, songs like 'Addicted To Love', precursors to the new, soft British male, were ushered in by a celebrity culture that had become stylistically diffuse. At a time when nonconformity was almost a cliché, it is intriguing how his 'look' was decidedly understated yet excessively engaging. Yet, as Walden notes, such capriciousness is 'not always to charm' (Walden 2002, p. 41), and this was certainly the case with The Cure, who we will turn to shortly.

What then makes an artist like Palmer dandified? And what are the socio-historical factors that account for this? Brummell's self-infatuation and fastidious preoccupation with clothes and presentation placed great emphasis on scrupulous detail and a modest style of elegance that would influence generations to come. Not so dissimilar, the Mods' downplaying of flamboyancy was instigated by appropriating dress codes that toned down outward ostentation. Deceptively, this elegant ordinariness would shape the history of pop. Spilling over to Britpop artists in the 1990s, it helped cultivate a laconic style that romanticized the egalitarian, if not mundane, emerging dominant class.[14] Following this lead, in yet another one of their numerous image shifts, Bowie, Ferry and Jagger adopted a look in the early 1980s that was understated to the point of asceticism, at least by comparison to what they were doing in the 1960s and 1970s. Similarly Palmer would nurture his style on an aesthetic that was theatrical yet modest and austere. This cannot be said, however, for all artists from that decade, such as the excessive fops, Leigh Bowery, Steve Strange, Marilyn, Boy George, John Galliano, Phil Oakey and others, who transformed and subverted many aspects of pop culture.

Lest we forget, performances in pop are tangled up with the contradictions of the music industry, which constantly revises its trends to suit its strategies. Precariously manifested by hype and titillation, the pop industry is underpinned by structures of cultural opposition and disputes over what constitutes creativity and commercial viability (Negus 1992; Toynbee 2000; Shuker 2008). One salient feature of this is located in the 'romanticization' of citizenship that goes into the marketing and production of British pop.[15] Given this, the regulation of the 'talent pool' of British musicians and artists (aided by a high population density within a relatively small geographical space) makes it easier to be visible and audible in the UK, with only one time zone and a more centralized media, than in the US. Plugging an act and broadcasting it at grass roots or nationwide (through relatively few outlets) has the advantage of accessing the entire country efficiently and swiftly. Two questions arise from this: first, what genres are promoted and marketed? And, second, who are the characters and prototypes selected and considered appropriate for accessing British audiences?

Market forces dictate the reception of the pop artist. For buying into the pop act is contingent on the myths that structure the idea of what 'our' music is like; the idea of whose music incorporates notions of belonging to a space that is culturally

---

[14]   My suggestion here is that the subversiveness of the Britpop dandy was confined to an unostentatious sense of fashion, which fused an ordinariness with a musical style that was all about poise and nostalgia. Yet, in this construction was concealed a glamorous element that was anchored in a luxurious lifestyle that routinely was made to turn on itself as a victim of high media visibility.

[15]   Over the years the music industry has been restructured in order to meet the demands of international pressure and technological developments, as well as the tendencies of state involvement. Furthermore, new approaches to cultural policy through government-oriented intervention have forged different links with the music industry. In a British context, that pop has occupied a main part of the economy is attributable to the media's maintenance of the music scene. Indeed, the media's construction of a star system, and its manipulation of this, has resulted in a pronounced influence on record labels and record sales. See Frith (1983, 1990, 2007) and Frith and Horne (1987).

recognized: suburbia, metropolis, countryside and the rural became the structures of an imaginary landscape. In this way pop songs function as anchor-points for the relocation and re-entry of the fan, socially and culturally, while the junction between national heritage and musical style authenticates those chosen moments through which people establish their places within a given cultural setting.

**Goth Dandies: 'Just Like Heaven'**

One such setting is British suburbia, a physical manifestation of a landscape where journeys between past and present propose something nostalgic. The Cure, formed by Robert Smith in 1976, will be remembered for the nervous anguish in a musical style that marked the end of punk. First called Easy Cure, and very popular in southern England, the 'easy' was dropped from their name when The Cure were signed to Chris Parry's Fiction label. With critical acclaim, their debut album *Three Imaginary Boys*, released in 1979, included the singles 'Boys Don't Cry' and 'Jumping Someone Else's Train'. Characterized by a morbid obsession with the darker side of songwriting and performing in the early 1980s, The Cure's signature would owe much to Smith's style.

Following on from the provocative album *Pornography*, released in 1982, Smith's songwriting took a more pop-oriented direction with bouncy beats and fun grooves.[16] As the 1980s wore on and the 1990s dawned, The Cure's popularity increased, with hits such as 'Just Like Heaven', 'Friday I'm in Love' and 'Lovesong', which made it into the Billboard Top 40 charts in the US. By 2007 the band had produced 30 singles and 12 studio albums and had sold over 27 million albums. One of the first alternative rock bands to gain such commercial success, The Cure had a dandy as their front man. This helped.

Distinguishable by the musical traits of melodic bass lines, strained vocals and pensive lyrics, The Cure's sound captures the melancholia of Goth.[17] As well as an acoustic guitar, a six-string bass, Solina string sounds and, of course, Smith's inimitable voice, keyboards featured prominently in the album, *Seventeen Seconds* – most of the material was written on a Hammond organ in Smith's parents' home. The keyboard-oriented style conjured up a sense of romanticization and deep-felt

---

[16] Consisting now of only two members, The Cure needed a new direction, opting for a more pop-oriented, cheesy single, 'Let's Go To Bed'. Promoted by a flamboyant video directed by Tim Pope, this song helped launch the band's new direction towards an electronic, groove-based style with the two singles from 1983, 'The Walk' and 'The Lovecats'. The following year the album *The Top* was released, prompting a world tour, at which point the band's members increased to five (with the return of Porl Thompson, the original guitarist from the Easy Cure days).

[17] Many of the band's songs were conceived by bassist Simon Gallup and Smith, who would put down the drum and bass parts first, before taking them into the studio for production.

nostalgia, transported by a morose style and Goth sensibility that made The Cure enormously popular in Britain during the 1980s. Such was his appeal that Smith would emerge as a well-known public figure over the years, crossing over into film and television.[18]

Best remembered for his messy black hair, smudged lipstick and deathly white complexion, Smith later modified his image to shorter spiky hair and polo shirts as The Cure's aesthetic moved from a depressive gloominess to psychedelia. Yet in the early 1980s The Cure's suburban Goth and post-punk inflections would provide a mundane, apolitical precursor to the ironic and glitzy pop bands such as Frankie Goes to Hollywood and the Pet Shop Boys. Rebels against flamboyancy, their dandyism sported the Baudelairean blackness of dress.[19]

Becoming a buffer for resistance against disco and the boom in fashion, The Cure would inspire a large sector of Thatcher's youth to reject mainstream pop. Not unlike the Teddy boys a couple of decades earlier, the Goths adhered to an alternative form of representation that was suburban and provincial, where 'young men and women with heavily powdered faces, mourning clothes and Robert Smith's hairstyle would be seen at domestic ease in towns like Littlehampton and Ipswich' (Bracewell 1998, pp. 119–20). Smith's standing as post-punk Goth dandy cannot be overstated, as his subjectivity emerged on a wave of Gothic revivalism. Embodying everything about the alternative pop star, he signified, in Bracewell's words, 'a pseudo-occultist, pallid romantic, trapped in the haunted semi of his unbearable memories' (ibid., p. 119). When performing it was not just his voice that stood out, with its monotonous and mournful sensibility, but also an image of the disaffected, bored and depressed young male. Lacking the veneer of urbanity, Smith mastered a seductive mawkishness that spelt out an apathetic temperament; a temperament through which a yearning to deny modernity was manifested in a personalized style, which hinted at resentment, leading nowhere.

With the release of *The Top* in 1984, Smith had not only written most of the material, but also had played all the instruments (apart from the bass). Experimental by comparison to their previous albums, *The Top* is probably the closest one comes

---

[18]   His appearance in the final episode of the *Mary Whitehouse Experience* (a British comedy radio and TV show, which started in 1989 and consisted of surreal sketches featuring pairings of Rob Newman and David Baddiel, and Steve Punt and Hugh Dennis) involved Smith punching the character Ray and imitating his famous line, 'Oh no what a personal disaster'. And in the animated series *South Park*, Smith would appear in an episode where he went into combat against a huge, mechanized Barbra Streisand.

[19]   Baudelaire's clothes were tailored to the minutest detail. Understanding the symbolic relevance of dress, he would appear completely in black (including cravat and waistcoat) as if marking an age of mourning. This refinement in costume, as Moers points out, was Baudelaire's means of marking his 'superiority to the aristocratic world' as well as his 'scorn of the bourgeois' (Moers 1978, pp. 272–3).

to a 'Robert Smith solo album'.[20] Written as a nostalgic tribute to Smith's wife during a visit to Beachey Head, a seaside location in south England, 'Just Like Heaven' would be the group's first US Top 40 Hit. Directed by Tim Pope, the video for this song, shot in London's Pinewood Studios in late 1987, paints a narrative of wild, windswept cliffs as the band members, dressed in black, are filmed performing in blustering open-air conditions. Much of the visual narrative is borrowed directly from an earlier video, 'Close to Me', consisting of cliff scenes, waves and water and shot at Beachey Head. During the bridge section, Smith's girlfriend (and future wife), Mary Poole, appearing in a dazzling white dress, quite ghost-like, dances with Smith. Angelically, her dress codes stand out in dramatic contrast to the Gothic clothes of the band members, who are framed by a bleak landscape. Bizarrely, the music in 'Just Like Heaven' is euphoric in its energy.

Based upon the bright tonality of A major, the main chord progression, I-V-ii-IV, supports a descending guitar riff that binds the verses together while contrasting starkly with the muddied sound of the rhythm guitars. Prominent in the mix are keyboards, with a piano riff entering in the second verse and bridge passage. Once the introduction of the song establishes the up-tempo mood, Smith enters on the lines 'Show me how you do that trick, the one that makes me scream'. Describing his joy when baffling friends with basic magic tricks provided the impulse for this opening. Smith has acknowledged that the 'trick' relates to a seduction device he turned to much later in life. In the video, the opening lines are sung and delivered with the camera skirting around Smith, with long shots of him and the rest of the band. Only in the second verse do we catch sight of him, although it takes up to the chorus before his face comes into full view. When he finally confronts the camera's gaze, he delivers the seductive lines 'You, soft and only, You, lost and lonely'. Catching the paleness of his face against the black eyeliner and deep red lips, with hair blowing in the wind, the camera follows him crawling on the ground, revelling in the emotions of musical elation. 'The song', Smith claimed, 'is about hyperventilating – kissing and fainting to the floor.'[21] That the band was falling apart during the recording, which took place in the south of France, with a keyboardist so drunk he could hardly stand let alone play, resulted in a weird vibrancy, a *joie de vivre*, a far cry from the austerity of the video's setting. This type of ironic distancing I have addressed in earlier studies of the songs of the Pet Shop Boys and Morrissey (Hawkins 2002).

Subjectivity in 'Just Like Heaven' can be problematized through a complexity in male representation that raises questions relating to how meaning is mediated according to the context in which it is inscribed. Smith validates his performance by revealing the stylistic codes of his music through a discursive network that is culturally grounded. The narcissism, the androgyny, the indifference and the nihilistic stance of

---

[20]   This was followed by the album *The Head on the Door* (1985), and its successor, *Kiss Me, Kiss Me, Kiss Me*, released in 1987, with four hit singles, 'Why Can't I Be You', 'Catch', 'Hot, Hot, Hot' and 'Just Like Heaven'.

[21]   http://www.blender.com/guide/articles.aspx?id=515 (last accessed 2.10.07).

his subjectivity is wrapped up into one entity, his temperament, which enables him to break the stranglehold of bland formalism in order to lay claim to revolutionary utopianism. Smith stands as a symbol of his own rejection, of a history he was tangled up in. Most of all, there is something distinctly Baudelairean in the sombre elegance he exudes and the way he fashions his desire to reform and transcend conventions.

Consider the eccentric signifiers that constitute the pop persona. What defines the performance strategies of a group like The Cure, and how did they emerge in the aftermath of punk? First and foremost, the notion of the 'cult of the self' lends itself to a voice that was hypnotically monotonous. Bracewell points out that it was a voice that could make monotony 'malleable', through a quality that 'granted [Smith's] somewhat boneless performances a sympathy and energy which his singing, by rights, denied' (Bracewell 1998, p. 117). Lacking the glamour of Siouxsie and the Banshees, The Cure were the 'alternative' boy pop group whose striking Gothic aesthetic helped revive Victorian style. Dominating this was a look sculpted by the use of cosmetics arguably in an unfeminine way. Beautifying oneself, Baudelaire would insist, revealed the tendency to 'rid the complexion of those blemishes that Nature has outrageously strewn there' (Baudelaire 1964, p. 34).

Taking upon himself the task of expounding the beauty in modernity, especially through the rites of artifice that portrayed women's elaborate dress, Baudelaire concluded that artifice could not lend charm to ugliness. Indeed, the cosmetic markers, such as 'artificial black' and rouge that he referred to, had an uncanny resonance in the Goth look:

> Red and black represents life, a supernatural and excessive life: its black frame renders the glance more penetrating and individual, and gives the eye a more decisive appearance of a window open upon the infinite (Baudelaire 1964, p. 34).

Smith's arresting look in the early 1980s conveyed a coldness that emanated from a resolute determination not to exhibit much emotion: this was a beauty that comes from a monstrous self-conceit that partakes more of gloom than happiness. Thus, if temperament shapes the pop text, then subjectivities are located in an extraordinary range of categories – from the space-cowboy, pirate, ghoul, neo-mod, guy-in-the-street, to the bored, doe-eyed Goth, all of whom remind us of the dynamics of pop masquerade. By invoking playfulness by dressing up and wearing make-up, pop dandies have as their mission the task of tempting us with their own disguise.

## Conclusion

During the course of this chapter the debates presented in Chapter 2 have been extended by turning to the strategies employed by pop artists in a collection of songs and videos. The crux of my argument so far centres on the calculated intentions of the star's 'naturalness' at the same time as his uniqueness. A central paradox of pop dandyism lies in its phenomenon as something far from fixed. And, more a phenomenon of flux, dandyism varies from one subjectivity to the next in terms of an expressive aesthetic.

Songs embroil us, the listeners, through sonic immanence.[22] Spurring us on through the structures, functions and moments of musical detail, they promise pleasure with every repetition. As we have seen, the sense of the 'real' is coloured by the out-of-ordinariness of the temperament of the subject. Music can never explain the visual spectacle alone; it only contributes to it by becoming part of form and content, subjectivity and objectivity, and self and other. Musical expression escorts the listener through a profusion of sonic events in order to assimilate the ideals of individualism in the act of performance. A pounding bass line, an explosive guitar riff or a wailing vocal scat are powerful because they touch us physically through the bodies of those who produce them. Such gestures of musical expression operate as open-ended disclosures of the performing subject, implying that working out the identity is feasible through an aesthetic evaluation. After all, the subjectivity of an artist when musicalized gains its significance through its correlation to other texts. Which returns us to the problem of the process of identification and the ways we engage ourselves with music dialogically.

The foregrounding of the artist's voice in the recording constitutes the most personal of listening experiences. For the voice is always vulnerable, offering the promise of intimacy. Also voices are gendered, evoking desire by capturing our attention through the phrasing of a tune during the movement of one tone to the next. Added to this are the sonic qualities of the body that implicate the listener in terms of emotional response. Seduction forms a main function of this process, taking place through the charm of the sung voice.

A typology of the pop dandy, I believe, is required to articulate the interrelationships that lead to the final effect. As well as this, it is the encoding of gender through the listener's recognition of the singer's voice. A strategy of pop performance is to convince the fan that they have direct access to the 'real' self. Persuasion in such a strategy is constructed through the control of representation on-stage and in video recordings. The singer exposes his performance to a 'gaze' that puts him under the spotlight as an object of desire. In this way, the singer becomes feminized or even 'unmanly' via the gaze of the onlooker. A key aspect of this is the balance of activity and passivity that upholds the structures of hegemonic masculinity. Clearly we need to consider to what degree genderplay normalizes masculinity in pop texts, in the same way that whiteness upholds dominant power structures within the music industry. Given the pop star's tendency towards self-aestheticization, I think there is an argument to be made for genderplay and its close interconnection with homosociality as a performative strategy. This phenomenon is taken up in the next chapter, as I point to the possibilities of masculinized address for the sake of musical pleasure.

---

[22]    See Rycenga (2006, pp. 238–43) for an enlightening discussion on 'sonic immanence and form' in her readings of P.J. Harvey and Yes, where the queering of form is theorized through notions of formal function.

Fig. 1 (left)  **Adam Ant**.
S.I.N / Alamy

Fig. 2
(below)  **Morrissey**
performing at
The Belfort
Eurockéennes
Festival, France.
Lebrecht Music
and Arts Photo
Library / Alamy

Fig. 3 (left)    **Robbie Williams**. Content Mine International / Alamy

Fig. 4 (below)    **The Jam**. Pictorial Press Ltd / Alamy

Fig. 5 (left)    **Sid Vicious** from the
                 Sex Pistols. Pictorial
                 Press Ltd / Alamy

Fig. 6           **The Kinks**, about
(below)          1965, Pictorial Press
                 Ltd / Alamy

Fig. 7
(left)

**Pete Doherty**
from
Babyshambles
at XII Festival
Internacional
de Benicassim,
Castellon,
Spain, July
2008. Lebrecht
Music and Arts
Photo Library /
Alamy

Fig. 8
(right)

**Marc
Bolan**.
Pictorial
Press Ltd /
Alamy

Fig. 9     **David Bowie**.
(right)     Pictorial Press Ltd /
            Alamy

Fig. 10     **Jay Kay**
(left)      from
            Jamiroquai.
            Content Mine
            International
            / Alamy

Fig. 11 (left)  **Jarvis Cocker** performing at Connect Music Festival in Scotland. Jethro Collins / Alamy

Fig. 12 (below)  **Bryan Ferry**. Pictorial Press Ltd / Alamy

# Chapter 4
# With a Twist of the Straight: Dandyism and Gender Revolt

> Sexuality itself was being manipulated in a way that England, looking on with fascinated ambivalence and primal hostility, had not witnessed since the indictment of Oscar Wilde.
>
> Michael Bracewell[1]

Re-enter the pop dandy, he who queers for the moment of a three-minute song, a video performance, a live act or the crackle of a melodic strand on a car radio. Nowhere is masculinity more put-on-display than in the masquerade of pop. One reason for this is that pop depicts gender in quite extraordinary ways, often driving home the arbitrariness of sexual categorization. For the MTV generation of the early 1980s, the playfulness of dressing up, wearing make-up, behaving differently, and not giving a damn about how others might perceive you, would certainly leave its mark. One might say the success of MTV in the early years resulted from the fact that pop music representations were never displayed along a single axis of identification. Rather, on offer would be a sense of something for everyone. Much of this has to do with the consciousness of male representation, which can be traced back to the dandy in the eighteenth century and the gender revolts that have ensued hitherto.[2]

The link between MTV and sexual politics is an integral part of any discussion of masculinity and how male artists are represented through musical styles as symbols of desire. Why specific types of subjectivity are mediated as more 'normal' than others is a phenomenon that has been theorized through the gendered gaze (Mulvey 1975; Kaplan 1987; Hawkins 1996; Dyer 2004; Jarman-Ivens 2007). Notably, the artists presented in this book are constituted as icons through their projection of sex appeal: Bowie (androgyny), Smith (effeminacy), Morrissey (ambisexuality), Tennant and Almond (gay), Jagger (bisexuality), Ferry, Kay and Palmer (heterosexuality), and Williams, Doherty and Draper (bisexuality/straight).

---

[1]   Bracewell (1998, p. 194).

[2]   Since Theophile Gautier's publication of his famous novel *Mademoiselle de Maupin* in 1835, gender-bending has been associated with dandyism. Starting with dandyism as a form of social pose, Gautier's novel ends by proclaiming that dandyism can only be expressed in works of art. Notably, Gautier had a profound influence on writers such as Baudelaire, Wilde and Flaubert, and remains a point of reference in art, literary and theatre criticism.

As Roy Shuker puts it, 'popular music is also a significant area of culture in which sexual politics are struggled over' (Shuker 2008, p. 252).

By debating the issue of sexual politics in mainstream pop it is not my intention to draw up a long list of weird and queer artists; such an exercise would be redundant in the framework of pop dandyism. Rather, my objective is to examine how the dandy might be read as queer. After all, queering has a long history in Britain and is culturally complex; it changes over time and is integrated in the histories of musicians, their songs, videos, websites, concerts, documentaries and interviews. One aspect of intrigue in queer identification is that it inscribes meaning in contrasting ways, acting as a catalyst for variants of gendered expression (Cleto 1999; Summers 2004). As such, the role of queering in pop and genderplay seems a productive starting point for further considering dandified behaviour.

As we have seen so far, strategies of enactment are decisive in the masculinization of pop expression, which privilege the gaze as much as the vocal sound and other musical signifiers. Indeed, the valorization of masculinity is seldom far from the project of queering. For the homosociality of boys performing relates directly to the styling of performance, affording an opportunity to map out the different forms of behaviour that latch onto genre and style (Fast 2001). Judith Halberstam's work on queer alternatives and subcultures verifies the 'safe alternative' for 'straight' boy bands, such as Backstreet Boys, where their sublimation of sexual explicitness 'keeps at bay the erotic relations' (Halberstam 2006, p. 22) between the boys on the one side and the girls on the other. Heterosexual boy bands, Halberstam insists, depict gender and sexuality in ways that 'allow us to think of boyhood, girlhood, and even tomboyhood and riot girlhood not as stages to pass through but as pre-identities to carry forward, inhabit, and sustain' (ibid.). Halberstam's critique of queer subcultural activity serves as a cursory reminder of the binary of adolescence and adulthood, which not only structure but also constrict communities, such as lesbian subcultures and subcultures of colour. Halberstam also points out how lesbian involvement in punk subcultures has altered our perceptions of the punk movement, forcing us to rethink the universal narratives of youth culture.

The excursions taken by Halberstam in linking queer subcultures to musical performance underline the necessity for more critical work on mainstream queer identity and difference, as well as identifying, musicologically, the links between gender, sexuality and music (Solie 1993; Brett and Thomas 1994; Halberstam 2006; Whiteley and Rycenga 2006; Middleton 2006; Jarman-Ivens 2007). Accordingly, the crux of my argument in this chapter addresses the pop artist's entry into mainstream culture by way of the 'queer backdoor'. While many of my arguments on male identity are built on earlier studies (Hawkins 1997, 2002, 2006, 2007a, 2007b), it is the dandified figure who now takes centre stage as I examine the strategies of containment that regulate his queerness. Implicit in my discussion is an overriding conviction that there are valid reasons for contesting the motives behind queering one's performance act.

Queering identity can be better understood as a marker of behaviour that presumes both opposition and compliance within a heteronormative (as much as a homosexual) framework. A basic tenet here is that all pop artists encounter some controversy surrounding their sexual identity.[3] This goes with the territory. Press interviews and articles abound that testify to the dynamics of sexuality as artists frequently 'kiss and tell' as part of their publicity stint. Confessions of one's private life, as I discussed in Chapter 3, open up the possibilities for constructing and modifying the self through narratives that are regularly construed as contradictory. In other words, the staging and manipulation of sexual identities is part of the trope of subjectivity in pop, which is conveyed through a long tradition of norms that mobilize sexual politics. Signifying one's queerness, as I want to argue, is also a form of appropriation that produces meanings that are intentionally ambivalent, and, moreover, that aspire to a queer utopia.

My contention is that the tendency towards the desirability of a resistance to the norm is the *raison d'être* of queering. Many of the concepts around queering and gender politics taken up in musicology stem from the seminal text *Queering the Pitch*, edited by Brett, Wood and Thomas in 1994, which has had a profound impact on music research. It took just over a decade for another volume dealing with queerness, this time in popular music, to be published, *Queering the Popular Pitch*, edited by Whiteley and Rycenga (2006). In this collection of essays a more interdisciplinary approach to subjectivity and sexual politics would form the main focus. Significantly, academic studies aligned to popular culture have denoted a turnaround from the cautiousness of the 1980s, with a marked effect on the queering of acts in the pop arena. Female artists, such as Siouxsie Sioux, k.d. lang, Melissa Etheridge, the riot grrrl punk bands, Michelle Shocked and Madonna, continued to chip away at misogyny in the industry, while a string of male artists, Neil Tennant, Michael Stipe, George Michael, Marc Almond, Rob Halford and Stephen Gately (of the popular Irish pop group Boyzone), would come out (more) publicly. By the end of the century it was as if 'queer' had turned into a token term for those who did not want to conform to normative representations, to the point that one might be forgiven for believing that prejudices had vanished from the pop scene, and that all was 'fine and dandy'.

But what is the relationship between 'dandyism' and 'queerness'? And how do concepts of sexuality relate to the act of entertaining? Up to the end of the nineteenth century the word 'dandy' was synonymous with something unsettling and repelling. Loaded with meaning, it reached its apotheosis in 1895 with the public punishment of the 'social body' as a sign of degeneracy. At least in the English-speaking world, Wildean subjectivity turned into a referent for a peculiar, subversive and problematic human condition. Closely affiliated to 'homosexual', a mid-nineteenth century discriminatory construct, the 'queer' would emerge as a

---

[3]    By no means does this just apply to male artists. The problematics of sexualization and queering have been addressed in relation to Britney Spears, whose queering of gender is a strategy for mobilizing a parody of the 'normative'. Invariably, the politics of queering can be read as contradictory, as exemplified in the sound, text and iconography of Spears's video 'Toxic'. See Hawkins and Richardson (2007, pp. 617–20).

species that bypassed the ontological categories of normality. But, in the short space of one century, Wilde's martyrdom would have made its mark, turning queerness into an inclusive, positive signpost. Or so this might seem, at first glance.

Queerness, as a category of identity, takes its own convoluted route. For any proclaimed queer representation renders problematic the subjectivity of the persona who plays out different gendered roles.[4] With its oppositional ontology and value-laden implications, the term 'queer' exposes the potential of subjective agency and, moreover, accentuates ideals that are impossible to achieve in any absolute sense. Nikki Sullivan's analysis of queer performativity starts with the idea that there is no way to decide the meaning of a particular performance as 'it will signify (often contradictory) things to many people' (Sullivan 2003, p. 91), and therefore remain open to multiple readings. If we concur with Sullivan, the term itself does not necessarily belong to those who feel marginalized as a result of sexual preferences. For 'queer' in its usage today also has the effect of '(mis)representing us as one big happy (queer) family' (ibid., p. 45), thereby privileging the values and desires of one group of people while overlooking or even silencing those of another.

Wary of these pitfalls, my discussion adheres to the following premise: for the pop dandy to exist, he must be *constituted* within a framework of gendered representation that breaks with conventions. And, along the way, music subjectifies sexuality. But before turning my attention to the plight of a number of pop artists with reference to their music, I am keen to probe further at some of the ideals that have institutionalized male identity and have led directly to the phenomenon of pop dandyism.

**Physical Ideals: Institutionalized Male Identity**

Bowie's Ziggy Stardust character must be the ultimate example of the flaunted queer identity, firmly imprinted in the memories of those of us who were around in 1972. I recall the jumpsuit of red, black and cream painted leather, and the costume of black and white quilted vinyl, with exaggerated pants flared out to the sides, worn with the red vinyl boots designed by Kansai Yamamoto. Bowie's look would have a tumultuous impact on scores of British artists: the punk bands, the New Romantics, indie and Britpop groups, boy bands and artists such as Morrissey, Sylvian, Almond, Doherty, the Pet Shop Boys, the Divine Comedy, and many others.[5] Revolutionary for his time, Bowie was one of the first pop stars to 'draw

---

[4]    For a study that deals specifically with the essentialization and appropriation of the term 'queer', see Lance and Tanesini (2005).

[5]    In pop video productions few directors have broken into the mainstream who do not adhere to aesthetic ideals of gender representation. Two notable exceptions, though, are found in the work of Chris Cunningham and Michel Gondry, whose pop videos and commercials break with many of the constraints placed on directors working with

our attention to the fact that a person could *play* the part of a rock star before actually becoming one' (Buckley 2000, p. 147 – author's emphasis). Challenging notions of representation, his reference points were grounded in a Warholian sensibility that made British pop radical for its day. Liberating and potent as a force, Bowie's entrance into the pop world would symbolize 'the marriage of alien and dandy giving birth to the ultimate outsider figure for the modern age, the queer messiah from space – the definitive rebel' (Bracewell 1998, p. 198).

Conventional representations of the Western male are traceable back to the ideals of manliness in the eighteenth century, whose antecedent was in the ancient Greeks. Not only was the gymnasium a place for boys to learn to use their bodies (sexually and physically), but also it was the context for acquiring power and knowledge in the form of oratory skills that would contribute to their community's democracy (Foucault 1980). As the body ideal started to dominate discourses of masculinity (with the muscular body as an emblem of power and perfection), so boys were encouraged to compete with each other and become good fighters; hence, the gymnasium as the site for marshalling the body's fear into muscles during middle to late adolescence, a phenomenon that was later ubiquitous in Victorian Britain, where athletics provided a means for displaying a male body that was pliable at the same time as being desirable.[6]

That the queering of the body in a British context is so commonplace today raises few eyebrows. Yet, evidence shows that US critics and audiences have traditionally perceived music from the UK as feminized and effete, especially when it comes to rock (Marsh 1999). The vitality of American rock (so the argument goes) highlights the affectation and superficiality of English 'art' rock, whose preoccupation with gender-bending and theatricality contrasts heavily with the white, normative masculinity of straight rock groups – of course, the Stones, The Who, The Kinks and the Beatles are exceptions to this (Meisel 1999). Wrestling with issues of gender in *The Sex Revolts*, Simon Reynolds and Joy Press (1995) have unravelled many instances of normative yet queer representations through a range of male pop and rock artists (in particular, Morrissey, Jagger, Bowie, Ant and Vicious). Perhaps most revealing in their study is how passivity is attached to performance style, gender and nationality; the outcome of which is that the artists most associated with 'feminization' are British musicians.[7]

---

mainstream artists. See *The Work of Director Chris Cunningham* (DVD, Palm Pictures, 2003) and *The Work of Director Michel Gondry* (DVD, Palm Pictures, 2003).

[6]    John Tosh's research (1999) into masculinity in Victorian England identifies the social dynamics between the home and masculinity. Tosh points out the contradictions and paradoxes in the practice of Victorian fatherhood through a discourse of gender that sheds light on how men's lives were shaped by the Victorian ideal of domesticity.

[7]    See Robert Walser's seminal study of heavy metal (1993), which has made a significant inroad into the debates surrounding masculinity in popular music and the overlap of heavy metal with classical music. The value of Walser's study lies in an astute

Aligned to discourses of masculinity, pop texts also reflect the historical lineages of manliness as an institutionalized construct in the narratives of opposite-sex attraction. 'Falling in and out of love', a dominant cultural phenomenon (and central narrative in pop songs), is characterized by possession and control, where monogamous intention excludes the possibility of another partner (at least in a normative acceptance of the process).[8] Over time, though, as pop songs verify, the queer and/or 'feminized' male has delineated a range of desires and pathologies that transgress the 'natural' binarisms.[9] In Britain, where charges were waged against Wilde on the grounds of same-sex desire in 1895, it is noteworthy that by 1995 countless songs would gain massive popularity by virtue of their trivializing sexually based prejudices. Wilde's persecution, Michael Bronski argues, symbolized much more than just radical sexual politics; he was put on trial just as much for his 'vocal espousal of aesthetic theory and his flamboyant public persona' (Bronski 1998, p. 85). Like Brummell, Wilde's breaking of rank upset the ideals of civilization by his insistence that beauty was an end in itself:

> As a young man he favored scarlets and lilacs, in later years elegantly cut black velvet suits. It was not simply Wilde's ostentatious display of 'effeminate' dress that got him into trouble but that such behaviour, particularly in conjunction with his nonutilitarian philosophy, was increasingly seen as indicative of homosexuality (Bronski 1998, p. 86).

Albeit briefly, Wilde's trials would send the new, emerging 'gay' community underground, and for the 15 years following the First World War significant changes in masculinity took place. Much of this was down to a literary circle of British writers and poets who contested the traditional values of gender and social class. Among them were Evelyn Waugh, Noël Coward, Siegfried Sassoon,

---

theorization of male behaviour, where the complexity of homosociality is addressed in conjunction with the social relevance of musical virtuosity.

[8] Freud pointed out in his work on sexuality that normal opposite-sex attraction and male sex drive and conquest is inherently unstable and not easily tenable through the presumption of monogamy. Freudian analysis also showed that in the psychoneurotic there was always the tendency to shift from one sexual gaze to the other. Moreover, that a range of so-called perverse identities existed that symbolized the antithesis of the acceptable male heterosexual – fetishism, sadomasochism, paedophilia and exhibitionism.

[9] Who would have believed (Wilde's friends might have exclaimed!) that by 1994 a British band would be satirizing the gender norms and sexual codes of heteronormativity. Blur's 'Girls & Boys', the band's first Top 5 hit, a hedonistic celebration of pansexuality and party culture in the UK, did just this. Thematizing gender neutrality in British youth who flocked to places in southern Europe, such as Faliraki and Kavos, to get drunk and debauch, this electro-pop song would satirize the arbitrariness of sexual categorization.

Wilfred Owen, E.F. Benson and Rupert Brooke, all of whom addressed the phenomena of new social orders and the sexual manifestation of gender.[10]

The Victorian period would also produce researchers, such as Richard von Krafft-Ebing, whose idea of the third sex created a stir. In his 1886 study *Psychopathia Sexualis: a Medico-Forensic Study,* Krafft-Ebing claimed that a female soul could reside in the male body, and that the heterosexual male was distinguishable from the homosexual by the signs of his effeminacy (Sullivan 2003).[11] Muddled into such categorizations of the 'passive male homosexual'[12] were exaggerated gestures (speech, walk, laughing), emotions (crying, rage, temper), as well as unconventional tastes in dress code, all of which contravened the acceptable masculine. The passive male homosexual's femininity would be essentialized by his preference for subjects at school, such as music, art, languages and history,[13] while in the case of the 'manlier' homosexual, with male-based subject interests, it was still suspected that a latent 'female personality' lurked somewhere.[14]

---

[10] Notably, women in Britain during this period started breaking out of their social straitjackets, paving the way towards an upheaval of norms that destabilized gender identity and correct behaviour.

[11] With the belief that homosexuality was congenital and symptomatic of neuro-psychical degeneration, so the persecution of the male homosexual would continue its plight throughout the twentieth century. That his condition was pathological, a notion that sat comfortably with dominant Christian beliefs, was widely accepted, while studies into body types and appearance by medical researchers in the early 1930s would be substantiated by deviant behaviour related to variations in body proportions (see Krafft-Ebing 1965). Absurd findings on physical characteristics of deviance were established through the identification of physiological 'abnormalities', such as a feminine distribution of pubic hair, smaller than normal penises and testicles, lack of hair on chest, face and back, narrow hips, high-pitched voices and mannerisms that were unmale, like the deportment of arms and legs at pronounced angles.

[12] See Terman and Miles (1936). Also note that the 'unnatural' condition of homosexuality was endorsed by Freudian psychoanalysis.

[13] See Susan McClary's reference to this in her introduction to *Feminine Endings* (1991).

[14] From this a discipline of sex endocrinology emerged, which focused on the biological indicators of masculinity and femininity in male homosexuals. Routine tests to locate female sex hormones in men suspected of 'indecent sexual relations' failed, however, to produce any strong evidence of significant differences, while other theories, still widespread today, suggested differences in the brain might elucidate sexual orientation. Such findings proposed heterosexual men might possess larger clusters of neurones in the hypothalamus than homosexual men, a premise for ascertaining same-sex desire as 'other' and, therefore, not normal. By and large, the corrective or normalizing efforts of such research circumvented the case for examining the select 'norms' of heterosexual behaviour, which have always nestled comfortably within a range of biologically deterministic arguments (LeVay 1994).

Links between music and masculinity have revealed much gender trouble, afflicting musicians as much as scholars (Frith and McRobbie 1978; McClary 1991; Citron 1993). Brett and Wood have argued that '(t)he art of music, the music profession and musicology in the 20ᵗʰ century have all been shaped by the knowledge and fear of homosexuality' (Brett and Wood 2002, p. 3). Males exhibiting an ardent interest in high arts, such as opera and classical music, in particular have been the main suspects. Even in recent times the artistically inclined male continues to be denigrated by derogatory terms, such as effeminate, poofter, pansy, and worse. In her studies of gender and music, Susan McClary makes the charge that this stretches as far back as the 'recorded documentation about music', and has to do with subjectivity and 'music's association with the body (in dance or for sensuous pleasure)' (McClary 1991, p. 17). A preference for music lessons over being on the sports field positions the artistic male as 'outsider', threatening him with emasculation. When it comes to popular music, the matter of discrimination is subtle. Rock musicians, for instance, are viewed differently from pop artists, country singers, R&B musicians, hip-hop artists, white boy bands, and so on (Walser 1993; Fast 2001; Bannister 2006). Unquestionably, MTV's reinforcement of gender stereotypes has opened up for masculine prototypes. With few exceptions, video performances since the early 1980s have been about stereotypical representations, grounded in musical style as much as in the choice of clothes, shoes, hats, hairstyles, and make-up. Framing body types along the lines of race, gender, ethnicity and sexuality,[15] music videos are instructive by means of gendered display in walking, strutting, dancing, instrumental virtuosity and holding the microphone. Pop music is therefore actively imbricated in the narratives of gender roles.

The development of the gendered look is crucial to any debate on subjectivity. Whereas clothes, make-up and earrings might have been indisputable signifiers of femininity in earlier decades, the advent of pop and rock and roll disturbed this. Consider Jagger's display of masculinity. Undoubtedly a political component of his apparel, his image has been as provocative as his songs. What will remain in the minds of many is the giant red, white and blue silk cape worn in 1981, designed by Giorgio de Sant'Angelo, with the American flag depicted on one half and the British Union Jack on the other half. Flashing this around in performances at the height of the Reagan–Thatcher era, Jagger flaunted his body in political protest. His brand of sexiness was further accentuated by the wearing of skin-tight, chest-exposing velvet jumpsuits designed by Ossie Clark, and American-style baseball–football costumes designed by Antony Price.

Not unlike Jagger, Bowie's physicality has always been slight, his mannerisms affected, as he flirts with Otherness. Particularly his artistic identification with

---

[15]    See E. Ann Kaplan (1987), who provides one of the first studies that problematizes the role of music television when it comes to essentializing gender and sexuality. Also see John Docker (1994) for a detailed critique of the postmodern conditions that affected popular culture.

Mod culture and lifestyle played a decisive role in his turning to fashion. Blending fashion with narcissism, he alluded to a queer sensibility that expressed a weird representation in the form of Ziggy Stardust in 1972 (Buckley 2004a; Auslander 2006; Stevenson 2006). Mostly, it was his role as a bisexual space alien that queered his performance. Positioning himself opposite the conventions of gender representation found in rock, he invented his character through transvestism and theatricality linked up with space travel. Ken McLeod evaluates the Ziggy persona as 'emblematic of [Bowie's] bi-sexual alienation from the heterosexual male-dominated world of rock music' (McLeod 2003, p. 341), the symbolism of which would be embraced by others in the years to come. Moreover, the space-alien creature provided recourse to experimentation through the male performer extracting himself from a range of norms. Bowie's sexual difference and extraterrestrial status, according to McLeod, united fans 'with a common "other" that transcend[ed] divisions of race, gender, sexual preference, religion or nationality' (ibid., p. 354).

The intricacies of Ziggy Stardust would be extended into another troubled, 'insane' boy-character, this time targeted at a different market. The album *Aladdin Sane*, released in 1973, was destined for the US, and contained many of the lyrics and musical codes celebrating American popular culture. Bowie's character, Aladdin Sane, further accented a sexual ambivalence, his music comprising a mish-mash of jazz, rock and ballad styles. For its time, the performance by Aladdin Sane lacked any firm definition generically, begging the question, 'where the "real" Bowie begins and where the fabricated image ends' (Stevenson 2006, p. 65). For Nick Stevenson, this character was positioned as a 'postmodern image floating free of surrounding context' (ibid.), affording Bowie room to regulate his identity well beyond normative codes and assumptions.

Early live concerts and film footage testify to Stevenson's assertion, drawing attention to the issue of homosociality. Performances by Bowie and his lead guitarist of the time, Mick Ronson, parodied all the conventions associated with cock-rock. Bowie's 'feminized role' as lead singer was mapped against Ronson's manly, virtuoso guitar hero role. Alongside Ronson, he feigned a romantic and erotic act that best exemplified queering in the making. A live performance of the song 'Moonage Daydream' stands out. Philip Auslander provides the following account: 'Bowie and Ronson shared a microphone while singing, Bowie gazed fondly and smilingly at the guitarist, and gave him an affectionate kiss (Auslander 2006, p. 141). Examples of homosociality are abundant in rock, as Susan Fast also demonstrates in her analysis of Led Zeppelin. The chemistry of the relationship on-stage between lead singer Robert Plant and guitarist Jimmy Page both feminized and masculinized their roles (Fast 2001, pp. 44–5). Calling into question the hyperbolic coding of performance, Fast and Auslander confirm, in their respective studies of gender, that rock performances are homosocialized in an overstated way. Bowie's displays of genderplay during the Ziggy Stardust era would be linked to his sexual identity, as 'performative and, therefore, lacking in foundation' (Auslander 2006, p. 146). And, in his transformation from Mod to hippie, from Ziggy Stardust to Aladdin Sane, through the avant-garde rock style of *Low* and *Heroes* to the pop dance style of *Let's Dance*, his queering renegotiated masculinity.

## Queering Antics and Negotiating Masculinity

Investigating homosociality and its impact on gender politics has been a prime aim of Queer theorists (Butler 1993; Petersen 1998; Fraser 1999; Maddison 2000; Thomas 2000; Sullivan 2003). Historically, the epistemology of sexuality is dominated by the hetero/homosexual binarism and the arrangements of identity categories. Hence, the concern for working out how the management of sexual difference has policed individual behaviour (Foucault 1980). Generally it is argued that the unitary labels for categorization all too swiftly bypass the fluidity of sexual difference. Because the body is a contested *site*, its 'truth' is uncovered at various stages in life. Mariam Fraser claims, '(b)lack, white, male, female: these are identities which appear to be "given" (at birth?) and to exist "on" the body for *all time*' (Fraser 1999, p. 109). While sexuality develops over time, through puberty and adolescence,[16] Fraser also suggests that race and gender are in competition within the sexual politics of Western culture.

By the mid-1990s a scepticism had seeped into white middle-class experiences of sexual difference, which questioned many of the traditional beliefs and doctrines that classify sexuality. Nonetheless, as a discursive construction, sexuality was still perceived as functioning as a normative regulator for control. This has been taken up in various men's studies, where the distinctions between race, sex, gender and ethnicity are viewed as critical aspects for evaluating masculinity (Shneer 2007; Thomas 2000, pp. 11–44; Segal 1990; Hearn 1992; Petersen 1998). Dominant types of masculinity, however, are considered exclusionary,[17] and the dualistic approach to 'natural' and 'socially constructed attributes' enforces a silence that circumvents important experiences. Drawing attention to the fluidity of identity, however, exposes the risks of imposing one identity over another. Queer theorists have been keen to stress that there are no resolutions to the problem of categorization. Accordingly, renegotiating masculinity as a construct is a tricky exercise.

---

[16]   See Mariam Fraser's enlightening essay (1999) on the close association between seeing and knowing in Western culture, where the author considers how the political and theoretical tools of analysis deployed in one context may have inverse and very different implications when applied in another context.

[17]   In musicology the critique of heteronormative assumptions found in areas such as music theory only began in the 1970s (Brett and Wood 2002), while feminist inquiries into absence of women composers and gender-related issues only took off with Susan McClary's *Feminine Endings* (1991).

Another dimension of Queer theory has involved the scrutiny of the politics of 'coming out' and 'outing'. The pressure of gay politics in the 1960s and early 1970s to 'out' individuals resulted in conflicting views on the demarcation between personal and public spheres; for heterosexuality is a paradigm of the public space, while homosexuality is a paradigm of the private space. This binarism helps shed light on configurations of power and control, a point Foucault (1980) argued. If the reification of sexuality is deeply entrenched in theoretical and historical models of sexuality, we cannot ignore the intersections of social class, geographical space, generation, race, ethnicity, within different periods and different contexts (ibid., p. 62). Foucault's examination of the practice of confession through the 'coming out' ritual aided the establishment of a more stable sexual identity, which, by definition, referred to a state of essential difference.

*Not* coming out (of the 'closet', that is), however, has presumed the location of the Other. A problem here lies in the fashioning of the self that did not exist before 'coming out' or 'confessing' became a norm. From one perspective, confessing blocks the visibility of power structures, as Foucault has asserted (1980, pp. 62–3), implying that the sense of liberation that arises from this ritual, paradoxically, lies in its very failure to disclose one's inner secrets. A ritual of discourse, the confession is part of a power–knowledge relationship that induces 'intrinsic modifications' (ibid., p. 63) in the subject. Promises of salvation, therefore, exercise a controlling function in the modern history of sexuality, not least through the disciplinary powers of self-government among individuals. Foucault's illumination of the pathologization of sexuality, then, reveals the socio-historical context of sexual liberation and confessional therapeutics; hence, the deep scepticism surrounding the merits of 'outing'.[18]

In the wake of the effective political action of sexual liberation in the 1970s, 'outing' was a central force during the following decades, characterized by a range of tactics. Rife with controversial 'outings', many British public figures have fallen victims along the wayside.[19] Strategies of 'outing', gender theorists have insisted, have often been in direct conflict with much gay political theory, emphasizing the 'imperfect fit between sexual desire and behaviour, on the one hand, and sexual identity, on the other' (Petersen 1998, p. 108). That self-truth is identifiable in any

---

[18]   An overarching issue here relates to ethics and the intrusion of 'outing' on human rights and privacy. In the mid-1990s there was much media reaction to the 'outing' of British bishops by the group OutRage. Notably, the gay organization Stonewall condemned this act on the basis of the rights to privacy.

[19]   One case in point is the fate of the Nigerian born, British league player Justin Fashanu, the first million pound black footballer who played for Norwich and Nottingham Forest. While still a professional footballer, Fashanu came out on the front page of the *News of the World* in 1990, under the banner headline, 'I'm GAY'. A spate of frenzied articles followed which linked Fashanu to politician boyfriends in the House of Commons and ultimately to an alleged sexual assault of a 17-year-old. In May 1998 he was discovered dead, hanged in a lock-up garage in east London.

one fixed group is a grossly over-simplistic presumption, which Alan Petersen labours when arguing for a politics of difference that steers away from essentialism at all costs. Indeed the extent to which queer politics can challenge the power relations of gender, sexuality, class and 'race' (ibid. p. 108) is relevant to this debate. Queer theory thus has the potential to upset gender politics and unsettle established views on sexuality, where a tolerance towards 'difference' instates a pluralism that necessitates a strategic essentialism.[20] We might say that gender, if and when queered, needs to be conceptualized as a surface that accommodates the multiplicity of voices within a culture. Such a deconstructive position is useful for understanding the function of gender representation in popular music.

**Signifying and Flaunting Queerness in Pop Expression**

Questions linked to the concessional categories of dandyism, I would suggest, lead onto an inquiry into what signifies queerness in masculinity. Softer male characters, or reconstructed males as some might have it, started appearing in prime-time British programmes during the 1990s, which were mainly women-centred.[21] Rather than a political intent to heighten gender consciousness, it was market economics that aided this softening-up.[22] Tested out in ways not seen before in Britain, gender-ambivalent coding would renegotiate traditional masculine values through tactical queering, paving the way forward for celebrities to gladly flag up their differences. As a form of appropriation, the practice of queering swiftly substituted for a range of norms in gender behaviours; queer performance, after all, undermines the subversive side of gender politics,[23] which has its parallels in race, ethnicity and class. From another perspective, though, signifying queer is a lot more about maintaining tensions than resolving them, a point I have argued in earlier studies, where I have concentrated on the performance strategies of Robbie Williams, Justin Timberlake and Richard James (aka Aphex Twin) (Hawkins 2007b; Richardson and Hawkins 2007).

---

[20] Addressing the pitfalls in gender theory, numerous queer theorists have engaged in an approach that upholds the tension between identity and difference, insisting that identity, as a category on its own, might be kept permanently open. See for example S. Seidman (1996).

[21] The UK afternoon talk show *Richard & Judy*, presented by married couple Judy Finnigan and Richard Madeley, is a prime example of this.

[22] In recent years this trend has coincided with higher numbers of women working and being away from home during the day. In a fascinating analysis of such trends, see Steve Craig (1993).

[23] Many studies have taken up this important issue. For example, research into Madonna's appropriation of queerness, homosexuality and androgyneity has been addressed by a range of feminist scholars, including Susan McClary, Pamela Robertson, Freya Jarman-Ivens, Vanessa Knights, Sheila Whiteley and bell hooks.

The particularity of queering one's act gives rise to several issues. All too often acts of entertainment parade the arbitrariness of gender and its social construction at the expense of marginalized groups. As the 'self' creates the Other, so bending the norms redefines straightness on its own grounds. In most pop forms of the late twentieth century, performance is instilled through gender on display. Accordingly, the body inscribes ideals of gender and sexuality that are part of the process of politicizing style and expression spatially and temporally. The body politics entailed in configuring pop narratives allegorize libidinal positions of desire that ritually marginalize dominant groups from Others. This is discernible through most music videos. I am therefore keen to consider how representation politics operate via the technical and stylistic codes of sound and production,[24] an issue I mould into Chapter 5 in my interpretation of vocality and corporeality.

Entering the queer debate from another angle, it is worth considering the expressive space between 'sex' and 'sexuality', through which popular culture has become urban, bold and postmodern, and at the same time transgressive. Much of this is attributed to the early 1980s when, as I have already suggested, pop stars owed much of their success to MTV as the prime televisual platform for addressing a culture of shifting gazes. Originally established for promoting pop songs and pop artists, MTV enunciated a wealth of different desires and subjectivities,[25] and, as I have taken up in Chapters 2 and 3, its impact is predicated upon the convergence of audio-visual codes of display. The fetishization of bodies through music produces meanings that are intertextual, which raises questions around the objectification of men and women in new social and cultural spaces (Whiteley et al. 2004; Richardson and Hawkins 2007). Yet what constitutes desires and notions of 'reality' in pop varies considerably from one person to the next, dependent on geographical space.

As a transgressive mediator of audio-visual codes, queering is an agent for social and cultural order, prescribing difference at the same time as upholding dominant values. My point is that the queer pop artist cannot be taken at face value when he or she designates an act of transgression. The ambiguity inherent in queering, I have noted, corresponds to aspects of dandyism in the nineteenth and early twentieth centuries that paved the way for celebrity culture in the late twentieth century. Graeme Turner has addressed the cultural function of celebrity status, exploring it as a discourse 'marked by contradictions, ambiguities and ambivalences' (Turner 2004, p. 109). Consumption practices, which are highly individualized, are characterized by a wide variety of responses:

---

[24]   In the first chapter of *Settling the Pop Score* I take up a discussion of musical codes and their compositional design by advocating an approach that is concerned with how codes attach arbitrarily to the discourses that construct them (Hawkins 2002, pp. 9–12).

[25]   Steven Drukman has insisted on MTV's 'gay draw' to videos that expose identities as fictional and inauthentic. Drukman points out how through the dreamlike experience of viewing MTV, '" reality" and "appearance" are thrown into question'. See Drukman (1995, p. 88).

> (S)ome sections of the audience appear to be quite gullible about the 'truth' of
> what they see, hear or read; whereas others seem extremely well informed about
> the industry processes and therefore about the constructedness of what they see,
> hear or read (ibid., p. 110).

By moving from classifying celebrity practices to the social function of gossip, Turner provides an evaluation of behaviour and norms. Concluding that the celebrity is processed as a 'spectacular commodity' (ibid., p. 118), he insists that the establishment of community through gossip is a 'multi-faceted activity', whereby sentiments of 'admiration, class-envy, revenge' and rumours can wildly circulate.

Like their counterparts in film, television and sports, pop stars are formed by consumer trends, where the pressure to be glamorous is as much the male's concern as the female's (Dotson 1999). Fashioning masculinity therefore has far-reaching implications for understanding the aesthetics of style and temperament. Seldom do pop celebrities expose themselves as much as when they play on difference and originality. In another typology of masculinity, Robert Heasley (2005) describes the stylistic 'straight-queer' as highly coded in terms of fashion consciousness: haircut, clothes, accessories and facial treatment. This, he insists, makes men not only attractive to straight women, but also to gay men and straight males. Heasley, like Turner, emphasizes consumer practices in this process, as much as the commercial gain of celebrity status. With huge profits in appropriating marginalized communities, straight-queerness designates a type of behaviour that does not quite fall outside an idealized framework that is legitimized by assumptions and norms.

Somewhat precariously, though, queering works across a sliding scale, extending from the 'very' queer to the straight, metrosexual queer. And while straight-queers might elect themselves to be queer for a career in the pop industry, the act of thinking straight while performing queer involves a cunning configuration of personalized boundaries. Calvin Thomas (2000, pp. 11–44), in his perspectives on straight-queerness, extends Butler's ideas, and for that matter Heasley's, on the compulsory character of the norm. Thomas argues that any political value in the straight-queer aspiration may be to 'assist in working the weakness in the heterosexual norm' (Thomas 2000, p. 31). Conversely, though, queering also allows straights to 'sidestep interrogations of their own sexual practices' (ibid., p. 17), which becomes an indicator of privilege in itself. From all this a crucial matter looms large: does queering constitute the disavowal of specified sexual identities? And, if so, is queering a legitimate 'vehicle' for expressing an affiliation with anti-homophobic politics?

Icons such as Bowie, Jagger and Prince (a non-British, African American dandy) have successfully negotiated the movement between queer and straight, exhibiting the sensational possibilities of sexual identity as fluid on their terms. But queering as a strategy for 'letting go' (or even confessing) differs vastly from the performativity of non-heterosexual artists. Numerous pop dandies depend on their iconic status to deploy strategies of Otherness that move from the gay to the androgynous, the self-parodic to the glam-rock, the drag act to the surly neo-Mod, and so on. This is how the intentionality inscribed by queering forms an integral part of mastering the staging of subjectivity (Whiteley and Rycenga 2006). Thus, in the democratized domain of the pop act, any challenge to sexuality might rather be read as a denial than a challenge. Nonetheless, being queer and being dandified are not mutually exclusive, and neither can necessarily lay claim to being Other – for queering in pop customarily offers a dramatized instance of renegotiation.

So, if the qualities of being dandy are classified by the creativity of one's persona, a defining feature must be the nonchalant, defiant approach to performance. Unconditionally, pop dandies are masters of such characteristics. Through musical style they reinforce dandyism's triumph over an indifference to originality. It is as if this radicalizes pop artists' detachment and coolness by making the commonplace their own. Undoubtedly, creating something as commonplace – as Baudelaire notes in *Fusées* – is a stroke of genius, as there is no higher accolade than to have been imitated or reproduced. And, as we will see, queering the 'ordinary' can attest to the most profane aesthetic sensibility.

**Norms, Assumptions and Paradoxes**

Male queering involves the put-on display of masculinity; it signifies something out-of-the-ordinary.[26] Given the centrality of gender in musical performance, it is worth considering how 'normative masculinity' functions, especially through the star system. In Ian Biddle and Freya Jarman-Ivens's discourse on masculinity (2007), its 'alteritous formation' is mapped against notions of femininity and 'antinormative' masculinity. Emphasizing the fragility of gender formations, Biddle and Jarman-Ivens maintain that 'normative gender formations somehow manage to sustain themselves in some kind of robust form, naturalizing themselves such that they close themselves off to question' (ibid., p. 13). In a late twentieth-century British context, there is plenty evidence of this in the perpetuation of role

---

[26]   This is borne out by disciplinary areas such as psychoanalytic studies, which have normalized heterosexuality and reinforced the standardized bias of evolutionary theory, which would explain why Freudian notions of reproductive consequence are still ubiquitous. Such positions idealize heterosexuality as a conventional norm. Likewise, heterosexism is found in sociology – one of the main disciplines influencing the direction of men's studies, a field where critical questions relating to assumptions of sexuality are frequently ignored (Seidman 1996). On this matter, Seidman has argued that the bias found in the epistemology of sexuality is heterosexist, where there has been a failure to employ various terms in a social and historical light. Also see Barrett and Whitehead (eds) (2005) for a collection of essays that arouse key debates on masculinity: violence; homophobia; sport; male power; Black, Chicano and Latino masculinities; schooling; gay relationships; and subjectivity. Taking a sociological view, this Reader acknowledges the global changes of male behaviour, questioning a wide range of problems in the gender order of masculinity.

models when it comes to 'exalted brands of masculinity' (ibid.). Yet subjectivities are always malleable formations of gender.[27]

Queerness, in this sense, is a way of circumscribing gender through the discursive networks that are musically, culturally and historically generated. Baudelaire's political objectives of the anti-hero dandy, point to the virtues of masculinity that were not particularly mainstream. By suggesting a blurring of norms in the male, Baudelaire would single out the force of hegemonic masculinity in the cultural and historic space. Dandyism, for Baudelaire, thus designated the potential to open up new horizons through artistic originality rooted in temperament. In pop, the destabilizing of gender norms presents an opportunity to reflect on difference and opposition, although, as I have already intimated, the transgressive intent of queering is not without its problems.

Transgression breaks down barriers and reverses the status quo or makes it circular, but no sooner has one set of boundaries been crossed than a new set crops up. As Clare Hemmings (1995) insists, transgression of the status quo can consolidate rather than undermine the dominant discourse. In this way transgression disempowers difference:

> There is no guarantee that a postmodern focus on difference within sexual politics (queer, SM, etc.) is not simply setting up an alternative opposition that equates difference with the post-oedipal, the rejection of the mother – and hence sameness/difference dichotomies are maintained. Difference can end up being privileged for its own sake, and the necessity for analyses of power and possibilities of community or coalition may frequently be ignored (Hemmings 1995, p. 48).

Hemmings suggests that transgression dodges the risk of spiralling into an endless set of binary oppositions. Yet, because identity is contingent on the existence of fixed categories, binarisms must be structured from a position of sameness. Identifying the Other is therefore a complex process and constitutes a crisis in feminism (Butler 1990). Because theories of difference present new ways of expressing old arguments, 'the more things change the more they stay the same' (Hemmings 1995, p. 49). For Hemmings, binarisms of sameness and difference inevitably privilege 'outsider' status.[28] Thus, while bisexual theory might critique sameness and difference as mutually exclusive categories, there is a tension in the

---

[27]    See, for example, Bradby (1993); Walser (1993); Green (1997, 2002); Whiteley (1997, 2000, 2004); Fast (2001); Burns and Lafrance (2002); Fouz-Hernández and Jarman-Ivens (2004); Richardson (2005).

[28]    Turning to her own bisexuality and psyche, Hemmings (1995) reads the operation of binaries as a reconstruction of what she claims to deconstruct empirically. The intention behind this is to demonstrate that by maintaining an 'outsider' position, there is a compulsion to reproduce the binarisms that have nothing to do with the subject.

privileging of sexual Otherness. Location, then, becomes a critical determinant for working out sexual politics through transgression.

For all intents and purposes, identifying queerness in pop dandyism opens up a range of issues connected to genre and style, which has a historical relevance. Let us take one genre as an example. Much of British pop lies in its historical connection to the musical, which has always held a special place for queer identification. The works of American and British songwriters and composers such as Coward, Cole Porter, Lorenz Hart, Arthur Laurents, Leonard Bernstein and Stephen Sondheim, all gay and bisexual men, have largely determined the course of West End and Broadway popular culture. Brett and Wood have pointed out, however, that the narratives spelt out in many productions have been 'as heterosexist as those of any other representational form' (Brett and Wood 2002, p. 10), only to be decoded on the basis of a 'knowing' audience. Queering abounds in musicals, evident in the tomboy Maria's role in *The Sound of Music*, in Coward's song, 'Mad about the Boy', and in Mary Martin's cross-dressing role in Peter Pan. In addition, the Academy Award-winning film, *Cabaret*, from 1972, articulated a masking of homosexuality in the characters of Brian Roberts, a reserved English scholar and writer, and the playboy baron, Maximilian von Heune, while more recent musicals, overtly bent in their innuendos, include *A Chorus Line*, *Fame*, *La Cage aux Folles*, *Priscilla Queen of the Desert*, and the trilogy of musicals by Baz Luhrmann, *Strictly Ballroom*, *Romeo + Juliet* and *Moulin Rouge*.

From these examples a high degree of genderplay has spilled over into pop culture, and vice versa. The ubiquity of queering in pop music, as with musicals, can account for significant changes in gender identification and sexual politics. Petersen (1998) describes how heteronormativity has formed part of a conventional project that emphasizes the self as unitary and pre-social. Resulting from this are 'cultural assumptions about men, their desires and their identities' (ibid., p. 113). Petersen, like other theorists, probes at the implicit heterosexist biases of sociology and psychoanalysis in their normalization of the masculine, for the arbitrariness of a conventional sexual taxonomy, where notions of normative sexual orientation are difficult to sustain, becomes problematic. As we will now see, denaturalizing the natural not only becomes part of queerness, but also a perturbed renegotiation of gender. Enter Pete Doherty.

**Fixity and Phantasmatic Play: Pete Doherty as 'Prince Alarming'**

Attributable to a range of strategies, male performances are usually constructed around the organization of homosocial behaviour. Whether we are talking of music hall, opera, film or pop performance, representations change over time according to social trends and customs. In recent years, masculinity has been shaped within a buoyant cultural context, where the phantasmatic free play on the fixity of the body is obvious in popular culture. Indie-pop star and front man of the English band Babyshambles, Pete Doherty, is a good example. In 2005 *Vanity Fair* ran an article on Doherty, concluding with the following assertion:

> Already, Doherty is like a performing bear. On stage, he receives bigger cheers when he smashes a bottle on his head than for singing. Asked if he's received any wisdom in all this, Doherty gently quotes from 'Can't Stand me Now': *'Cornered, the boy kicked out at the world/The world kicked back, a lot fucking harder.'*[29]

Describing himself as bisexual (in his flirt with Otherness), he constructs his narrative around the idea of the 'troubled soul' (Yates and Samson 2005; Hannaford 2006). Doherty, in interviews, refers to the literary influences of works by Jean Genet, Baudelaire and Wilde, all dandies and homosexuals in their own right. His biography is further spiced by confessions of an addiction to hard drugs. Disorderly behaviour, in an Iggy Pop vein, is borne out by brawls, detentions, public outbursts of crying and heartfelt declarations of love for his girlfriend, supermodel Kate Moss. Over-hyped, the BBC documentary *Who The Fuck Is Pete Doherty* would pay a back-handed tribute to its subject, romanticizing queer, poetic virtues all the way through. Moralistic and nostalgic in tone, the film underscored the British media's obsession with a smack-fried, tragic figure. Symbolically, Doherty has been ripe for the picking, policing and pillaging.

An unruly temperament can conveniently be read as a gender revolt – against prescribed norms. What's more Doherty's claim to bisexuality and allegations of his time as a rent boy have positioned his masculinity precariously. Well, at least on first impression! Following in Bowie's footsteps, the interface between Doherty's claims to sexual diversity is a template for paradox; the British public in 2005 voted him 'coolest man alive'.[30] Quite aptly, Doherty's nickname, 'baby-shambles', illustrates the little-boy-lost, screwed up, distraught and *signifying* queerness.

Couched in a genre far removed from the polish and flawlessness of mainstream productions of artists such as Williams, Kay, Ferry and Draper, Babyshambles' music is about raw simplicity, shaped by a neo-indie idiom and impression of 'ordinariness'. Again, vulnerability and naivety are the ingredients of a temperament that is dandified. Extending from the songs from his first band, the Libertines (when he paired up with Carl Barat as a songwriting duo) to Babyshambles, Doherty's aspirations for an Arcadian ideal remain at the forefront of his style.

Tuneful, with simple harmonic progressions and unpretentious rhythmic patterns, Doherty's songs accentuate an introspective, lyrical hyperbole. A sense of vulnerability always permeates Doherty's lyrics and reproachful performance style. And it is through the hopeless romantic that dreams rather than reality matter.

---

[29]   *Vanity Fair*, July 2005.
[30]   *The Independent on Sunday*, 6 February 2005.

Plundering the depths of his soul in the song 'La Belle et la Bete', Doherty's quest for liberation and justice is passionate. This, the first track from the album *Down in Albion*, is about a nightmare, as he sings, 'It's the story of a coked-up pansy, who spent his nights in a flight of fancy'. Throughout the song, the protagonist's plight (as doomed rock star) is positioned alongside his supermodel girlfriend of the day, Kate Moss. Stylistically, a blend of indie and Britpop, reminiscent of early The Cure, is structured around a surf riff,[31] dominated by an F sharp minor arpeggiated chord. Emotionally overcharged, Doherty's singing is contrived as he wallows in the dilemma of being a God-forsaken rock star.

Much in the musical performance is dandified and, for that matter, queer. Alex Hannaford claims that 'La Belle et la Bete' 'is an ironic and very British ditty' that highlights Doherty's 'lyrical dexterity' (Hannaford 2006, p. 310). Rhythmically, passages alternate between fast quaver figures and sudden abrupt moments of long, as well as sustained, chords that flirt with metrical consistency and stability. Characteristic of many British rock productions, the drums sit fairly low in the mix (hi-hats and snares in the foreground), while the guitars are distributed in terms of their backing and lead activity. Often the bass part is brought up to double with the melodic riff. Throughout Doherty's vocals are foregrounded, highlighting his erratic approach to vocal rhythm. Sticking to the beat, and doubling the instrumental lines at times, he works against the rhythmic flow of the band by inducing off-beat inflections in order to overemphasize parts of the Brechtian-type lyrics – 'why did you do it to so many people' – he sings, affectedly, with a heavy inflection on 'peo-ple' (3:56–3:59). Rhythmic articulation in such lines is enhanced by stark dynamic contrasts that dramatize the song's narrative.

The performance style in 'La Belle et la Bete' is further impassioned by the subtleties of overproduction in the recording, which comes across highly monitored with tightly controlled feedback. What sounds likes a no-nonsense, DIY approach is nevertheless calculated, profiling the lead vocals sufficiently to prevent this from being a rough mix. An overall impression is that little is obscured in the mix. That the performance feels rough and shoddy, with sniggering and scatting in the background, is quite another matter as Doherty's out-of-key phrasing and unhinged pitching works as an obvious marker of authenticity. Moreover, the numerous 'wrong notes', sloppy pitching and 'slips' between the bass and guitars, not to mention a degree of careless drumming, all work to authenticate the brilliance of his lyrics.

Moss's unlikely contribution to this song in all three of the chorus sections should not be underrated.[32] Entering the first chorus (1:24) with 'Is she more beautiful',

---

[31] Surf music is considered to be genre-specific, and under this category falls surf rock. Surf rock is intentionally a contradiction in terms, as it designates a new name for an old music that fans use to refer to the opposing idioms of surf culture and rock 'n' roll. Classic examples of surf rock are found in The Beach Boys and Surfaris.

[32] This was not Moss's first appearance on a pop recording. Earlier, she had added vocals and tambourine on an Oasis re-recording of their B-side 'Fade Away', which also

her voice exaggerates, if not parodies, her femininity through a child-like tone that is ever so slightly off-pitch. Heralded by a sudden drop in dynamics and decrease in instrumental activity, her entry is preceded by an unexpected two-bar kit solo on a shuffle figure (1:17–1:21). Immediately following her chorus part, a four-bar instrumental break ensues in the form of a guitar riff that is rhythmically punctuated on the off-beats (1:38–1:46). Typical of a standard rock production, two guitars are used, one panned to the left, one panned to the right, while during the second chorus Doherty assumes an affirmative role by joining in with Moss on segments of the melodic phrases (2:13–2:38). Then, taking over and completing the chorus with heartfelt delivery, he asks 'is she more beautiful, is she more beautiful, is she more beautiful than she'. That the personal pronoun at the end of this line is 'she' and not 'he' or 'me' is loaded with innuendo, given the narcissistic positioning of the male protagonist in a song that seems to be all about 'me', the male. Moments like these take Doherty's buffoonery to the limits of an incorrigible romanticism that reveals his deep-seated yearning for love and approval. Complementing the lyrical content, his musical performance accentuates his dilemma of being trapped between heaven and hell. By the final chorus (4:31–5:05), Doherty interjects less than before, in a feeble-sounding timbre, as Moss circles around the hook, 'is she more beautiful' – a delicately rounded moment that promises every sign of resolving gently at the start of a gradual fade-out. In the very last seconds, though, all pleasantries are dispelled as, without any warning, the next track bursts forth with the most penetrable guitar jangle drone imaginable. 'Fuck Forever' is the track's title.

Doherty's transgressive behaviour works as a socializing agent, where 'performing out' gains its currency by the physical possibilities of what we imagine we see when we hear. Sonic markers in 'La Belle et la Bete' are processes of queer identification, and the artist knows intuitively what will appeal to his audience. Audio recordings get us to imagine the reality of the performer. This means that in intended ways, a performance style can signify the ideals of what listeners aspire to. A song like 'La Belle et la Bete' functions as a vehicle for creating imaginative spaces that aestheticize the peculiarity of individual agency.

Doherty's blatant narcissism and nonchalance creates a fantasy that is objectified through music. Worth stressing, in this context, is his play on the plurality of signification especially when it comes to gender. When pop icons borrow from queer chic, however, their gender-ambivalence is not without its problems.[33] For transgressive performance strategies need to fuel the desires of the music industry.[34] Because the transference of intimacy between fans and their pop

---

featured her boyfriend of the time Johnny Depp on guitar.

[33]    See John Gill (1995) for an in-depth discussion of queer tactics in pop.

[34]    Addressing this issue, Paul Burston (1995) has claimed that the manipulation of homoerotic imagery during the 1980s was largely due to the increased availability of nude male images in advertising.

heroes needs to be powerfully instated on many levels, codes of sexual ambiguity often feel safely regulated.

That is to say, the erotic potential of the male performer is stabilized, even in queering. Which brings up the question of deviance in the form of autoerotic pleasure. What I mean by this is that if the pop dandy is confronted by his own homoeroticism, then he has little choice than to regulate the response on his own terms. As I have so far been suggesting, Doherty's risk-taking is a prerequisite for transgressive strategies. Passing for 'straight-queer',[35] he navigates a course of self-centred autoeroticism that is anchored in a biography full of contradictions and melancholic stories. Queer performativity, he shows us, guarantees little stability as the dandy reinvents himself. In other words, his subjectivity activates a narrativity that is full of surprises yet still prescribed (Hawkins 2002; 2006; 2007a).

Satirizing norms and assumptions linked to gender and sexuality, then, Pete the dandy's mission can swiftly become a shambles. For only up to a point do queering antics convince. Strategies that mobilize difference often lay bare the constructedness of conventional masculinity. Ostensibly, artists such as Doherty, Morrissey and Almond are imbued in a strategy of self-mockery that is self-deprecating, where their behavioural codes are the outcome of music's interaction with dialogue, narration and characterization. What, then, is the purpose of such fickle genderplay, and how does this measure up politically in the name of fame?

## Melodramatically 'Kitsch': Marc Almond and David Sylvian

Preoccupied with posturing, the dandy is an expert in guarding his own turf, releasing the force of his subjectivity as social commentator. For he knows that songs reach fans in intended ways. The pop 'star system' is about these intricate mechanics of performance, where queering has a long tradition, at least in British popular culture – cross-dressing, camp and drag can be traced back to the Elizabethan stage, as much as to Victorian melodramas and burlesque forms of extravaganza. Over now to the next artist.

---

[35]   In an important study that identifies the strategies of 'straight-queers', Robert Heasley has come up with a typology of masculinities that captures the ways in which the characteristics of heteromasculinity are queered. Heasley explains how 'stylistic straight-queers' develop and display a specific aesthetic in order to attract the interest of gay men, as well as straight males who can identify with border crossing identities. In addition, the aim is to grab the attention of straight women who find themselves attracted to what is perceived as a 'gay' aesthetic or a 'gay' sensibility. See Heasley (2005).

One of the members of the synth duo Soft Cell, Marc Almond helped to establish a style that was a unique blend of kitsch, camp and melodrama.[36] This seemed a natural precursor to a sensibility rooted in France's most revered singers, Edith Piaf, Jacques Brel and Monsieur Serge Gainsbourg. As well as owing much of his style to Bowie, Roxy Music, Brian Eno, Lou Reed, Alice Cooper and the New York Dolls, Almond's palette has drawn on Russian romance songs, electronica, disco, New Wave and Northern Soul. His eclecticism is further demonstrated by close collaboration with artists such as Antony and the Johnsons, Jools Holland, Nick Cave, Siouxsie Sioux, Jimmy Somerville, Patti Smith, King Roc and others, a token of Almond's creative standing within British pop. All told, Almond's performance style is an original blend of European cabaret, mainstream pop and British music hall, with much emphasis on cultivating the 'look':

> I suppose as a pop performer I do tend to exaggerate the image side of it. I've been through some pretty androgynous periods, and I've been through periods where I've adopted a more aggressive look. (…) But what I present on stage is a part I play. It's a very conscious thing, something to hide behind. People meet me and they say 'oh you're not at all like I thought you'd be'. I find that really bizarre (Almond in Burston 1993).

Melodrama is a chief ingredient in the song 'Kitsch', from the album *Stardom Road*, released in June 2007. Musicalized by means of epic film scoring, with loud orchestral stabs, the song is quite over the top. The protagonist tells us that 'kitsch is a beautiful word' in a world where 'all we need is rock and roll'. A cover of Barry and Paul Ryan's 1970 hit,[37] the song is camped up (à la Eurovision), with a schmaltzy chorus and brassy quote from Richard Strauss's *Also Sprach Zarathustra*. Kitsch abounds, as is evident in the references to 1970s glam-rock, 1960s full orchestral sounds and a crooning style of singing that is reminiscent of the 1950s, with more than a touch of Charles Aznavour and Jacques Brel. Dandically, the song personalizes Almond as 'celebrity moniker', who insists

---

[36]   Almond's gay sexuality, however, was not strongly advertised during a period where the increasing conservatism of the music industry would closet artists and their music. See Brett and Wood (2002).

[37]   Yorkshire-born Barry and his twin brother Paul signed up with Decca in 1965, releasing singles 'Don't Bring Me Your Headaches' (1965), 'Missy Missy' (1966) and 'Have Pity on the Boy' (1966). Later becoming a singer/writer duo (with Barry as solo artist and Paul as songwriter), they were signed up by MGM Records and were successful with hits such as 'Love is Love' (1968), 'The Hunt' (1969), 'Magical Spiel' (1970) and the song analysed in this chapter, 'Kitsch' (1970). Barry Ryan's popularity spread to Germany, where he recorded numerous songs in German, such as 'Zeit macht nur vor dem Teufel halt' (1972).

that everything we experience is 'pointless grandeur, failed seriousness and a celebration of mediocrity and banality'.[38]

A camp sensibility in Almond's voice has always disclosed a tendency towards satire and neo-burlesque. Masking his act by deviating from an array of norms, Almond addresses themes that are comical, pastiche and controversial. His description of 'Kitsch' qualifies this point:

> It had to be utterly overblown, a colossal colorful tasteless ride to nowhere. It reminds me of the strange situations I've been in, the surreal stages I've performed on, and the insane people I've had to endure in order to promote my music. (...) Above all though, it is great fun in a chintzy, tasteless and garish kind of way.[39]

Set to a pounding disco beat, the performance of 'Kitsch' is exuberant, with full-throated vocalization as Almond soars over the swells of the orchestral sweeps and backing vocals. With great panache his singing is choreographed by every compositional and scoring detail, and in contrast, say, to Doherty, he satirizes all notions of 'ordinariness' by over-stylization and tackiness. Much of this is attributable to a glossy production that emphasizes the ephemerality of his style. Further, his sentimental criss-crossing of a range of stylistic idioms renders the song, in Almond's words, as 'bad taste'. Unlike Doherty, though, Almond's brand of performance tends towards cabaret, where the open acknowledgement of one's own artificiality signifies a different type of queering; a queering that revels in an emotional and sexual catharsis.

Organized around a structure that consists of intro–verse–chorus–verse– extended chorus–verse–extended chorus–outro, 'Kitsch' is a sophisticated tongue-in-cheek take on Ryan's original. Camply, the song includes two extended choruses with material directly lifted from the legendary chorus coda of T. Rex's hit 'Hot Love', as well as the Strauss motif which I have already referred to. Intertextually, Almond's musical ideas reveal an approach that is reflective and full of surprises. His hyperbolic style communicates the presence of a staged personality, gaining credibility through the peculiarity of its expression. Imitating the original in an exaggerated manner, then, is central when conveying parody and pastiche.[40]

With Almond's singing style there is much regulation of pitching and breath control, which aids his precise diction. Like Bowie, Tennant, Cocker, Ferry and Morrissey, Almond's vocal articulation is 'white' and English, with little trace of a local accent or the Americanized inflections (found to varying degrees in

---

[38]   http://www.marcalmond.co.uk/ last accessed 13 June 2007.

[39]   Ibid.

[40]   Allan Moore picks up on a similar point in his discussion of Bowie and Ferry, whose output, he argues, indicates that the use of parody and pastiche in their performances are integral to their working practices. See Moore (2001, pp. 201–11).

Jagger, Williams, Justin Hawkins, Rod Stewart and Jay Kay). Far removed from Doherty's performance style, Almond's is 'trained' and mannered, a 'true' measure of his affectation. To be more precise, his vocal flamboyancy is exhibited through techniques such as regulated vibrato, clipped pronunciation and ornamentation on long notes in his mid to high range that highlight the meaning of selected words in an exaggerated fashion that comes over as camp.

At the start of 'Kitsch' the first trace of this is on the word 'come', that is elongated over four bars (1:09–1:14) with little sign of faltering. The forcefulness of this demanding phrase culminates with an upward mordent. In such moments Almond is afforded the opportunity to savour his own vocal virtuosity. As such, something 'put-on' and fake marks his queerness. In the end, the hefty dose of showmanship in 'Kitsch' is determined by the body's erotic charge, a teasing tactic that ignites imaginative engagement and makes the music pleasurable.

Moving from Almond's style of singing to the visual markers of another glamorous dandy, I want to pick up on the theme of homosociality aired at the beginning of this chapter. Music provides the male performer with recourse to self-expression in restricted zones that fall outside the confines of 'normative' masculinity. In effect, the visual representation of music can establish a resistance to norms in everyday life by feeding off the spectators' own ability to imagine, fantasize and renegotiate otherwise prohibited areas of desire.

My final example deals with the post-glam, New Romantic dandy David Sylvian, whose queering stems from Bowie, Roxy Music, T. Rex and the New York Dolls. Sylvian, like many of the other British dandies, would change his image from the flamboyant to the straight-queer over a long, productive career. In ways that espouse a swishiness, Sylvian's heyday in the band Japan was staked out by a display of straight-queering. For the purposes of this part of my study, I have selected two of Japan's earlier videos, 'Adolescent Sex' and 'Bamboo Houses/ Bamboo Music', both of which embody the glamour of visual representation.

Grounded in glam-rock, New Wave, Krautrock and punk, the New Romantic movement was soundtracked by synth-based electro-pop. In addition to Kraftwerk, Can and the Japanese band Yellow Magic Orchestra, the British bands Landscape and Ultravox introduced electronic, computer-based synthesizer styles into the pop scene. And, in the aftermath of punk, the New Romantic male emerged unperturbed about his feigned masculinity. Fearless of his effeminacy, he beautified himself with make-up, fashion and attitude, coming over queer. Sylvian, a forerunner of this trend, would set the precedent for a look that was subsequently adopted by other bands, such as Duran Duran.

Japan's first album in 1978, *Adolescent Sex*, not surprisingly did not sell that well in the US and Britain, although its title track single went down well in Asia, the Netherlands and Canada. On the track Sylvian almost imitates Bowie, leaving the listener to wonder if this is a send-up or for 'real'. In the video 'Adolescent Sex', which I will turn to now, the band's iconography says much about masculinity for its day: effeminate futurists beautified in a way that matched the perfection of their synth-pop style. The combination of elegant suits, hairstyles, heavily made-up eyes and lipstick were heightened by vibrant musical codes: mesmerizing beats, modern keyboard sounds and funk bass line. Telling us to 'just keep dancing, whatever gets you through the night', Sylvian's vocal performance is laced with erotic innuendo. Further enhanced by a high dose of reverb, sighs and experimental synth timbres, the music cuts to the beat at certain points. Toward the end of the song, Sylvian's outpouring culminates in the phrase 'take it much higher', a cliché phrase in disco and house.

In terms of the homosociality of the spectacle, two-thirds of the way through the video (2:09) Sylvian puts his arm round the bass guitar player's shoulders, fervently singing 'Oh, when we were out on the streets, with lovers infections, Count impossibilities by illumination'; what's unusual about this is the bassist, who cannot take his eyes off the lead singer, whose gaze is directed at the camera the whole time. Such moments of awkward male bonding are exacerbated as the camera pans over to the nonchalant keyboardist Richard Barbieri, who looks ahead disinterested while he plays.

Reminiscent of Pink Floyd's *Dark Side of the Moon*, a bubbling effect is produced by an LFO control of the volume and dispersed attacks on an envelope (2:39–2:47). In just a few seconds the keyboard playing, futuristic for its time, takes the performance to another plane. An ascending keyboard riff (D–B/D sharp–D/E–E/F sharp) on straight minims, with an undulating tremolo effect, becomes the central feature, whose affective charge provides a sense of 'getting higher'. When released from the minor tonality of the verse, this chorus riff, in the major key, signifies a sense of great relief.

So far, I am suggesting that the song's success depends not only on the contrast between the verse and chorus material, but also the keyboard and bass riffs that ground the musical textures and give support to Sylvian's voice and the backing vocals. Poised camply in the video, Sylvian and the bass player share the same microphone all the way through. Their performance is, however, simulated. We are reminded in an instant that queering is registered by the nuances of homosociality. Let me elucidate. In contrast to Sylvian's flirtatious relation to the pretty bass player, it becomes imperative for him to distance himself from the traditionally relegated femininity of the male keyboard player. In contrast to Barbieri's intense labour at the controls, tweaking the knobs, albeit by simulation,[41] Sylvian looks on bemused. Alone this reveals a narrative of instrumental stereotypes, as the keyboardist's 'less masculinized role' (at least in the hierarchy of rock music) signifies abjection. Similarly, Sylvian's marked disinterest in Barbieri is a demonstration of gender politics, bringing into relief the performative aspect of instrumentation. Rendering 'feminized masculinity' as 'natural' (in terms of his look and mannerisms), Sylvian

---

[41]    My thanks to Richard Barbieri from Japan (correspondence) for clarifying the point that the performance was synced, and also for identifying the instruments which were used on the track of 'Adolescent Sex', namely a Micromoog synthesizer, Solina String ensemble (synthetic strings), a Wurlitzer EP200 electric piano and an acoustic piano.

absurdly reinstates gender-order in a male hegemonic context that marginalizes the keyboardist.

Portrayed as a New Romantic aesthete-dandy in the video 'Bamboo Music', Sylvian provides an overtly camp style of performance that is juxtaposed against shots of the exotic Other, including images of Buddhist monks, untouched forests and different lifestyles. Iconographically, these representations are symbolic, occurring in monochrome with Sylvian and the other performers illuminated on a minimalist white set. Emerging from this video and 'Adolescent Sex' is an erotically charged androgynous display that is a provocation. As a style and trend, the idealism of New Romanticism was grounded in the celebration of a subversive inscription of masculinity, something ambivalent and disturbingly implicated in structures of post-punk representation. Subversive implications of this type of male drag are addressed by Judith Butler, who differentiates between gender performance, gender identity and anatomical sex. In *Gender Trouble*, Butler distinguishes the anatomy of the performer from their gender by arguing that performance is 'a dissonance between sex and gender, and gender and performance' (1990, p. 137). Butler's standpoint on the denaturalization of deviant sexualities raises an important objection, namely that of the play on feminized masculinity and its intentions.

Sylvian's iconography and mannerisms are a sophisticated cultural construct that desubliminate the type of femininity that glamorizes mainstream female pop artists. In both these videos his representation is not that far removed from female artists of the day, such as Kim Wilde, Kate Bush, Annie Lennox and others. After all, the task of repetition (during transformation and resistance) is to 'displace the very gender norms that enable the repetition itself' as Butler argues (ibid., p. 148), although the conditions for this need to be culturally assimilated. Queering gender, as evidenced in these early videos, then, not only confronts, but also appropriates aspects of sexual identity and cultural authority through parody.

Drawing on parody to imitate style through acts of cross-dressing, genderplay and camp display, the New Romantic renegotiates hegemonic structures of masculinity. But there might be more to this than meets the eye. The privileging of feminized masculinity in the early 1980s owes much to the liberation of homosexuality in the 1970s, without which straight artists such as Sylvian would not have been able to queer around. Andrew Ross maintains that the privileged site of androgyny was only made possible '*after* gender-bending had run its spectacular, public course' (Ross 1999, p. 326, his emphasis). Ross claims that this came about through 'David Bowie (the first and the best, although Jagger and Lou Reed of the Velvet Underground had been pioneers), Alice Cooper, the New York Dolls, Elton John, Iggy Pop, Marc Bolan, and other dandies of glam rock' (ibid.). As influential as the New Romantics, heavy metal artists of the 1980s heavily queered their acts to the point that the most masculinized images were 'spiced with miles of manicured long hair, risqué costumes, elaborate make-up, and a whole range of fetishistic body accessories' (ibid.). On this point, Walser stresses that the visual and musical codes of heavy metal would 'function to relieve anxieties about male power' (Walser 1993, p. 129) in ways that are not compatible with previous generations. For transgressive performances confront the gender constraints of maleness in instances where men on stage 'elevate important components of many women's sense of gendered identity' (ibid., p. 131).

Masculinity in popular music is without doubt spectacularized in countless ways, where music performance brings masculinity in close proximity to that which it emasculates. Given the instability of 'manliness', many fault lines are open to exploitation. From this, I would suggest that the inherent force of homosocial mechanisms and the paradoxical stability of queering in post-1990s pop emphasizes the agility of heterosexual masculinity, for the continuous repetition of queer identification involves a restructuring of pop that is intended to fascinate, intrigue and entertain.

## Conclusion

Pop dandies have given music volume and sexual attitude. Be it in songs, interviews or public appearances, queering one's act says much about the development of the pop phenomena. Performing, after all, is about playfulness, where acquiring roles and altering oneself is a main goal. Compelling is the projection of genderplay through the agility of queering. I am struck by how gender is queered in different cases of self-representation. Take Doherty's involvement with ambivalent sexuality and his championing of Kate Moss, Marc Almond's cultivation of a camp style that is over the top, and David Sylvian's coquettish antics of affected performance and peeved response to the keyboardist, all of which position gender as part and parcel of entertainment. Crafted pop performances reflect gender-ness, defining a social process that is entirely dependent on the rhetoric of bodily gesture and seductive pose.

The peculiarity of the pop performance is that it evokes impressions of desire, erotic impulse and fantasy through posing. Every performance becomes a channel for depicting identity, providing a pathway for being persuaded and entertained. Performance, Frith suggests, is 'a way not of acting but of posing' (Frith 1996, p. 205), and this is borne out by an audience's instinctive understanding and reception of the gendered body as object and subject. Meanings, then, shift in every performance space, articulating the polymorphous states of human difference and the particularity of pleasure. What I am suggesting is that while pop music frames its identities, the indefinable is there lurking, with all the inflections and nuances one chooses to afford it. This takes us back to the need for a queer discourse to focus on the qualities of difference and the complex layers of transgression found in so many pop texts. It is simply that gender-bending tactics have become mainstream in popular music, through a kind of enactment that draws our attention to the gendered body.

In the next chapter I consider how the recorded and produced voice mediates 'intimacy' and 'sincerity' through vocal costuming. 'Out-of-ordinariness', as much as ordinariness, and its relation to dandyism, is an aspect of pop I next examine in the voice, which, as I argue, denotes something thrilling. There are musicological and aesthetic reasons for studying how singing profiles temperament and profiles the persona, and the task is one of working out how to uncover these strategies through musical interpretation. So what should we take into account in the recorded performance? And how does vocality encode a song as dandified? These are just some of the questions addressed when examining the deep-felt pleasures of experiencing a dandified performance.

# Chapter 5
# Singing the Body Fantastic: Corporeality and the Voice

What's it matter?
The truth is in the songs.
So much is in the songs.
Morrissey[1]

Singing must be one of the most personal inscriptions of identity. From one artist to the next, vocal styles differ considerably, mediating the peculiarities of temperament. The voice can also be perceived as part of a strategy of linking style and composure. An underlying aim of this chapter is to extend some of my previous ideas on genderplay by considering singing and vocal techniques as an integral part of individual agency. In particular, I want to consider developments within the realm of technological reproduction and the positioning of the voice in the mix. As I will argue, techniques in recording have contributed to the 'produced voice', marking a special moment in mimetic expression. Becoming the site for interiorizing notions of identification, the recorded voice offers the listener access into a fantasy world. Sean Cubitt claims that the recorded song 'slips in under the censoring eyes of our social conscience' (Cubitt 2000, p. 156), allowing us access to pleasures that are otherwise unattainable. Implied here is the constructedness of the voice and its idyllic representation of self-image: for listening, once again in Cubitt's words, 'is the pursuit of that impossible reality along the trace of the singing voice' (ibid., p. 157).

If the pop voice designates narrativity, it raises the issue of personal intention: Why are voices recorded, mastered, and mixed in specific ways? And where does authorship in the process of recording lie? Actually, the recorded voice provides recourse for reflecting on the technical principles of singing and vocal recording techniques: the listener's immersion, the artist's presence and the processual conditions governed by the producer determine the pop performance. With few exceptions, the voices I have considered are marked by mid to high registers, where a low, bass range is not common. On this issue of register and pitch, I turn to Koestenbaum's study (1993) of the operatic trained voice and the discourse surrounding high register male voices which have been commonly associated with the feminine. With its obvious associations with castrati singers, the high male voice (spoken or sung) always teeters on the edge of emasculation. Yet any notion

---

[1]  In Woods (2007, p. 217).

of androgyny in these high-pitched voices differs significantly from that found in styles such as rock, metal and soul. The singers I consider in this chapter – Bowie, Jagger, Ferry, Morrissey, Justin Hawkins, Williams, Doherty, Draper and Cocker – all possess high-pitched vocal virtuosity, which connotes different variations of masculinity. When choosing these artists to write about from a dandified perspective, some way into this study I concluded that one of the artists, in fact, proved to be hardly dandy at all. This will be revealed during the course of the chapter.

Meanwhile, I want to stress that the male voice in pop is not just determined by register. At the time of writing, popular Antony Hegarty, who sings in a mid-range register, has created a bit of a stir through his androgynous voice. Interestingly, the degree of gender ambivalence in his vocality is commonly interpreted as 'unmanly'. Why? Is it that Hegarty's voice unleashes a sound through its over-abundance of vibrato that is too unsettling? Or is it that his iconography and openly declared gayness instantly charge his voice with something Other? Not unlike the castrato singer, albeit it in a lower register, Hegarty's voice is angelic, brimming with soulfulness, at the same time as it is contrived. Non-straining, nasal, with a sound produced by a head-tone, his voice is unique. It would be hardly possible to go further on in this discussion without linking his voice to the genre of pop he turns to. For generic choice is all-defining, and, as Middleton argues, Hegarty's tendency towards 'torch song' is significant as this is 'in origin and by tradition a female genre' (Middleton 2007, p. 103) and appropriated by a number of gay singers. Conversely, the tautness of vocality, produced by the stridency of a falsetto tone, in much heavy metal is suggestive of the phallocentricity associated with conventional masculinity (Walser 1993; Fast 2001). Precision of pitching and rhythmic inflection is commonly aligned to virtuosic guitar-playing, measured by its technical polish. Without doubt, the coding of guitar-playing in rock is gendered differently from the quiet jazz piano backing of ballads by Hegarty, such as 'I Fell in Love with a Dead Boy', 'For Today I Am a Boy', and numerous songs from the second album *I Am a Bird Now*. Thus, the stylistic coding of this voice is predicated upon a range of devices that shape notions of self-representation. There can be no doubt that his voice is a queer one; as Erik Steinskog puts it, a voice through whose queerness we hear 'different kinds of subject-formations' (Steinskog 2008). So, what of the recorded dimension of vocal address? And what makes it dandified? Hegarty's voice most certainly is not.

The recorded voice has everything to do with the advent of electronic and digital equipment during the twentieth century, where the powerful connection between singing and the ever-changing domain of music technology has illustrated the continuously mobile terrain in pop aesthetics. During the past 50 years, changes in the recording studio have profoundly affected vocal production. And, in more recent times, the transition between analogue and digital technology (especially with the advent of the compact disc in 1982) has had a strong bearing on how pop music is consumed. Thus, the creative ramifications of the modern recording studio account greatly for the recorded voice's integration into the compositional fabric of pop songs.

When it comes to recording techniques, the meticulous choice and positioning of the microphone in relation to the lead singer provides that intimacy we expect and become accustomed to. Technical manipulation of the human voice is crucial. As Timothy Warner (2003) points out, the vocal 'drop in' during the recording process has much to do with enhancing and even altering the quality of the voice. Multitracking recording means that the voice can be edited, recorded and 'staged' a segment at a time by dropping in and out of the recording mode. The effect of this is that 'each phrase, each word even, can be dropped in several times until it is judged suitable' (Warner 2003, p. 31). Recording techniques therefore contribute to enhancing musical accuracy and intensifying expression in quite unnatural ways.

As well as microphone placement and vocal 'dropping in', many other techniques profile the voice in the mix. Consider the effect of 'riding the fader' and subjecting the lead vocal part to dynamic compression: the result being that the voice is regulated in accordance with the other parts and tracks. In pop productions the voice fades in and out of the mix in ways that have 'no parallel in the acoustic domain' (ibid., p. 33). The issue of presence in the tangible reproduction of the original voice is of great relevance here. For recordings attest to a performance that reproduces the artist's body in ways unattainable outside the environment of the studio. Thus, the pop aesthetic derives from an artificial context that feels 'real' and becomes the authentic location for identification. Yet not only style, but also temperament make their impact on the listener.

Mindful of such matters, I now lead this debate in various directions during this chapter, arriving finally at the question of camp vocality, a vital clue to the dandified performance. My discussion revolves around the sensibility of camp (or, as Koestenbaum puts it, the 'camp glow'), which emanates from the moments of spectacle that are dependent on intimacy and empathy. Because vocal closeness is mediated through the recording, any critique of it needs to involve considering vocal expression alongside the performative inscriptions of the body. Interpreting the dandified voice, then, lies in working out its conviction and propensity for negotiating pleasure.

## Voices in the Mix

Always a matter for interpretation in the pop performance is sincerity, and, in musical terms, this has to do with being convinced by the singer or not. Responding to a singer's voice entails some evaluation of the persona presented in a song, and one might say that the act of singing takes on numerous roles that mediate narrativity through processes of masking (see Chapter 6) that do not necessarily imply inauthenticity. The listener's position is activated by Frith's concept of putting on the 'vocal costume' (Frith 1996, p. 198). Useful for working out temperament, style and intention, the vocal costume is what we, the listeners, turn to when we respond to the voice as a carrier of meaning. Because singing reproduces the artist's body through the imagination, it is through the voice that we get in touch with the artist first on an intimate level.

To gain a better sense of how this works, I consider the recorded voice as predicated on its technical as well as its cultural construction. My argument is that vocality works through intersubjective dialogue, and, as a trajectory of desire, the sung phrase is polysemic, its function being to convert aural representations into multiple meanings. To demonstrate this I have chosen a number of singers and their songs: Bowie ('Slip Away'), Jagger ('Hideaway'), Morrissey ('At Last I am Born'), Justin Hawkins ('I Believe in a Thing Called Love'), Williams ('Millennium'), Ferry ('Don't Stop the Dance'), Doherty ('Albion'), Draper ('Wide Open Space') and Cocker ('Common People').

*David Bowie: 'Slip Away' (2002)*

Bowie's performance of 'Slip Away' on his album, *Heathen*, released in 2002, is retrospective, traversing a range of stylistic possibilities and mannerisms that are melodically melancholic in their mood. The entire album has what Buckley calls 'melodic clout', as Bowie finds 'a new accommodation with the more melodic side of his songwriting' (Buckley 2004a, p. 112). Reminiscent of his Ziggy days, the song 'Slip Away' leaves one in little doubt of Bowie's legacy over a three-decade span, as his vocal expression comes across as invigorating as ever. In a song that is dark and atmospheric, Bowie revels in the contours of a simple and beautiful melody. Much of the mood in this song has to do with Tony Visconti's input as producer, where the elegance and theatrical weight of Bowie's voice is captured by a chilled aloofness in the recorded sound. Caught up in lines, such as 'Don't forget to keep your head warm, Twinkle twinkle Uncle Floyd', Bowie's voice soars into its high register, with a wealth of strenuous inflections, as he reminisces back to the 1970s with fond recollections of the TV-cult film, *The Uncle Floyd Show*.[2]

Example 5.1: 'Slip Away'

---

    [2]   Cryptic references are made to this show from 1974, which was popular in the late 1970s and 1980s in the New York City area. It featured two puppets, Oogie and Bones Boy, mentioned in 'Slip Away', as well as the host, the veritable Uncle Floyd Vivino.

A main clue to Bowie's subjectivity lies in nuances of musical expression, such as the heavy vibrato on lower, sustained pitches, and a wavering in pitch control on the high notes, which produce a sense of mournfulness. The pristine vocal sound is the result of the choice of microphone, the EQ-ing and compression on the voice and backing. In addition, his melodic phrasing hosts an array of emotions that are enhanced by flurries in the guitar part, the sustained chords and twirls on a Stylophone synth,[3] featured on 'Space Oddity' (1969). Another feature is the undulating contours of the fretless bass that cushion a voice that croons and booms on every word, as the protagonist urges the subject of the song to 'keep his head warm'. Looking back to the year 1982, the song's narrative is profoundly nostalgic as the protagonist recalls how life was better in his youth.

Teasing things out in this song showcases a landscape that is quintessentially British and artified. Contributing to this is timbre, diction and a sensuality that has its roots in androgynous 1970s glam. The pizzazz of this musical arrangement enables him to seduce and cajole, and, narratively, the song is about the loner, the anti-hero, as Bowie explains:

> Heathenism is a state of mind. You can take it that I'm referring to one who does not see his world. He has no mental light. He destroys almost unwittingly. He cannot feel any Gods presence in his life. He is the 21st century man. However, there's no theme or concept behind Heathen, just a number of songs but somehow there is a thread that runs through it that is quite as strong as any of my thematic type albums.[4]

Finally, 'Slip Away' is an elliptical song, paying homage to R.E.M.'s 'Man on the Moon' and Bowie's earlier Ziggy Stardust period. The most flamboyant marker[5] of this song is Bowie's voice, which owes much to Visconti's knack to get the best out of his singing style. Buckley claims that while Visconti's masterpiece is probably the astonishing vocal in 'Heroes', on *Heathen* 'he comes close, capturing that big, full, booming voice perfectly' (Buckley 2004a, p. 113). So, behind the scenes is

---

[3]   Bowie describes the Stylophone as the most loony of pre-synths, saying that 'it was really cheap and the tone is nasty as hell'. Playing only one note at a time, one has to use a stylus to get at the keyboard. See http://www.concertlivewire.com/interviews/bowie.htm (accessed 5 September 2006).

[4]   http://www.concertlivewire.com/interviews/bowie.htm

[5]   In the now famous 1972 *Melody Maker* interview, his declaration of gayness, despite being a father and married to a woman, is undoubtedly one of the most heated debates in British pop history, not least for the shifting positions Bowie assumed afterwards. For instance, in the *Playboy* interview from 1976 he would qualify his earlier claims by categorising himself as bisexual rather than gay. As cultural, political, and social conditions changed in Britain, so his persona altered, and in the 1980s and 1990s he gradually distanced himself from his former self.

the producer, whose crafting of the voice has everything to do with shaping and masking temperament.

*Mick Jagger: 'Hideaway' (2001)*

Another artist rich in eccentricity is Jagger, who, rather than slipping away, chooses to hide away. On the heels of a long career, Jagger expresses himself with great aplomb in the collection of romantic and spiritual songs found on the album *Goddess In The Doorway* from 2001. Delivered with humility and pathos,[6] 'Hideaway', the fourth song on the album, starts off in a Sam Cooke style, ending up by becoming tinged with an Al Green flavour. Wyclef Jean, working with Jagger on this track, allegedly changed the feel of the song by giving it a reggae-like Caribbean groove and hip-hop feel. The impassioned hook, 'Hide away, hide away', opens the story with someone who has made it big, got it all, and yet who longs to disappear. 'I'm out of everybody's reach, Out on some twisted beach, I'm gonna hide away', he laments, with more than a hint of U2's 'Where the Streets Have No Name'. Longing for that place where he can 'disappear to and never come back', the protagonist says, 'I'm gonna wear some fake disguise' (1:12–1:17).

Example 5.2: 'Hideaway'

Heavily inflected, the vocal rhythm adds much to this phrase (Example 5.2), over-accentuating the lyrical rhyme. Rather than hitting the first beat on the word 'wear', Jagger chooses to over-emphasize 'I'm gonna' on the weak beat of the preceding bar, and, in turn, the weak beat of the next bar on the second syllable of 'dis-guise'. Syncopated devices in phrasing heighten a sense of expectancy. At this point in the song Jagger's register is mid-range as he pitches his melody with a gentle touch of glissando on cadence points. The only time falsetto is used is on the repeated words 'hideaway', where Jagger is dubbed with Wyclef in falsetto an octave higher. In keeping with his laid-back, earnest style, Jagger's inflection on 'hideaway' emphasizes the 'ai' sound in 'hide', assisting the hook to float in and out of 'audio' sight through a careful control of dynamics and microphone distancing.

---

[6] Drawing on a pool of other artists for the *Goddess In The Doorway* album, such as Bono for the song 'Joy', Lenny Kravitz for 'God Gave Me Everything', Rob Thomas for 'Visions of Paradise', and Wyclef Jean for 'Hideaway', Jagger enlisted support from Matt Clifford, former Stones keyboardist, and Marti Frederiksen from Aerosmith.

Intensity in melodic and rhythmic phrasing, with all the idiosyncrasies we associate with Jagger's voice, is about immediacy; the rawness produced by a maximum constriction of the muscles in the throat and the raising of the glottis, making his vocalization throaty and nasal at the same time as producing a raspiness. Such details emphasize his rebellious cause. For decades, Jagger has delivered to rock fans a style that is subversive, raw and exciting, and always on the edge. His strength is to inject unbridled energy into ordinary words and clichés so that they mean something. Borne out by an enunciative mannerism, Jagger's vocal presence is part of a process of melodic phrasing that alludes to intimacy, sexual provocation, and camp.

Yowling on 'I' in 'I'm gonna fly away or wear some fake disguise or rent a small hotel', Jagger positions himself, albeit as protagonist, in close relationship to the listener. Obvious in its playfulness, the phrasing of 'I'm gonna' underlies a passion that is located on an imaginary plane. Moments like these hold a clue for what it is that makes his voice endearing and sincere. Is it that Jagger's vocal expression is one of self-parody? If so, to what end? Traditionally, a virility, a crude variant of cock-rock, exhibits the physical properties of Jaggerian vocal rawness. This is exuded through a timbre and style of singing that elicits the star's gender-ness, his Britishness, his generation and middle-class status. Jagger's vocal sound is the result of arrogant sloganeering, a process that is steered by a larger-than-life ego. Above all, this is greatly assisted by the studio production.

Using his vocals to signify physicality, the effete dandy entices us into the intimate space of the recording. In contrast to Bowie (who also grew up loving American culture and music) (see Buckley 2000), Jagger's vocal mannerisms are more directly associated with African American singing traditions and styles, which are exemplified in 'Hideaway' in the friendly dialogue between Wyclef and Jagger. Vocal tendencies in British beat/R&B bands of the early 1960s and beyond (especially in reference to the Beatles and the Rolling Stones) have their foundation in black American antecedents, which developed into a heterogeneous British style (Moore 2001, pp. 71–3). Appropriation of the black voice by white artists in popular music resonates with cultural signification. As Frith has claimed, while no listener in the 1960s would have perceived Jerry Lee Lewis or Jagger as black, 'every listener realized that they wanted to be' (Frith 1996, p. 198). For as early as the 1960s, the British tended to stylize American popular music from the 1940s and 1950s – blues, R&B, rock 'n' roll – packaging it in their own way. This is a salient point when considering the origins of voice-types, which draws our attention to the body as a domain of indolence and pretension; in Jagger's case a white body lacking in 'blackness'.[7]

---

[7]    Usefully, this point was supported by Robynn Stilwell, who also drew my attention to the fact that the dandified British voice, often thin, nasal, fragile and whiney, is distinct from the piercing nasality of the American Appalachian style that has its roots in an Irish style.

*THE BRITISH POP DANDY*

*Steven Morrissey: 'At Last I Am Born' (2006)*

Void of Jagger's African American vocal inflections, Morrissey's singing style is of a very different kind. Its traits are derived from the New York Dolls, The Kinks, Sandie Shaw, Dusty Springfield, Patti Smith, The Velvet Underground and The Byrds. For Morrissey's eighth album, *Ringleader of the Tormentors* (2006), which reached number one in the UK album charts,[8] Visconti was asked to be producer. And in addition to Visconti, an impressive line of musicians and composers, such as Jesse Tobias, Alain Whyte, Boz Boorer, Gary Day, Mikey Farrell and Matt Chamberlain were invited to take part. Perhaps most unlikely was the choice of legendary film composer Ennio Morricone. Morricone's scoring would provide the colourful backdrop for the soul-wrenching sentiments on the track 'At Last I Am Born'.

Well known for his attraction to stories of glamorous thuggery, especially through the plight of the underdog, Morrissey turned to songs from *Ringleader of the Tormentors* that are awash with cunning tales of sensuality and erotic innuendoes. Uncharacteristically, though, a narrative of sexual liberation besets 'At Last I Am Born'. Pompously introduced by an orchestral fanfare, the song's mood is sculpted by an expansive and lush vocal tenacity. Almost three decades after he started his career with The Smiths, there is a sense that Morrissey shirks off any evasiveness by rejoicing in finally being 'born'.[9] Made memorable by stylistic inflection, clipped pronunciation and cadential elaboration, the central hook, 'at last I am born', transports the listener into a drawn out climactic coda that gently dissolves into a couple of sporadic gestures before its fade-out. Conveyed through a catchy tune that is set to witty lyrics, the beguiling lines, such as 'I once was a mess of guilt because of the flesh, It's remarkable what you can learn, Once you are born, born, born', display Morrissey's ingenuity as lyricist and whimsical performer. Exaggeration, the prime marker of his vocality, occurs through incessant repetition, as much as intonation. Alone, the word 'born' is delivered 28 times, embellished to the extent that it builds up to five pitches in descending motion. Such musical variation is characterized by different intervallic structures that reinforce the modal identity of the melodic material (Example 5.3). Over several bars, 'born' is stretched out by glottal shakes and a quivering tremolo

---

[8]   Ironically, the album cover alludes to the Deutsche Grammophon record cover logo and design, with Morrissey posing as a violinist after the classic photos of Jascha Heifetz or Yehudi Menuhin. Recorded in Rome, it was released internationally on 3 April 2006, and one day later in North America.

[9]   Throughout the 1990s the caution exerted in the 1980s, during the AIDS decade, was shirked off, as openly lesbian and gay musicians emerged in mainstream pop. In addition to Neil Tennant, Michael Stipe and George Michael, Judas Priest's front man, Rob Halford, demonstrated that it was possible to transfer gay leather culture into metal contexts without losing one's fans. By the turn of the century most gay and queer bands had a crossover following, which paved the way for many rock and pop artists to 'at last' become 'born'.

that provide a boost to his crooning.[10] Elated, Morrissey reaches his final 'born' towards the end of the song (3:09 onwards), which is followed by a children's choir bridge passage. Forced well up into its high register, as well as the mix, Morrissey's voice unleashes his final outpouring on 'born'.

Less chagrined than before, his vocal buoyancy seems steadfast, enhanced by Visconti's recording techniques that sensitively offset Morrissey's close-miked voice against the finely balanced mix of the strings, march-like, triplet snares and guitar licks.

Example 5.3: 'At Last I am Born'

Based upon patterns of long notes, extended cadential points and intervallic leaps, Morrissey's singing embodies not only the song's narrative, but also the intricacies of his persona. Vocal articulation involves different types of physical exertion, such as straining up to a falsetto register. Overall, the intimacy in this style is attributable to the specific positioning of the voice in the mix, which extracts the qualities of timbre, volume and resonance that personalize his style. Evidenced by a tendency to stagger his vocal pitches with chords, Morrissey overtly enunciates through a delivery that balances between sung and half-spoken phrases. Elegantly paced, his melodic phrasing reaches a climactic point with him scatting around the word 'born'. In these moments his voice discloses a transgression that seems worlds apart from the virtuosic style associated with the British band The Darkness,[11] and their lead singer, Justin Hawkins, who we will now turn to.

*Justin Hawkins: 'I Believe in a Thing Called Love' (2003)*

Rooted in the glam-rock of the 1970s, with undisguised references to Queen, Kiss, AC/DC, Led Zeppelin, Def Leppard, T. Rex, Judas Priest and Van Halen, Justin Hawkins's virtuosic musical performances complement his image: tight catsuit, long coiffured hair, glitzy accessories and, of course, make-up (Walser 1993). Launched in 2003, The Darkness's debut album, *The Darkness – Permission to*

---

[10]   Distinguishing between tremolo and vibrato is not an easy task. One of the useful definitions I have come across is Alan Lomax's: 'any quaver of the voice, which is audible as such, is considered tremolo. If the undulation is so finely controlled and so narrow in pitch (as in normal vibrato) that it is heard as a constant aspect of the singer's voice quality *rather than* a quaver of the voice, it is not tremolo' (Lomax 1968, p. 69 – author's emphases).

[11]   From Lowestoft in Suffolk, the two brothers Justin Hawkins (vocals and guitar) and Dan Hawkins (guitar) met up in London with childhood friends Frankie Poullain (bass) and Ed Graham (drums) to form their dream band, The Darkness.

*Land*, reached number one in the UK. Slickly produced, their style, like their performance, is pure pastiche; a nostalgic take on glam-rock, with an ever-so-slight touch of metal. All the ingredients are in place for revisiting the 1970s, with much emphasis placed on passion, self-indulgence and defiance. Flamboyant in every way, Justin Hawkins struts his course as a parodic glam-rock star, singing about sex, love, Satan and drugs in a shrill falsetto that is supported by the tightest of latex unitards.[12]

The fourth track, 'I Believe in a Thing Called Love', an instant number-one hit in 2002, consists of an aria-like delivery with one exaltation after the other, executed through faultless vocal and guitar solo pyrotechnics. The song's aesthetic lies in the soaring gestures of the phrases, as much as in the vocal agility of the lead singer. Lines such as 'touching you-ooo, touching me, touching you-ooo, God you're touching me' include daring intervallic leaps and pitch embellishments that are unavoidably hyperbolized (Example 5.4). Moving rapidly upwards and downwards pitch-wise and sliding between a natural register and forced-out falsetto, Hawkins's agility in melodic phrasing follows the contours of his guitar playing. One could say that the sheer force of his high pitching through a powerful falsetto range signifies a masculinized passion. Miller (2003) makes the point that the 'falsetto voice does not mimic the female one, but it grants an expressivity to male singers, allowing them to articulate and communicate a frenzy of precise emotions to the auditor'. Rock performances usually involve the male artist moving beyond his 'real' voice to his 'false' one, in order to express genuine emotion. In 'I Believe in a Thing Called Love' Hawkins's emotion is blatantly obvious. The rapid alternation between the natural voice and falsetto at the end of each short phrase on the words, 'you, me', is marked by the fussiest of ornamentation (see Example 5.4), counterbalancing longer lyrical phrases, 'I believe in a thing called love, Just listen to the rhythm of my heart', with the tricky leap of a major sixth between 'love' and 'just'.

Example 5.4: 'I Believe in a Thing Called Love'

Integral to hard rock, metal, soul and funk are the pyrotechnics of technical posturing. On the distinction between the mad and violent leanings of heavy metal and the less extreme macho posing in hard rock songs there is much to say. Moore points out that while the high-pitched male voice characterizes hard rock, in heavy metal the style is 'less concerned with vocal theatrics, polished tone and harmony voices' (Moore 2001, p. 149).

---

[12]  A unitard is a single item of clothing, a highly stretchable garment, with or without sleeves, that covers most of the body, from the feet to the neck.

Verification of this can be found in Hawkins's rock-inflected voice and the numerous techniques used, such as frequent glissandi, extreme register fluctuation and vocal stretching. By stretching I am referring to the vocal oscillation between the closed, tight and narrow positioning of an expansive open-throated tone, as found on the phrase 'just listen to the rhythm of my heart'. Here the technique is one of navigating the falsetto range with a head tone that is extraordinarily high. Technically, the constriction of the glottal region and opening of the throat creates a tension, producing a high-pitch wailing that steers the melodic contours. In such moments, the high tessitura of vocal phrasing blends perfectly with his guitar solo passages and vice versa, paying homage to previous artists and songs, with a great deal of tongue-in-cheek. Uncannily, the raucous, chunky guitar parts, as well as the sung phrases, bear a striking resemblance to those in the Scorpions' legendary song, 'Rock You Like A Hurricane'.[13]

Hawkins's overstated gestures mostly underlie a showmanship that is almost too contrived to be dandified.[14] His phallocentric style falls short of parodying this most masculine of genres, signifying a vacuous, polished copy of an original. While such a strategy shows off one's virtuosic style, it falls short of the political objective of metal 20 years on! As I interpret it, the perfectly controlled falsetto and technical proficiency ascribes to an exclusive identification that frames the 'I' by allegorizing the performer's mimicry. This type of performativity, a 'put-on queering around with style', is manifested in the 'relation of being implicated in that which one opposes' (Butler 1993, p. 240), which, in the end, establishes a show of political resistance that is not oppositional. The track 'I Believe in a Thing Called Love', with its deployment of dazzling vocal techniques, rearticulates the very phallocentric ideals it occasions through drag. Butler concedes in her studies that drag is about performing out the 'sign' of gender, 'a sign that is not the same as the body that it figures' (ibid., p. 237). In this sense, the hyperbolic dimension of Justin Hawkins's performance, its knowing insincerity, is as haunted by its own inefficacy as its gender imperative. Invariably, such constructions result in their own insubordination. He is no dandy.

---

[13]     In her analysis of this song, Sheila Whiteley also makes the point that Justin Hawkins appropriates and embodies an element of rock excess and 'although his camp gestures and falsetto evoke memories of Mercury', there is strong evidence of past heroes such as 'Ian Gillan (Deep Purple), Jon Anderson (Yes), Thijs van Leer (Focus)' (Whiteley 2007, p. 30).

[14]     I am indebted to Sarah Niblock, who pointed out that the 'camp, drag look' of the flamboyant hard rock guitarist does not necessarily signify dandyism. Justin Hawkins's parody of phallocentricity as resolutely phallic (in the same way as Led Zeppelin) is a strong defence against being seen as feminine, and his spoof on gender-bending is a mere token gesture.

*Robbie Williams: 'Millennium' (1998)*

Socially and historically grounded, vocal articulation tells us much about how musical genres are established. Vocality concerns the details in the voice – the signifiers of the body – that render singing possible. As I have been pointing out in this chapter so far, strong distinctions define voices and stylize them, where the distinctive speech physiology of an artist establishes subjectivity. Williams's voice, a marker of impertinence, comes across through attitude, accent and a put-on Northern-ness. In comparison to Justin Hawkins, I would argue that Williams possesses a style that is distinguished by charade, and, hence, is more original. Aided by a heavy vibrato on long notes that connotes a sense of gloating, Williams draws on the many codes of British rock and pop. From the album *I've Been Expecting You*, released in 1998, the third track, 'Millennium', is crammed full of vocal techniques that make for a camp performance.[15] Built around the famous sample of Nancy Sinatra's theme for the James Bond film *You Only Live Twice*, the song epitomizes a dandy-in-performance. A close second to Prince's '1999', 'Millennium' became a hit for heralding in the new millennium. Vocally, several strategies extract the sentiments of this song. For instance, fluctuations in register not only create an expression that is fun-seeking, but also heighten a sense of dramatic delivery. Further idiosyncrasies in 'Millennium' are conveyed through a standard mid-range and falsetto tone, as Williams sneers and jeers through a quasi-spoken voice in his natural register. Starting with the phrase 'We've got stars directing our fate', this high-pitched full chorus enters at the end of the fourth bar of the introduction melody (Example 5.5). In the verse sections, less use of effects than in the choruses are employed as the voice is mapped closer to the kit and bass lines. Later a fuller, more reverbed sound in the chorus sections releases the emotions of the lyrics, which are supported by the introduction of strings and multi-vocals. Later on, the bridge passage (2:08–2:28), 'Come and have a go if you think you are hard enough', consists of a registral shift to falsetto, with larger intervallic leaps and staccato accents resolving ceremoniously to the word 'millennium' (Example 5.5). The three bars of melodic material preceding the resolution to 'millennium' consist of tricky octave and major seventh leaps. Rapid intervallic rising and falling of this kind enables an outburst of emotions. Rhythmically, the melody is jerked off by its syncopation, contributing further to the build-up in tension and energy in the voice. The effect is one of hyperbolic animation.

---

[15]    Notably, while this remains one of Williams's most popular songs in Europe, the story is different on the other side of the Atlantic, where its reception has been lukewarm. British camp does not always travel easily.

Example 5.5: 'Millennium'

Languidly, the word 'millennium' is articulated by a full-throated sound, with deft vibrato punctuating its final note. Accenting the fourth syllable (instead of the second in normal speech), Williams milks the symbolism of this word by inflection and ornamentation (Example 5.5). Set to five pitches (not including the B natural as this is a downward grace note on A flat), 'millennium' comprises variable angular intervals and melodic fragments, while the diction of this word ensures a clarity that brims with innuendo. Vocal phrasing playfully delivers a superficial storyline in an arrangement that shifts texturally from a sparse to dense textural carpet.

In the mix, Williams's voice is kept continuously mobile, either immersed or left raw and exposed. Overall, the recorded-image is determined by details of vocal inflection, underlying an attitude that not only has to do with what is being sung, but also what is intended for his fans. Dynamically inflated in the final verse (3:03–3:10), his vocal tone is mocking, 'I often think we were born to hate, Get up and see the sarcasm in my eyes'. The deliberate accenting of the words 'hate', 'sarcasm' and 'eyes', suggests a faking of earnestness (Read: 'Don't take me that seriously'), as once again, connotation is felt by ornamentation, hyperbole, and the specific accent of pitches. Finally, when the instrumental intensity of this passage increases, Williams's vocal input, multilayered, is altered in an obvious way with him reverting to a more elaborate form of syllabic embellishment.

Flashy on all counts, 'Millennium' is the over-the-top camp offering of the late twentieth century, epitomizing in every way the dandified prankster. This performance thrives on pastiche and parody, as Williams accents his own theatricality and contrivedness. Indeed, something very British characterizes his act. He is an expert at moving in and out of characters, inspiring pleasure by larking around. Regularly framed by glitzy arrangements, Williams puts on his voices, some 'natural', some overly affected. Yet, while the clown character he depicts might be an endearing character, his folly is not always convincing; a pivot point of my discussion of masking in Chapter 6.

All of this means that voices fulfil the function of negotiating pathos through register, mannerism and production processes. Unlike Justin Hawkins's pyrotechnics that exhibit a more impressive display of agility, that involve swooping up and down the register and hitting his pitches spot-on, Williams's vocal display is more measured and assisted in the production with a different form of technical virtuosity. I would say that the main conditions of his vocal coding relate to the charge of a polished style. Effortlessly, he conjures up a wealth of associations we have with generic posturing, and from this, then, Williams's vocal mannerisms determine the type of empathic and emotional charge of his musical style. His containment of subjectivity in vocal sound, and the fooling around with masculinity, serves to reassure fans of the 'sincerity' of his performance.

*Bryan Ferry: 'Don't Stop The Dance' (1985)*

This last point also becomes operative when working out Bryan Ferry's demeanour, especially in the post-Roxy Music period.[16] The track 'Don't Stop The Dance', off his sixth solo album *Boys And Girls* (1985), consists of a lush, sensual groove that transports the velvet-like croon of Ferry's vocal delivery; yet another poignant sign of the times. For many Roxy fans, however, the glossy studio techniques and faultless productions that the band turned to on their last album were a huge disappointment.

The mid-1980s were very competitive years for British pop artists, and, while *Boys and Girls* went virtually unnoticed in the USA, it soared to number one in the UK with critical acclaim.[17] Dedicated to the memory of Ferry's late father, *Boys and Girls* contains many musical references to Roxy Music's final album *Avalon* from 1982. 'Slave to Love' and 'Don't Stop the Dance' are momentous landmarks in Ferry's post-Roxy era. With meticulous attention to the smooth production, the iconoclastic sound associated with Roxy Music is always evident even when Ferry dims the lights.[18]

His vocal timbre furnishes a style of crooning that maintains just the right degree of detachment. Quivering in his mid-range, Ferry enters 'Don't Stop The Dance' with the lines, 'Mama says the truth is all that matters, lying and deceiving is a sin'. From the outset, the song has a dance club feel despite its slow, drawn-out tempo and romantic lyricism. Elegant and richly evocative, Ferry's vocal part is alluring, encapsulating the era of the New Romantics. His register and resonance, plus a large dose of reverb, create an eerie, melancholic raspiness in vocal colour that comes across in a soft-focus kind of way. The song also consists of clean synthesizer parts that are placed in the mix at a medium volume level and pitch. Cushioning the melody, they introduce a sense of state of the art technology and modernity. Complementing the synth parts a gentle, bouncy bass allows the riff to groove in a cool, laid-back manner, always with just the right levels of control. Mostly, Ferry's over-produced vocal sound is a marker of the fashion and design-oriented end of the market, symbolizing the rise of the New Man in the

---

[16] As lead vocalist for Roxy Music in the 1970s, Ferry pursued a parallel solo career until the group finally disbanded in 1983.

[17] For example, albums by Sting (*The Dream of the Blue Turtles*), Phil Collins (*No Jacket Required*), Tears For Fears (*Songs From the Big Chair*), Bryan Adams (*Reckless*), Wham (*Make It Big*) and Dire Straits (*Brothers in Arms*).

[18] Ferry also enlists well known artists on this album, such as Dire Straits' Mark Knopfler (guitar) and Guy Fletcher (keyboards); Pink Floyd's David Gilmour (guitar); Nile Rodgers (guitar); and jazz musicians Marcus Miller (bass) and David Sanborn (saxophone).

1980s.[19] Vocal virtuosity in his case is of a very different kind from the other artists I have considered so far, located in an attitude towards singing that is caught up in pitch control, vocal width, phrasing, and rhythmic articulation. The phrasing in 'Don't Stop The Dance' is so airbrushed that it can hardly fail to ensnare the listener; for every breath he takes, he enhances the seductive signifiers of an aurally configured body. What, then, can this tell us about the art of vocal seduction?[20]

Example 5.6: 'Don't Stop The Dance'

Strategies of performing seductively involve beautiful melodies that are angular and not overtly challenging in their intervallic structures. The verse's tune in 'Don't Stop The Dance' (Example 5.6) almost drowns in the effects of its production, profiling Ferry's voice as sensual and vibrant (at least in the context of the 1980s). A velvet-like purring quality in the diction works with the timbre and 'grain' of a voice, and is so full of sensuality that it might well be taken for phone-sex. But it would be missing the point to detach the histrionic elements of Ferry's style from his reception and the audience he addressed. Stylistically, his smarmy delivery reflects not only the purity of performance and studio production, but also that of its social context in Britain of the 1980s. I am referring to stylistic codes that are vastly different from others during the same period, such as indie rock. Conversely, the indie-influenced singer of the 1980s would be less polished than Ferry, and more rhythmically suspended in melodic phrasing, sounding 'natural' (Bannister 2006). And such a prototype of this vocality is found 20 years on in another British dandy, Doherty, whose singing unfurls in an 'ordinary', raw and sensitive manner, where an edgy tone belies a temperament that is unashamedly self-indulgent, even by Ferry's standards.

*Pete Doherty: 'Albion' (2005)*

The Babyshambles' song 'Albion', from their first album *Down in Albion*, yields something poised and defiant. This is all down to Doherty. Performed as a lullaby,

---

[19]    In other studies, I have explained the effect of changes in the marketplace on male pop artists within a British context (Hawkins 2002, 2006).

[20]    If Ferry is only performing, is he still classifiable as a hysteric? Qualities of the hysteric are taken up in Middleton's discussion of the performer that draws on Lacanian issues of embodiment. See Middleton (2007, pp. 114–16).

this song, a reference to the ancient name of Great Britain (in Ptolemy *Alouion*), commences with a violent, distorted instrumental jam introduction of one minute's duration. After this, the song settles down into a mundane, steady slow tempo with conventional chord progressions. The topic of Arcadia is ubiquitous in a narrative that oversentimentalizes England: 'so come away, won't you, come away, we could go to, Deptford, Catford, Watford, Digberth, Mansfield, ahh, anywhere in Albion'. The affect of this delivery is derivative of The Clash, The Kinks, The Smiths, and the Stones.

Poetically, 'Albion' lends itself in every way to a pop–indie style, where one of the many features of vocal presence hints at a childlike regression. Attentive when it comes to lyrical enunciation, Doherty extracts his narrative through a vocal technique that is premised on 'ordinariness', a point I will elaborate on later in this chapter. Beginning the song with a vocal tone that is chesty, he uses little exertion from the diaphragm to produce a mellow, gentle and rounded tone; the effect is one of vulnerability. But, as the intensity of his delivery increases and his range extends upwards, so his timbre becomes more nasal and thinner with far less resonance. In such melodic passages subtleties of sloppy pitching are discernible, especially in the straining-up to a high pitch and never hitting it square on. Such intonational carelessness seems in keeping with a nonchalant style.

Example 5.7: 'Albion'

Doherty's phrasing involves him straining up to high notes in his 'natural' voice, exhibiting all the traits of effort that go into being confessional and personal. Alex Hannaford points out that Doherty has been intent on using his songs on *Down In Albion* to tell stories, well aware that 'his tortured soul was laid bare on this album' (Hannaford 2006, p. 309). Technically, Doherty's voice goes a long way in affording credibility to the nostalgic, the mundane and the ordinary, as he mythologizes England's pastures green. Much the same type of vocal expression characterizes the other tracks from *Down In Albion*, where the dandy comes alive through the choice of material and performance antics. Not without some deliberation, the track 'A Rebours' ('Against the Grain'), borrowed from the French novelist Joris-Karl Huysmans's 1884 novel *A rebours*, depicts the life and tastes of the prime character Des Esseintes, a reclusive, vulnerable dandy and anti-hero who despises nineteenth century bourgeois society.

Doherty's stylistic references on 'A Rebours' can be traced back further than just punk rock to the skiffle form of the 1920s, which refers to British bands who substituted expensive instruments with homemade instruments like the kazoo, washboards and tea-chest basses, to draw on black American roots music. This influenced John Lennon, and is inherited by other English bands, including Doherty's former band The Libertines. Once again we are reminded that the revival of styles within a British context has an intricate genealogy that gains credibility in various ways from one artist to the next. Nine years Doherty's senior, Paul Draper's approach to singing exemplifies this in quite another way.

*Paul Draper: 'Wide Open Space' (1997)*

Influenced by Bowie, Robert Smith and Kurt Cobain, Draper's style is also derivative of Frankie Goes To Hollywood, Prince, Duran Duran, George Michael, and a touch of The Clash and Soft Cell. In the wake of the Britpop craze, Draper, lead singer and rhythm guitarist for Mansun,[21] a guitar band, would produce a sound collage that looked backward and forward in a postmodern kind of way. Combining hard rock with the stylishness of the New Romantics, with a touch of indie pop, Mansun would take over from Blur with their debut album *Attack of the Grey Lantern* in 1997, becoming one of the most acclaimed new British groups. Mansun's success, however, was short-lived, not only due to an over-zealous eclecticism, but also because of a lead singer who might have just got it wrong.

Discernible as much in his vocal sound as his image, Draper's identity would change vividly from one song to the next. Mansun's DVD *Legacy*, released in 2006, profiled the track 'Wide Open Space', the fifth track off *Attack of the Grey Lantern*. This exaggerated performance is supported by starkly contrasted melodic phrases, driving guitar riffs and a spacious mix swamped by reverb. Draper's highly compressed voice extracts the essence of the lyrics through melodies that are elegantly sculptured and overlaced with reverb, while the effect of his pitch and register is perfectly balanced and controlled in a way that comes over as effortless and glossy. Affected in a Britpop way, Draper's vocal expression is warm, albeit detached and superficial: 'I'm in the wide open space, it's freezing, You'll never go to heaven with a smile on your face from me'.

Example 5.8: 'Wide Open Space'

---

[21]    Mansun were formed in Chester in 1995 and disbanded in 2003. I am grateful to Shara Rambarran for introducing me to Mansun during a guest lecture at Oslo University, and for her useful feedback on my ideas about Draper's style of performance.

Living up to its title, everything about the song's production feels expansive and chilled. Not only do the backing vocals enhance Draper's whining style, but they also intensify the timbral colouring. In particular, the multilayered vocals and instrumental parts merge into a space, ensnaring the listener into a virtual world that offers escape. Draper's treatment of the lyrics of 'Wide Open Space' include colourful vocal gestures, such as impressive intervallic shifts from one voice type to the next. Aided by a loud echo effect, his voice exudes a tenderness that is girly and contrived. This is largely due to a falsetto tone that is brought to the fore of an overproduced recording, with an abundance of digital delay on the guitars and the other instrumental parts. In addition, the overwhelming sense of textural depth creates a sensation of vast, endless planes that are swamped by the blurring of all the instrumental and vocal components. The perceived motion between events in the near and the far distance through panning suggest that 'sense of space' (Moore 2001, p. 164) typical in rock productions, with the polarization of variable tempi evoking openness in a sumptuous way. Thus, overindulgence might be an apt term for describing the particularity of Draper's dandyism. Ultimately it is the production that aestheticizes the original voice.

*Jarvis Cocker: 'Common People' (1995)*

So far I am suggesting that studio production shapes our perceptions of vocality. Another fitting example of this is Pulp's single 'Common People'. One of the legendary Britpop anthems, it reached number two in the UK singles chart in 1995.[22] In a song that brought class matters to the fore, Cocker's performance is a powerful critique of social slumming on the part of individuals who seek to glamorize poverty. Derisive lines, such as 'I want to sleep with common people like you', form a fitting riposte from the smart side of working-class culture who get their kicks from 'birds', 'footie' and thug films. In the song the protagonist claims that his female friend from Greece will never be like 'common people' because in the end she is of a different class.[23] During the course of the song, the girl is taken to a supermarket to enter an imaginary world with no money: 'You will never understand, how it feels to live your life, with no meaning or control'. Social condemnation becomes a satirical rendering of humiliation.

Set against rising keypads, the catchy four-bar single-finger synthesizer riff (played by Pulp's keyboardist, Candida Doyle) is offered short respite by two drum breaks. Musically, the upbeat tempo and rhythmic charge makes the melody

---

[22]  'Common People' also appears on Pulp's 1995 album *Different Class*. Notably, in the single, which lasts approximately four minutes, the final verse, 'Like a dog lying in a corner' is not included, although it appears on the album version. This includes a climactic point, where the singer whispers and parodically refers to the life of common people.

[23]  In the video of 'Common People' there is an appearance by actress Sadie Frost and a cross reference to the Eleanor Rigby sequence in the film *Yellow Submarine*, where everyday people are positioned in repeating loops lasting less than a second.

memorable, as Nick Banks's tight drumming underpins Cocker's phrasing. Hewn over the rigid beats, his vocal delivery is characterized by ragged timing and erratic change-ups. Hinting at a mish-mash of stylistic influences – New Wave keyboard idioms, 1970s-type rock drumming, and fuzzy glam guitars – 'Common People' follows in the wake of The Who and The Kinks in many different ways. Layered with instrumental lines that build up texturally to the shattering climax, Cocker yells out, 'You will never understand, how it feels to live your life, with no meaning or control, and with nowhere else to go'. Not unlike Morrissey, Cocker's retort lies in the gleaming observations of British social life, as he confronts the anxiety, struggles and uncertainties of everyday incidents through a singing style that progressively escalates in terms of emotional sentiment.

Example 5.9: 'Common People'

Bearing in mind that such readings are based upon the recording as score, attention to recording techniques is vital. For instance, the specific microphones chosen, and the blatant use of 'issing', assist the sense of intimacy and sincerity, thus enhancing Cocker's vocal positioning in the mix. Starting off thin and soft in timbre, his diction is crisp, with syllables and starts of words, especially beginning with C's and T's, that crackle in the mix. All through the song, Cocker's singing is dynamically measured, with him moving from a quasi-conversational state to a full-throated style. Marked by an increased exertion as the register escalates, its straining upwards cannot fail to connote passion as he screams, 'You'll never live like common people, You'll never do whatever common people do, Never fail like common people, You'll never watch your life slide out of view' (Example 5.9).

In the coda (5:06–5:51) a manic edge to the voice culminates in his final outburst: 'I wanna live with common people like you'. Finally his voice cracks on the word 'you' in an extended three-note jam. On this climactic point he turns to yodelling, bordering on a hysteria that is reminiscent of the singing style of artists such as Steve Harley.[24] At this point, Cocker's vocal expression is also coloured by a Northern accent that befits his overtly mannered style, energized and hysterical.

---

[24]    Cf. Moore (2001) who compares Cocker's approach to Steve Harley's in Pulp's song, 'Sorted for E's and Wizz'. Moore also describes how Cocker and Brett Anderson, from Suede, show traits of an early David Bowie, especially in terms of 'near-hysterical forays into an uneasy falsetto', which are discernible in the singer Tony Hadley (ibid., p. 175).

As the word 'you' gives way to its vowel 'ooou', the audio space becomes blissfully non-verbal and texturally dense. Leading up to the final cadence point, a resolution to 'like you' involves vocal streaming on 'you-oo-oo-oo', as Cocker is freed from a deluge of ecstatic emotions. Narratively, an abdication of social responsibility through patronizing the girlfriend from Greece is crystallized in a moment that feels eternal.

In all these songs it is the manner of performing out lyrics that plays a major role in communicating temperament, engaging us, the listeners, directly with the performer. Regulated by compositional structuration and recording production, the singing voice operates referentially. Nowhere is this more prevalent than in the articulation of a tune. In Table 5.1 I have presented a catalogue that not only distinguishes one artist from the next, but also slots the voice into a context mediated by musical style. By this, I am suggesting that recorded voices are relics of the persona, where the nuances, techniques and stylistic inflections of the singing voice form part of individual agency. In pop, rules are learnt, shared and imitated according to circumstance. This process alone encroaches on the personal characteristics of performativity.

As my main aim is to identify the peculiarity of the dandified performance, a central part of my inquiry is directed towards attitude. Configured by timbre, inflection, accent and dynamic colouring that extract style, vocal properties are always aligned to the individual's register, gesture, timbre and production effects. With all the songs taken up in this section the voice remains contingent on recording processes, whereby the producer's role in the creative process is paramount. Staging the voice through the recording is about staging the personality, and this illustrates the painstaking attention to detail as masterminded by the production team. What this means is that the recorded voice is as much the outcome of the producer's input as the artist's, the difference being that the former is passive in his role while the latter active. As such, both parties inject their identities into the sonic space of vocal production, enticing the listener in through the full-blown seduction of performance.

Table 5.1    Features of Vocal Identity

| | Normal Range | Falsetto Use | Gestural/attitude | Timbre | Effects | Style |
|---|---|---|---|---|---|---|
| **David Bowie 'Slip Away'** | Mid-range | None | Heavy vibrato, quivering | Emotionally loaded & delicate | Variable use | Art rock |
| **Mick Jagger 'Hideaway'** | Mid-high range | Occasional | Growling, whining & over-emphatic | Thin, but hard-edged with Wyclef's timbre | Moderate use | Rock |
| **Steven P. Morrissey 'At Last I Am Born'** | Mid-range | None | Elated tone, exaggerated and parodic | Resonant, full voice | Moderate use of echo and reverb | Indie rock |
| **Justin Hawkins 'I Believe In A Thing Called Love'** | High range | High-rate occurence | Guitar solo imitative Hysterical | Strident, determined & full | High use of reverb | Hard rock |
| **Robbie Williams 'Millennium'** | Varying between mid and high | Alternating falsetto & natural voice | Scornful, cheeky & defiant | Deep, booming vs thin, delicate | Moderate reverb Heavy vibrato | Disco pop |
| **Bryan Ferry 'Don't Stop the Dance'** | High range | None | Sexy, gentle & trembling | Velvet-like, smooth and sensitive | Heavy echo and reverb | Synthesizer pop |
| **Pete Doherty 'Albion'** | Low range | None | Laid-back, nonchalant & passionate | Mellow, sonorous | Slight reverb | Post-punk |
| **Paul Draper 'Wide Open Space'** | High range | On certain cadence points | Affected, mournful, yearning | Fragile & affected | Moderate to high use of reverb | Pop ballad |
| **Jarvis Cocker 'Common People'** | Shift from mid-low range to high register | None | Angry, protesting & mocking | Rich, rounded & soulful | Heavy reverb and close-up miking | Britpop |

## Corporeality and the Affected Voice

How vocal style is aligned to image demands a closer consideration of the processes that go into singing. Pulling together the emotional, the cultural and the aesthetic through performance, the pop voice relies on imaginative forms and dramatized patterns of relationship. The pop voice, in obvious ways, is positioned in stark contrast to the classical, trained bel canto voice. Technically, pop vocality is rooted in a crafted approach that highlights a set of criteria that are predicated upon aesthetic norms. These are marked by the technical mastery of aspects such as balance, dynamic diversity and register control. That the pop voice is usually a recorded construction also distinguishes it from the properties of the 'live' voice outside the studio environment. For when it comes to recording practices, specific strategies stake out style and subjectivity. Broadly speaking, then, pop vocality is mediated through studio production and, only rarely, is performed live without any technological assistance. What I am getting at is that vocalization is a prime mediator of identity construction, connoting subjectivity through regularized norms that become the trademark of the artist. Within all forms of vocal practice, a personalized style is constructed in direct response to generic identification, and in this way singing is consigned to a musical coding that is almost instantly identifiable (consider the difference between Pavarotti's and Jagger's voices, or pop and classical boy bands Take That and Il Divo). The mediatory power of the voice and its idealized position in popular styles has everything to do with studio production and technological processing, which not only reinforces but also transforms vocal features. The recording is a reconstruction of subjectivity. And, defined through its relationship with everything else in the mix, vocal presence is projected in countless ways.

Seldom hovering far from being inventive, the pop dandy stages a fantasy around his own vocal construction. Pondering over the smooth crooning of Bryan Ferry, the acerbic edge of Mick Jagger, the woefulness of Morrissey, the edginess of Pete Doherty, the stroppiness of Robbie Williams, the declamatory magnificence of Justin Hawkins, the sarcasm of Cocker or the sissified allure of Draper, stark images spring to mind that are inseparable from the body. Because voices inscribe their own unique sense of composure, they console, entertain and delight by spectacularizing the body. Cowardian in its affectation, the voices of Morrissey, Tennant, Bowie and Williams might come across dandified because of their production, as much as the embellishments that underlie their technical proficiency. Indeed, every performance portrays some level of attitudinal adaptation, a particular response that is received corporeally.[25] Vocal production

---

[25] When it comes to the term 'corporeality' in musical expression, one of the proponents of this concept is Harry Partch. The large proportions of his self-created instruments induced movements on the part of performers in ways which Partch considered new: part dance, part theatre. His concept of 'corporeality' has to do with the attitude of the musicians performing live; that musicians have to use their whole bodies in performing

therefore functions as a vehicle for relaying the artist's persona. Which returns us to the central question: in what ways does singing encode the mannerisms of the body?

In some genres, the uncharacteristically high-pitched male voice might emasculate the subject or, at least, signify some loss of masculinity. But in pop and rock this is far from a simple matter. As we have seen in the case of Justin Hawkins, a high-pitched voice and screeching falsetto signifies a phallocentricity that is traditional and normative.[26] For vocal production is gestural and ineffable in its non-verbal quality, especially when the performance is a reaction to the primary state of the lived-body. When recorded, the body signifies a constant outward movement that is directed to its surroundings from a centre point that prompts participation. Musical meaning is therefore performed out in pop, where the recording process has a controlling role. That recordings not only reproduce, but also strive to eradicate human error raises important questions attached to authenticity. The aesthetic implications of this are intriguing. Equipment and software programs are designed to rectify flaws – that 'out-of-tune' phrase, the weak control of a sustained note, the stumbling onto a 'wrong' note, and so on. As such, the idealized performance is commonly the recorded one, aligned to modes of edition, through which the voice looms more real, more attractive and more sexy than it really is. No longer a part of a human body, the recorded voice is an altered state, having eradicated all traces of human imperfection. Studio engineers and producers work on perfecting a vocal part through the technical mastery of bodily control. Thus, those who work behind the desk produce an audio image that is merged into the subjectivity we imagine. A process of masking, which I return to in Chapter 6, is part and parcel of being a pop artist.

From this we might ask: if the 'real' voice is eradicated from musical production, how does the audio image reconstruct it? And what are the aesthetic purposes of reconstructing vocal types? Answers to this are obviously related to the artists in question, and their recourse to vocal performance. In his theorization of vocal staging, Serge Lacasse (2000) identifies two elements for interpreting the voice's evocative power: first, the voice's insertion within the recording and 'its relationships with all the other acoustic data', and, second, the context of '*when* and *where* the recording is heard' (ibid., p. 166 – author's emphasis). Lacasse insists that there is 'nothing *a priori* in the lyrics themselves', but rather that it is the connotations that 'emerge from the interaction between the performance, the

---

rather than just their arms. For Partch the visual conjoined the corporeal; the aesthetics of instruments on stage needed to be complemented by the musicians who were to be actively involved in the whole production. His idea of corporeal involvement is about the crucial physicality of the musician.

[26]   Musical gestures, as Tarasti notes, are 'like organs of a 'body'' (Tarasti 1997, p. 23), and in keeping with scholars George Herbert Mead and Maurice Merleau-Ponty, Tarasti argues that musical meaning is immanent in this respect.

lyrics and the voice's settings' (ibid., p. 236). If this is the case, what then conveys attitude, and how is this externalized vocally?

A primary component of vocal staging, attitude is predicated upon the precarious balance between artistic endeavour and temperament. Moreover, attitude is part of temperament, harnessed by the producer and engineer as much as the artist. In actual point of fact, the result of team collaboration is one of default. Someone dares to come forth, addresses another person, pleads, prescribes, demands, performs, and then records. As such, an element of chance in the entire compositional process determines pop aestheticization. In a bid to entertain, albeit often to their consternation, pop artists grasp that they are in peril that all might be in vain. In fear of being misunderstood or ridiculed, strategies in performance are about self-protection. Faking it, a main part of vocal staging, is about seducing. And to succeed, the artist must make clear his or her emotions. Expressed in another way, self-humiliation, one prime characteristic of the British temperament, involves the emotive correspondence of one's voice to another; the pop artist always strikes up contact with the fan through the recorded voice. Thus, contingent on the responses of others, he recognizes the veneer of his authority as integral to the total production and packaging of agency.

Paradoxically, corporeality is delineated by the recording, as the body conceals as much as it exposes. In all the artists we have looked at so far, vocal staging is about humility, where vocal delivery begs for recognitions through imagination. Identifying with the artist's voice, we, as fans, invest in a wealth of emotions that form part of the construction of vocal effect. That is to say, the formal qualities of vocal construction produce a fictive form of corporeality through personal identification. As a result, fantasy as a response emerges as the prime purpose of the recorded performance, while its attendant pleasures occur along an aural continuum that shapes the object of our desires. After all, the recording process suggests that the close proximity of the voice is illusory, and, as Cubitt puts it, the voice becomes the 'the site of a paradoxically simultaneous promise and denial of intimacy. (…) It is a re-presentation, a signifier, the grounds of whose existence is the absence of the thing represented' (Cubitt 2000, p. 147). Sensing intimacy in the voice, then, is about emotional responses that promise identification in countless ways. Whether it is the raw physicality of a shrill falsetto, or the soft crooning of someone waxing lyrical, vocality activates trajectories of desire and familiarity. In Miller's study of the falsetto voice, he describes how it 'extends a male's voice, moving beyond restraints, harking back to a boy's voice, and reaching forward to a woman's range, without ever sounding female' (Miller 2003, p. 147). This returns us to the matter of corporeality in vocality.

Connoting corporeality, the pop voice, in Middleton's words, makes 'available new routes of imaginary identifications and evacuating the too-easy conflation of sight and sound characteristics of live performance' (Middleton 2006, p. 95). In this sense, the recorded voice holds something of a symbolic order, something that is intangible and abstract, yet still, at least in many cases, authentic. Middleton's position, like Miller's, refers to the subjectification of the recorded voice, where the audio image increases the tensions in gendered display. Significantly, the 'acoustic mirror' effect of vocality plays out 'the dramas of reflection, identity and difference that construct subjects and their others'. In such interplay, representation is twice removed, resulting in a 'display of a display', where certain aspects are left to the imagination (ibid., p. 96). The technical details of the voice are thus objectified by the recording, foregrounding the constructed aspects of the pop persona. All this clears the way for trickery in the performative inscription of the body, which I consider as a process of masking in performance.

Recorded voices are an enactment of mimicry, codified and validated by the entire production. The pop artist's relationship with the producer is about an intimate collaboration, having a direct bearing on the shaping of temperament. For what a pop artist has to say through the recording is quasi-biographical, staged and glamorized. Well aware of the individuality of vocal display, the producer crafts the recording in a way that not only idealizes the audio image, but also casts the singer. Subsequently, an entire vocal track or strand or snippet can be enhanced, overdubbed and tweaked many times following the initial take. For instance, the multitracking of voices signifies transference of control from the pop artist to the editorial control of technicians and engineers. This is particularly evident in the production of Bowie's voice over the course of several decades, where various techniques define his sound and identity. Having worked with Bowie for many years, Visconti attests to the stylistic tailoring that goes into producing Bowie's voice. On numerous occasions Visconti has emphasized the Britishness of Bowie, the role it has played, and the differences that exist between the USA and UK when it comes to recording. Ostensibly, Visconti's approach to production and arranging has much to do with knowing Bowie well, as much as identifying with his compositional ideas.[27]

Minute details in recording vocals, Visconti has stressed, highlight the importance of detailed sound engineering. Selecting microphones that best suit the artist's voice, for example, has a strong bearing on the musical style and the final production: 'I used it [the Telefunken ELAM 251 microphone] on Bowie's voice, and he just sounded beautiful on it because he's got low end in his voice, but the high end on that mic is brilliant, too, so the vocalist leaps out at you. That's a dream mic' (Visconti in Massey 2000, p. 151). Continuing to explain that he always records vocals with compression, Visconti insists that he does not allow it to go beyond 10dB of compression at a 3:1 ratio. The reason for this, he adds, is that 'most of the stuff I do is rock, so that's acceptable', and on rock records one can let the compressor do the riding. For Visconti recording the vocals constitutes the most important part of the mix:

---

[27]   Visconti's sensibility in adjusting his approach according to the individual is borne out by his work with Bolan/T. Rex, The Moody Blues, Morrissey, Joe Cocker, as well as post-punk musicians such as Adam Ant, Iggy Pop, Thin Lizzy, the Boomtown Rats, Sparks and Hazel O'Connor. See Visconti (2007).

> If the vocal is poorly placed in the mix, it's going to defeat the purpose, it's
> not going to sell the music. People will remember vocals more than they'll
> remember the guitar licks – most people buy a record because it's a great song.
> My way of doing that is, again, to see where the vocal lives sonically. See where
> it lives and play with EQ until you find where the vocal is going to be really hot
> (ibid., p. 153).

The effects used, and their assignment to each instrument and the voice, expose a
wealth of details and subtleties that alter and enhance audio imagery. Describing,
for instance, his use of flanging, an effect that greatly contributes to Bowie's voice,
Visconti further explains:

> I'm still a fan of [mechanical] flanging. I'll still do it in the old-fashioned way
> if I'm in a studio that has enough tape machines. You can't beat it. There's no
> box in existence that can go forward and backward in time, which is what you're
> doing when you do tape flanging – it's actually a time machine you've created
> on a little scale (ibid., p. 154).

From Visconti's accounts, it is evident that his approaches to recording vocals are
a valuable aid for understanding the significance of production. For the dynamic
of the pop voice is contingent on a process that is studio-based, the result of
which is complex at a creative and technical level. As such, the producer becomes
integrated into the pop voice, a part of the characteristics of the artist. Moreover,
the producer's responsibility is to literally amplify the artist's voice, establishing
what Tagg (1981) has referred to as vocal stance – the communicative function of
transmitter to receiver, which is aligned to musical style, lyric subject matter, and
recording techniques. All of this positions the singer's attitude in relation to the
listener's reception. One consequence of such an interrelationship is that listening
experiences are a function of a collective cultural and historical purpose. From
this, it becomes clear that singing opens up a space where identity is located as
something unstable and fluid, invoking a multitude of responses that are retrieved
through the cultural idiosyncrasies of sound and style. Proceeding into the final
discussion in this chapter, I now turn my attention to one of the quintessential
British attributes of pop dandyism, camp, which owes everything to the process of
recording and production.

### 'Camp' as Vocal Address

Camp has played an important historical and cultural role in the development of
pop music, and remains a striking trait of British sensibility. So, what is camp?
Musicologists Brett and Wood describe it as 'a disruptive style of humour that
defies canons of taste and by its very nature evades any stable definition' (2002,
pp.5–6). I would go further by saying camp takes something ordinary – an object,

a phrase, a person or a situation – and turns it into something ironic, exaggerated and seriously defensive. Performatively, camp is intended as an allusion – which means it is up to the reader or listener to forge the connection. 'Being camp' is about making fun of oneself in order to prove a point; ostensibly this can be as provocative as it is pretentious, as political as it is frivolous. Neil Tennant of the Pet Shop Boys is an obvious case in point, especially when it comes to musical performance.

Tennant recycles any number of strategies of surplus value through a voice that is drawn out and exaggerated. Discernible in his singing style is the articulation of vowels, overtly elasticized and prolonged, which increase the tendency towards embellishment and melisma (see Miller 2003). Melodic phrasing in Tennant's style also hinges on points of release, where the artist succumbs to the music through the lyrics. Not dissimilar to Morrissey's approach, Tennant accents key words that appear weighed down by the sounds of the vowels themselves, rather than just the word. Inflecting vowels vocally highlights lyrical spots and puts them into 'exclamation marks'. Earlier I referred to Morrissey's inflection of the word 'born' in 'At Last I Am Born', where the sound 'or' takes on a timbral tone that heightens the communicative dimension of the song. The rounding of the vowel 'born' can be perceived as a marker of hyperbolic intention. Like Tennant, Morrissey is acutely sensitive to the onomatopoeic figurations of speech, which become part of a general aesthetic in his musical style. Wordplay, stretched-out vowels and affected intonation encode a temperament and sensibility that is decidedly British.

Camp, consequently, denotes a complex cultural process. It involves that chit-chat quality of dishing ridiculous retorts, silly put-downs and outrageous gossip. Identifying camp, then, denotes an attitude on the part of the listener as much as the performer. According to Koestenbaum, '(e)xperiencing the camp glow is a way of reversing one's abjection, and, by witnessing the depletion of cultural monuments, experiencing one's own power to fill degraded artefacts to the brim with meanings' (Koestenbaum 1993, p. 117). A camp performance says much about the personal interpretation, emotional response and intimacy of perceiving something/someone as camp. Yet there are subtleties involved: 'It's more sublime and more camp to keep quiet about joy and then rescue the story later, once everyone else has abandoned it' (ibid., p. 117).[28] Charged with a high dose of irony, the camp voice is not just a confirmation of the artist's personality,

---

[28]    Koestenbaum's reading of opera diva Maria Callas eloquently sums this up: 'Though it seems sacrilegious to call Callas's musically compelling creations *camp*, she performed the same kind of reversal that camp induces: she shattered the codes that separate dead from living works of art. To crosscut rapidly between yesterday and today is an effect that, in different circumstances, we recognize as camp' (Koestenbaum 1993, p. 145). The idea of Callas as camp can be applied to the aesthetic, political and historical positioning of the female dandy, especially in the case of pop artists (I'm thinking of Siouxsie Sioux, Kylie Minogue, Christina Aguilera, Ana Mantronic of Scissor Sisters, and Pink), whose singing styles often come about through hyperbolic inflection.

but also a revelation of the imaginative ideals gained through bodily representation. Because of this, camp has stuck as a British colloquialism and is employed as a description for temperament.

A performer camping it up reveals many intentions (Cleto 1999; Ross 1999; Tinkcom 1999). And given that the context determines the perception of camp, there are features in need of identification. In his close reading of the Finnish group The Crash, John Richardson (2006) refers specifically to lisping, 'correct' articulation, affect, emphases, exaggeration and theatricality. Seen from a British perspective, it is interesting that Richardson's reading of Finnish camp offers up an interpretation that might go amiss among the majority of the fans themselves. Koestenbaum has dealt in detail with the sublime dimension of this through pointing to the qualifying or corroborating intentions of the scholar with a queer eye (Koestenbaum 1993, p. 117).

In addition to the features Richardson identifies in The Crash's camp performance, I want to register three other categories: empathy, idiolect and drag. Rife with *double entendre*, innuendo and pun, is much British pop. Conveyed through sonic codes that strike up an empathy with the fan, the pop performance employs camp for the sake of humorous intent. The vocal styles of Bowie, Morrissey, Jagger, Tennant, Cocker, Williams and Draper communicate a sensibility that is different from one another's. For camp expression has to do with lyrical emphasis, allusion and style of delivery, where their abiding identities are constituted as part of their narratives. Notwithstanding these distinctions, and many more, artists regularly make fun of themselves (and others) in a very British way; this is what 'camping it up' means. Camp personae, however, depend on empathy, which is about accessing responses that are inextricably linked to idiolects – the words and sounds chosen that characterize the individual's idiosyncrasies. For example, as we have seen earlier, Morrissey's voice serves as an idiolect for his ambivalence towards many heartfelt matters. Modelled on the forlorn, mournful, dissident anti-hero of the suburban bed-sit, his self-loathing, Wildean-inspired narratives vividly equate ordinariness with glamour. Capitalizing on his camp appeal, Morrissey filters his persona through a vocal style that sounds vulnerable, often playing out the innocent victim in a struggle with himself as much as with those around him. His camp vocality suggests a unique approach to melodic phrasing that exposes a helplessness; poetic satire, smirking, an overuse of superlatives and vicious putdowns are his regular defence tactics. One effect of Morrissey's agency, as with Tennant and Bowie, is a satirical approach to storytelling, which belies a Cowardian penchant for wit and banter. In the tradition of Coward and others, Morrissey's persona is mediated through the affected mannerisms associated with the British music hall tradition that elicit surprise and delight.

Pop theatrics frequently ridicule the hypocrisy of the dominant culture. One might say that part of the dandy's idiolect is to challenge political, social and sexual values. This is verified by a string of artists who have gay connections (Liza Minnelli, Dusty Springfield, RuPaul, Boy George, Liberace and Glen Milstead (Divine)). To be sure, the camp display that Tennant exhibits is a send-up of his (and Chris Lowe's) gayness. Exaggerated aspects in their productions shape them as objects of desire, and, yet, distance them from the emotional content of their performance. The Pet Shop Boys' songs and videos can therefore be read as an allusion of their music, where the reality of performance is verified by a self-acknowledgement of their very pretence. And while camp is not necessarily sophisticated, the Pet Shop Boys' brand most certainly is, where their campness surfaces as a prominent marker of their aesthetic.

Among other things, the put-on vulnerability of the camp act is Baudelairean, in the sense that it becomes a defence of an aesthetic, in pop's case the by-product of postmodern art and culture post-1950s. Into the twenty-first century camp is so ubiquitous that it no longer is relegated to one particular group. Doherty's queer style, as we have seen in Chapter 4, eschews a host of conventions by taking the route of the whimsical, forlorn performer. His attitude is captured by an aesthetic that is based upon a renunciation of control. Foppish sloppiness and a cool demeanour, in his case, resists the glitzy disco-style of the Pet Shop Boys. Further, Doherty's vocal simplicity is rhythmically loose and kept low in the mix. Vocal staging for him centres on the de-emphasis of musical skills in the name of poetic brilliancy. On the whole, the transgressive aspect of the Babyshambles musical genre – post-punk, indie rock – articulates the latent melancholy of the artist's cause through a resistance to being outwardly garish, as in the case of Williams, Kay, Almond and, at times, Jagger. Bannister argues that 'melancholics are obsessed with the past', characterized by a masculinity that is associated with indie music in numerous ways (Bannister 2006, p. 138). In Doherty's case, a melancholic detachment from social and emotional investment, however, seeks its glamorization elsewhere, in the realm of excessive drug use and the attitudes of regression and passivity it provokes (Reynolds 1989).

Over time, a variety of tropes of cultural and social stereotypes have been moulded into camp, where the body and its gendered subjectivity denotes cultural production and notions of authenticity. In a Butlerian light, the pop subject is construed through processes of repetition that deal with sexuality, race, ethnicity and gender. By deconstructing gender binarisms and probing at the self-perpetuation of mimesis, Butler reveals norms as fictions and nature as culture.[29] In other words, gender, as performance, is a self-construction of subjective entity. Because the self is not stable, it is conditional on sets of relations that assume a reality through aspects of performativity. A type of *manière* typifies the dandy's vocal sensibility and mannerisms that fit into a dominant culture that stages a policy of recontextualization. To explain: the rare status of the dandified act thrives on a large cultural context, and as part of a fragmented subject, his access to the public domain is made possible by the musical force of cultural assimilation. Musical subjectivity is unquestionably an expression of deep-felt emotions that are conditional on cultural imagination. Thus, camp works as a critique of the

---

[29]    See Butler (1993).

entertainment industry, and I think the pop dandy signals a new critical episteme in the circulation of male identities.

Located within a performance context are countless ideals linked to self-expression and Western modernity. Warhol's employment of icons to contest the tensions within the dichotomy of high/low art confirmed that through camp there is no such thing as an original. For instance, constructing themselves for the consumption of others, pop singers are dependent on being adored by others, meeting their demands and desires on virtually every level. Camp aesthetics is determined by the rejection of essentialist identity, endorsing the performative self as a stylized act. It is through a fabrication of authenticity, deeply embedded in performance ideals, that dandyism is set to camp. As such, individual agency through musical expression reveals how the voice attends to the rhetorical demands of their peculiarity. The politics of camp in pop assume that musical gestures and performances are a put-on display of self-expression. In this sense, mannerism, language, theatricality and slapping on make-up are responsible for radical changes in the definition of masculinity. This is why dressing-up inscribes a symbolic exchange that sanctions the performer's intentions.

Camp in pop involves identification through musical coding. Critical to this process, though, are the extra-musical aspects of performance practice. Thus, it is the correspondence between musical codes and their delivery that activates empathic response. Pop music bridges the gap between frivolity and intensity as a locus of concentration. In the examples presented in this chapter, I find all the performances constitutive of camp in their own ways. In 'Common People', Cocker's vocal phraseology is characterized by a conversational structuring that draws on the English ballad tradition. Provocatively, Cocker's persona is loaded with connotations that are spiced up by the lyrics, by placing them in arch quotation marks. Inferences to 'everyday people' are about Cocker's own ego production as a carrier of the whiney Britpop lad, the construction of the subject who is in rebellion with himself. How can such a melodramatic retort fail to be camp?

Other markers of put-on rebellion occur in Morrissey's recording of 'At Last I Am Born', Jagger's 'Hideaway' and Bowie's 'Slip Away', where vocal delivery is heavily mannered and ornate. Predominantly camp, their melodic articulation gives credence to the lyrics, rather than vice versa, as vocal styling nurses empathy. From this, camp seems reserved for those 'with a high degree of cultural capital' (Ross 1999, p. 316), who have the confidence to define their taste on their own terms. At any rate, camp is tied up with the technical objectives of the recording production that not only authenticate identity, but also reveal the artist's own notions of self-aestheticization. Historically, Warhol's impact on 1960s pop made the pop artist camp. Bowie's voice, having always exhibited elements of exaggeration and hyperbole, conveys a playfulness that champions expressions of individuality through a camp sensibility. Invariably, his songs disclose a contrived quality that is wrapped up as much in his vocal sound as in his personality inventions (Ziggy Stardust, Aladdin Sane, The Thin White Duke, and others). Often with pointed irony, Bowie lets his fans know why he is assuming a new role, as he revels in borrowed styles, mocking the pretension of this as something trivial. Although his camp sensibility, as Nick Stevenson (2006, p. 53) argues, is most obvious in his early creation, Ziggy Stardust, it is also apparent in the *Hunky Dory* album from 1971. Also camp remains a trait right through all his work into the new millennium, as exemplified in *Heathen*. Mostly, Bowie's crisp enunciation projects a theatricality, where the manipulation of his voice produces a wealth of timbres and expressions. His intended self-parody brings to mind the idea that sound is actually no less camp than the imagery we associate with the artist: for to be camp in pop is to sound camp, and this is contingent upon a strategy of alienation. Singing, then, is always staged by a set of sonic codes that are definable by their purported effect. Of the range of elaborate effects, melodies and production techniques considered in this chapter, it is vocal effort that projects the individual's personal characteristics most. Singing is the most intimate inscription of identity and therefore has everything to do with the peculiarities of the pop dandy.

## Conclusion

If vocality translates into artifice, ostentation or even 'ordinariness', what makes a performance dandified through singing? And how does production influence the mannered voice, transporting it into our personal space? At the heart of this issue is subjectivity. By reference to a range of devices, I have attempted to illustrate how the pop voice is a powerful transmitter of subjectivity through attitude. Indeed, the mediation of attitude is a salient part of understanding vocal staging. As we have seen, working out vocal strategies helps advance the idea of dandification in pop. Through songs a performance exposes the contradictions that complicate gender positioning, and into this equation enters camp. Camp produces mixed signals that blur the motive or ideological agenda of the artist. For singing in the recorded form is not true to its source; rather it is a mask of an original.

Beginning with the claim that the pop voice implies narrativity, this chapter turned to a selection of songs and artists with special emphasis on musical style. Stylization lays claim to social and cultural indicators that inscribe what it is to be British, white and male in a given time. Staging one's persona through singing, though, is dependent on carefully calculated predictions of reception, as much as recording production. Is singing, then, the main constituent of the pop performance? If so, is it because its citational quality is formed by the particularity of temperament? One thing seems certain; the voice always arouses attention, as we look to the artist whose gaze is directed elsewhere.

# Chapter 6

# Jack-a-Dandy:
# Masking, Virtuosity and Mannerism

... but the comedy is tiring; a mask is painful and hideous, even for people of character.

Barbey D'Aurevilly[1]

But whatever lies behind this sense of difference, dandyism has been the method to gatecrash the visible world. Dandyism is both a pedestal on which to stand and a mask behind which to hide.

Stephen Robins[2]

Scotland in the 1750s: Jack-a-Dandy, the term used on the border to refer to a rake or cad,[3] also stood for an impertinent, foppish little person noted for their reckless spending of money, allure and promiscuity. By the late 1700s the 'jack' had dropped away from the 'dandy' to describe someone middle-class, aspiring to an aristocratic lifestyle and preoccupied with personal appearance, leisure and a refined manner of speaking. Yet there is more to this than the exterior reveals in the intellectual dandies, literary dandies, philosophical dandies, sport dandies and the great poet, dramatist and playwright dandies. In his *Peintre de la vie moderne*, Baudelaire noted that dandyism first and foremost is about 'the burning need to create for oneself a personal originality, bounded only by the limits of proprieties' (Baudelaire 1964, p. 27). Accordingly, the dandies of pop have partaken of the same characteristics Baudelaire reflected on. What started with the Mods extended the Brummellian tradition of contrived individualism into an aestheticized styling of the tailored look for the masses. At the same time, the genealogy of the Mod dandy owed a lot to the styling of African American youth culture of the 1940s, where the zoot suit worn by gangs signified a subcultural rebellion that would incite the Mods to take their look and attitude to extremes. Not dissimilar to the 'Regency bucks in the Row', with their horse-drawn carriages, the Mods would

---

[1]  D'Aurevilly (1988, p. 26).

[2]  Robins (2001, p. 4).

[3]  Etymologically, rake comes from Old Norse, *reikall*, imported into Middle English as *rakel*. On the origin of the word dandy, Robins has pointed out that the French word *dandin* was transferred to Scotland in 1548 as thousands of French soldiers went to war against England. Gradually the word 'dandy' was mutated, changing from a term of abuse into a 'term of grudging respect' (Robins 2001, p. 235).

career around town on Italian scooters, watch French films, listen to black American music, wear Italian suits and drink espresso (Robins 2001, p. 233).

It might be a truism to say that the visualization of pop has fetishized music and reinforced the body's coding. Very obviously, this has to do with the pop artist's own responses to musical style. With few exceptions, the body has spectacularized movement and mannerism through musical style. So what of dandified mannerisms and the musical gestures that aestheticize performance? In this chapter I will attempt to uncover some of the conventions that relate to physical responses to music. By pursuing the concept of the dandified performer to its conclusion, I argue a deceptively simple premise: that to see something we hear, and vice versa, is a guiding indicator of what music is about. Putting a spin on this, the performer's responses to music demonstrate an interpretive process that turns into an aesthetic matter. Let me explain. When performers abandon themselves for the recording, like an elaborately knotted cravat, a fancy arrangement is crafted. During this entire process masking takes place. Not necessarily, though, does this imply something cynical at work. McClary makes a similar point by arguing that flaunted artificiality can 'register confidence in the power of human signs to shape social reality' (McClary 2000, p. 153), where the effect is one of 'unmasking anything that tries to present itself as natural, centred, or authentic' (ibid.). During a musical performance, norms can be cast aside for the sake of the constructed act,[4] and as such the imaginative terrain of the pop recording is a ritual of masking. Let us say that to mask something is to place weight on that *which is not there*, or, more precisely put, on that which is incapable of being recognizable on first impression.

Throughout this chapter I consider what fuels the tropes of behaviour associated with the dandy figure. Much of the valorization of individuality, as I have already implied, appears in productions that are regulated for commercial enterprise. In this process, the cult of the pop artist is bound up in the entrepreneurial ways of working through ideas of creativity, especially in terms of sound and appearance. Pop, a predominantly youthful form, embodies talent in this way, working for and against established norms of conservative genres. Entering this equation is glamour, which corresponds to the ways that performers mediate their attractiveness. Music videos offer lavish spectacles of this, presenting the body in recorded form as a construction.

Strategies of seduction are about the prodigious value of original style, and to lack these would be to fail at being dandy. As we have seen so far, vast differences exist in the way pop artists express themselves musically. In this part of my study I consider how speech patterns and language affect our reception of music. As with music production processes, masking arises from the use of language in music. Lyrics always tell stories differently than in spoken form, and, in a British context,

---

[4]  For an informed account of this process, see Susan Fast's application of Victor Turner's concept of the subjunctive to music, where musical experience is comparable to the final phase of ritual liminality. At this point, the listener attains a position where notions of everyday-ness are suspended. See Fast (2001, pp. 54–55).

the differences between character songs, love ballads, rap tracks and rock songs reflect the diversity of approaches to singing and utilizing language (Frith 1996; Griffiths 2003).

Through the junctures of language and sound the fan must be convinced that innovation functions as an exponent of the persona, for the well-rehearsed narratives of success and fame in pop are all about displaying this. Tailoring the dandified subject is about manifesting desires within a site of contestation. From another vantage point, the profiling of the individual in the media involves a set of values. Musicologist Kevin Korsyn has considered the complex sets of cultural conditions that impinge on this by pointing out how 'signifiers, images, and fantasies that compose the subject circulate through the media' (Korsyn 2003, p. 143). Korsyn reminds us that it is the audio-visual recording, television, Internet, MP3, film (and other gadgets and gizmos) – the 'new modes of sociality' – that shape our impressions of the artist. Deliberating on the process of 'solitary listening', Korsyn insists that this is all about transformation. The sound recording directs attention differently in the absence of visual imagery, highlighting the role of the voice as an 'object-cause of desire and *jouissance*' (ibid., p. 147). Korsyn, like Koestenbaum, addresses the surplus of meaning generated by media conditions, where the juncture of technology and culture prompts specific responses on the part of performer and audience. An important issue here concerns the impact of sound in the absence of visual imagery, where the imagination generates reactions to aural markers. That is to say, the recorded performance corresponds not only to the produced sound, but also to its modification through listening. Which returns us to the matter of the recording and its masking quality.

Recording the body audio-visually is a complicated issue that demands explication,[5] and at this point it is worth stressing that my employment of the term 'masking' should not be confused with auditory or sonic masking, a phenomenon in psychoacoustics that deals with the ear's difficulty in perceiving sounds at extreme ranges.[6] Rather, masking in my application deals with sound as altered, concealed and, moreover, enhanced. Vocal flanging, for instance, constitutes a marker that is decisively different from its original, where the produced quality of

---

[5]  In styles that prompt dance, the performer or listener may deny any response in terms of movement, while in other styles that are more non-danceable, the performer might move or dance. From this, one could say the musical rules that subject one to dance are unpredictable. In this sense, dance is an endorsement of a particular identity and its agency. At any rate, dance is a way of seeking attention, an act of controlling the gaze, a concerted decision to move across space in time, and a mechanism for spectacularizing oneself. For my study dealing with temporality and corporeality in dance music (with specific reference to the New York DJ Joey Beltram), see Hawkins (2008, pp. 124–28).

[6]  Auditory masking involves the overpowering of one sound for another by making the latter indiscernible. Engineers working with audio compression turn to masking for determining the sounds that stand out in a composition for the purpose of retaining them, which eases the process of compression. Also see Katz (2002).

the sound teases in ways that are not necessarily true to its original. This is obvious when comparing the artist's everyday voice (in interviews, documentaries, chat shows) to the highly treated voice. At a general level, then, the recording profiles a particular moment in time, giving just *one* impression of the 'real' person.

What then are the technicalities that produce subjectivity during the recording process? Masking is self-referential, offering up the voice as the persona. As we have seen in Chapter 5, vocal intimacy is achieved through the emotive pull of auditory experience, mirroring the artist close-up as it promises corporeal intimacy. Vocal presence, however, is always illusory, for it is 'the site of a paradoxically simultaneous promise and denial of intimacy' (Cubitt 2000, p. 147), and, in its amplified state, the voice is a 're-presentation, a signifier, the grounds of whose existence is the absence of the thing represented' (ibid.). Uncannily, vocal sounds fixed in a song's mix denote something in the abstract, reminding us that a recording is a remarkably flexible category[7] ideally suited to masking. Jason Toynbee views the binary opposition between live and recorded music as based on 'notions of authenticity and artifice' (Toynbee 2000, p. 69), which is in danger of blocking our comprehension of what music technology signifies. He advocates a continuum, a 'technosphere', which stretches from performance on one side to the 'remote reception of sound on the other' (ibid.). Extending Toynbee's concept, it would seem that the technosphere is a domain of possibilities and limitations for framing the dandified performance. This is because reproducing the body through the recorded performance is an extraordinary phenomenon, and a vital component of technological reflexivity in pop, a key assumption in my debate, which I set out to apply to a range of musicians under the rubric of dandy.

## 'Who I Am Is Not What I May Appear To Be': Strategies of Masking, Gestures and Conventions

Quite consciously, the dandy plays on all the markers of identification that he can muster up. Like Baudelaire's dandy, the pop version is also *auto-idolâtrie*, a victim of the cult of the Self. I now turn to the visual display of the body in various performances, considering its particularity in relation to what we hear and see.

---

[7] Take rock and one of its offspring, glam-rock, which became popularized in the early 1970s, a more British than North American phenomenon. The New York Dolls, a proto-punk group inspired by the Rolling Stones, led glam-rock's popularity in the USA, and was mainly confined to Detroit and New York. Other major influences on US glam-rock were Alice Cooper, with his transvestite image, and Iggy Pop, who both came from the Detroit rock scene. In addition, Jobriath (the stage name for Bruce Wayne Campbell) was a glam-rock star from 1973 to 1974, and is credited as one of the first openly gay pop stars. A cult of pop star admirers in the UK have acknowledged his influence, such as Neil Tennant, Morrissey, Mark Stewart and Gary Numan.

Essentially, style and authorship are to do with the imagery of a performance. Take 'Children of the Revolution' by T. Rex, from 1972.

Credited for representing glam-rock at its best, this song is a landmark in British popular music and performed by one of the legendary idols, Marc Bolan. One version of this song is found in Ringo Starr's documentary film, *Born to Boogie* (shot in the renowned Apple Studios), depicting T. Rex at the height of their fame during a concert at Wembley in March 1972. During the scene, featuring a jam session, Marc Bolan places his head through the grand piano and flirts with Elton John, who eggs him on. I have singled out this clip as it vividly profiles the gestural mannerisms between instrumentalists, and the homosociality that exists in such interactions. Exaggeratedly, Bolan accents his downbeats with aggressive whammy-bar wide circles of the arms, while Elton John hammers away on repeated eighth notes that involve the full weight of his arms on each attack, creating a shuddering effect. Bolan responds with the characteristic head-banging movements associated with rock guitarists, strutting his course back and forth in time to the beat. Elton John's role is more passive as he remains seated at the grand piano, looking demurely on with a tilt of the head. Meanwhile, in the background Ringo Starr is perched behind the drum kit, with stiffness in posture that is aligned to precision drumming and subtle fills. Together with other musicians (on guitar, bass and bongos), the visual spectacle of masculinity in this scene says a lot. Not only the visual, but also the musical dialogue is an important part of the dynamics that go into convincing us about musical performance. Furthermore, the physical responses we witness in this shot are formative when establishing the gender norms connected to Bolan's type of masculinity and rock. For many reasons, his performance in *Born to Boogie*, glam for its day, is a magnificent construction: glittery costume (a one-piece catsuit), with long, corkscrew hair and glitter daubed around his eyes and on his cheekbones. Moore has insisted that the 'private mythologies of Marc Bolan represent one aspect of the intrusion of the fantastic into progressive rock' (Moore 2001, p. 109), and linked to his style is the extraordinary, the bizarre and the weird. Yet there is more to this display than first meets the eye. Fast refers to 'the slippery issue of gender construction', where the strident masculine voice takes on 'feminine musical characteristics' (Fast 2001, p. 47). The scene I have described in 'Children of the Revolution' relies on the formal structures of choruses, verses, powerful riffs, bouncy rhythms, instrumental solos, cat-like vocal wails and composed breaks to bond the performers together. And as Fast claims, the rock performance is one of the few events that permits such blatant homosociality, as emotions are allowed to be 'openly indulged' (ibid., p. 47). In September 1977 Bolan died in a car crash in South-West London just before his thirtieth birthday. Not only would he be remembered for his top hats, feather boas and glittered cheekbones in the early 1970s, but also for leading the glam-rock movement in Britain and renegotiating masculinity. Bolan and T. Rex's influence would set trends in punk rock bands, Britpop, and indie bands, as well as open up the field for new forms of masculinity. Quite aptly, the final album by

T. Rex and Bolan was called *Dandy in the Underworld*, released just six months before Bolan died.

Long-time friend and rival of Bolan's, Bowie, also had his roots in Mod fashion. It is well known that the two frequented venues in London for their inspiration (Stevenson 2006). The swinging Sixties, their era, was a period when Beatlemania reached its height, establishing London as the world music capital. As much as embracing musical styles from American music from jazz to soul, Mod fashion and lifestyle brought with it a politics of stylization, where an obsession for detail in look, often feminized, would challenge conventional masculinity. And then there was the hair. As early as November 1964, Bowie had appeared on BBC television as the President of the Society for the Prevention of Cruelty to Long-Haired Men, where he claimed that calling long-haired men homosexuals just had to stop (Stevenson 2006). Effectively, the look Bowie adopted, with long hair and eyeshadow, bridged the gap between heterosexual and gay culture, leading to all forms of queering (see Chapter 4). Representations of masculinity in British Mod culture signified a masking of gender through a process of pluralizing, epitomized by pop stars such as Bowie, Bolan, Jagger, Ray Davies, and later Sylvian and Weller. Right from the outset, Bowie's appropriation of Mod culture symbolized his brand of Englishness through his urban locality of London. It would take up to the end of the 1960s for him to really find his voice. In July 1969 he made his major breakthrough with the single 'Space Oddity'.

Winding forward to 1977, with several character shifts behind him, Bowie moved, or rather escaped, to Berlin[8] where he 'literally fell to earth' (Stevenson 2006, p. 74) while attempting to step off the rollercoaster of fame. Paradoxically, this move would only increase his productivity. Collaboration with Brian Eno during the Berlin period resulted in three groundbreaking albums, *Low* (1977), *'Heroes'* (1977), and *Lodger* (1979), assisting Bowie to exorcize Ziggy and don the mask of an 'ordinary' person. First shown on television in September 1977, one of his most renowned songs, 'Heroes', turned out to be a simple affair, at least on the surface, camouflaging the elaborate details of the sound production. Visconti, who also produced this track, chose to set up three microphones at variable distances (9 inches, 20 feet and 50 feet) to capture a unique vocal sound. While all three mikes were opened for the louder, climactic passages, only the first was used for the quieter passages. As a result, a higher dose of reverb and effect enhanced the louder sections. Visconti describes how the mikes set up with electronic gates on them were only opened after Bowie hit a specified volume: 'It took about half an hour of David alternating between shouting and whispering, but it came off beautifully when I got the levels just right. The reverb you hear on "Heroes" is the natural but gated reverb of the room he sang it in" (in Buckley 2000, p. 323).

---

[8]    Sharing an apartment in Schöneberg with his friend Iggy Pop, co-producing three more classic albums with Tony Visconti, as well as co-writing with Eno during The Berlin Era (1976–1980), Bowie has acknowledged the influence of Krautrock and the minimalist style of Steve Reich.

Unquestionably, the expansive soundscape of 'Heroes' owes much to Visconti's creative handling of reverb; recording techniques such as this would define the performative aspect of this track. Visconti explains that it was the natural, yet gated reverb of the room in which Bowie was recorded that produced this spatial effect. The recording bears this out in a production that consists of multilayers of guitars, synthesizers and percussion, all regulated in tandem with a regular set-up of piano, rhythm guitar, bass and drums. The shuddering effect that dominates the mix resulted from Eno's use of the EMS VCS3, which introduced low-frequency, detuned tones and beat-frequencies from the synthesizers' three oscillators. And, positioned at various spots in the studio to alter the feedback pitch, the guitarist Robert Fripp provided a conglomeration of oddly sustained sounds to add finishing touches to this remarkable recording.

The mood of 'Heroes' comes from the innovative production techniques, or, better, the editing techniques. The way that the music commences – a soft, low/register, sung/whispered melody that merges into the guitar and synthesizer parts, and then gradually develops to take-off point – graphically captivates the song's narrative: 'that anyone can be a hero even if it's only for a day'. In the video performance, the techniques of filming deliberately downplay the glamour of Bowie's former videos. Dressed in a black leather open jacket, with low-cut T-shirt and tight trousers, and silhouetted against a brightly lit white background, he confronts the camera's gaze throughout. Notably, his way of standing and moving is feminized, and, in Stevenson's reading, it is designed to 'emphasize his bisexuality and otherness' (Stevenson 2006, p. 141).

A very different kind of iconography would be used a couple of years later in the video 'Fashion', from the second single on the album *Scary Monsters (and Super Creeps)*, released in 1980. Contrary to the experimental depth of musical ideas in 'Heroes', 'Fashion' comes over as contrived. The repetitive, onomatopoeic 'beep, beep' in the chorus riff, in particular, heaps scorn on those who set out to form a counterculture in order to become fashionable. This satirical take on the fashion world finds Bowie jeering at himself as much as others. Such cynicism is captured in the video, featuring the artist with his band performing to a crowd of apathetic onlookers, who ape his movements. Interchangeable with bizarre cameos of celebrities from British society, the band's performance is Warholian in a nondescript, send-up way. Bowie's occasional gestures imitate Fripp's guitar-playing, as he executes a series of whammy-bar arm movements (a common gesture that singers use in their reaction to guitar-playing).

In terms of the musical performance, it is Bowie's remarkable improvisatory flair in 'Fashion' that is most appealing. During the recording session, according to Visconti, a riff on the word 'Jamaica' was going around in Bowie's head incessantly, which only in the last minute was put down in the mix; this would end up as one of Bowie's most recognizable and legendary moments (Buckley 2004a, p. 60). Such is the unpredictability of the recording session. This helps explain why, when positioned alongside a rock riff in the guitar part, and clashing with the strong funk and reggae feel of the backing parts, Bowie's vocal phrases are as catchy as the histrionics of his enlivened gestures. Cool, aloof and self-assured, Bowie's presence is a shrewd result of a stack of musical colloquialisms that all merge into the physical manifestation of what Meisel describes as 'the body English.'[9] To be sure, the intensity of Bowie's physical display heightens the dramatic effect of his music, establishing a stylized vogueing that underlies his artistic intentions and musical curiosity.

### You're So Vain!

Bowie's menagerie of vocal types and costume changes never fail to fascinate. The youthfulness he has exuded since the 1960s contributes to a vitality 40 years on that is quite exceptional. Robins describes the dandy as a 'heroic young meteor, a shooting star for whom fatal burn-out is inevitable, an opulent social butterfly whose beauty and grace last only the shortest of seasons' (Robins 2001, p. 196); the point is, perhaps, that few stars grow old gracefully. Exceptions to this, Bowie and Jagger seem to have perpetuated the pop *esprit*, possessing all the criteria of a shooting star in slow motion. Barbey might well have labelled our dandies' identity as an English originality; an originality that imprints itself on a vanity that is 'anchored in the very hearts of the scullions' (D'Aurevilly 1988, p. 26). What makes artists so appealing from one generation to the next is the diversity of their performances, and their adaptation to new technologies. And while each artist performs and foregrounds their personae in quite different ways, it is their vanity that functions as a common denominator.

Carly Simon's 1973 hit 'You're So Vain' might well have been a reference to Jagger, one of her former boyfriends. If this is the case, we'll probably never know. Neither Jagger, who sang backing vocals on the track, nor Simon have ever confirmed this.[10] Whatever the case, the type of conceited male Simon describes in this song is a Jagger-type figure. At the time of the song's release, Jagger was on an assault course for achieving astonishing heights in male egotism. Hatched by the Rolling Stones (whose name comes from a line in a Muddy Waters song), Jagger's vanity has been musicalized by a raunchy rock style infused with R&B and other African American idioms (see Chapter 5). Over the years, the Stones' legacy has been built upon the display of Jagger's persona and performance traits,

---

[9]   Meisel's chapter on the 'body English' (1999, Chapter 9, pp. 115–28) is not without its problems as the author attempts to account for the impact of the British Invasion from 1964 to 1966 on North American culture. Meisel presents a complicated story of the deep affinity between American R&B and British rock without sufficiently distinguishing the English from the American body. What seems odd about this chapter is the lack of historical accountability for how the English body in rock evolved by means of its difference and eccentricity.

[10]   See Simon's comments at http://www.carlysimon.com/vain/vain.html.

making him a leading light in British popular culture. Guy Trebay provides the following account:

> Bowie was stylish. Bryan Ferry looked good in a suit. But it was Jagger who preened himself in a Mephistopheles cloak at Altamont; wore Ossie Clark jumpsuits split to the navel; and who appeared in a flounced neo-classical Grecian-style jacket to read Shelley at a concert after Brian Jones's death.[11]

Referring to the early days of the Stones, playing down their glamour, Jagger has claimed: 'we wore clothes very similar to what we wore offstage because we didn't have any money and that was the look'.[12] But from the late 1960s onwards, turning to an androgynous look, Jagger would transform himself into a dandified satyr. Not unlike aesthete and fop d'Albert, from Gautier's *Mademoiselle de Maupini*, ugly-handsome Jagger was on a mission that would release him from the constraints of bourgeois pressures, as he came out and struck a nerve in British culture.

Four decades later, still youthful and exceedingly wealthy, Jagger epitomizes the swashbuckling rock dandy. Through the 1960s and 1970s he would modify his style to accommodate skinny jeans, cropped jackets and tight-fitting, designer T-shirts. Freakishly skinny, his physical appearance is dominated by graphic facial expressions. Sensually masculine and feminine at the same time, his demeanour is marked by a middle-class accent that is tinged with an ever-so-slight American drawl. Breaking into the international market with the Stones' first hits from the 1960s, such as '(I Can't Get No) Satisfaction', 'Come On', 'Jumpin' Jack Flash', and 'Get Off of My Cloud', Jagger's temperament needs to be contextualized within a cultural space, where his display of permissiveness has inspired generations to come. In debt to Elvis Presley, whose effeminacy gave him the courage to address openly his own sexuality in a sustained and stable way, Jagger choreographed his masculinity with innate theatricality in a British way.

Many have been roused by Jagger's performance style along the way. In the 1960s Tom McGrath, editor of *IT*, the leading countercultural newspaper, urged people to find their inner voices and encouraged honesty and frankness during the Summer of Love in 1967, when hippies took to creative style in the forms of music, clothes, art and literature in order to counteract the frumpiness of the previous decade. Framed by the Beatles, the Stones, Mary Quant and Vidal Sassoon, Biba and Habitat, British popular culture would achieve new aesthetic standards. No longer could high culture lord it over as British icons reconfigured female beauty (Twiggy), male beauty (Mick Jagger, David Bowie, Ray Davies), artistry (Lennon and McCartney) and heroism (James Bond). In fact, the individual's right to pleasure was fused by a permissive sexual revolution as British youth engaged themselves

---

[11]   http://www.iht.com/articles/2006/11/24/features/jagger.php.

[12]   Op. cit.

in a festive breaking of taboos.[13] Mostly, it was freedom, sexual liberation, and various types of spirituality that would prompt a rethinking of religion in the form of a new morality or moral relativism.[14]

Rebel dandies such as Jagger, by leading the way, surely deserve their dues.[15] Undoubtedly, his path to fame in the Stones signifies a pivot point in the mythology of the pop star, demonstrating that glamour takes on many guises according to identity and genre. Through his most recent solo project (at the time of writing this book), *The Very Best of Mick Jagger*, released in 2007,[16] Jagger has managed to stay at the top, and although his solo career might seem dwarfed in comparison to the Stones' output, the material he draws on in his solo albums highlights his dandified status. Quite void of the tensions that have characterized his relationship with the Stones, his solo albums involve the luxury of hand-picking celebrity friends and associates to flank him in a rollicking self-send-up way. Setting out to personalize his success in the *Very Best*, Jagger's motives are revealed in giveaway titles, such as 'God Gave Me Everything', 'Old Habits Die Hard' (from the soundtrack of the film *Alfie* (2004)), 'Lucky in Love' and 'Charmed Life'. Retrospective and inward-looking, these songs, like the photos one discovers in an old family album, include 'Dancing in the Street', which Jagger and Bowie recorded for Live Aid in 1985, and 'Too Many Cooks (Spoil the Soup)', produced by Lennon and recorded by Jagger in LA in 1973. Most of all, *Very Best* testifies to the consistency of Jagger's narcissism, egocentrism and alluring temperament. Although his solo efforts are viewed as sell-outs (numerous critics have dismissed his messing-about with styles outside the rock domain), they do profile a man who is unmistakably self-deprecating and outrageously over-the-top. For Jagger customarily throws himself into solo roles with a devilish recklessness that he knows is not possible with the Stones. The track I turn to now illustrates this superbly.

---

[13]   In 1965 Kenneth Tynan said 'fuck' on television, following which four motions were tabled in parliament, in the same year that the first drug reference appeared in a Beatles song. The prosecution of *Lady Chatterley's Lover* in 1960 turned it into a bestseller, while Christine Keeler's nude body became the defining image of the Profumo Affair of 1963, as did Marianne Faithfull's in a similar role during the 1967 Redlands drugs trial.

[14]   While the liberal Bishop of Woolwich reshaped Christianity around 'situational ethics', where nothing could be labelled as wrong, humanists saw permissiveness as part of a process of secularization that took off in the 1960s and continues to this day. Despite the unfashionable turn permissiveness took in the 1970s during the Winter of Discontent, the vision of a Britain, embracing freedom, individualism, iconoclasm, pluralism, frankness, pleasure, creativity and a post-Christian morality, at the onslaught of the twenty-first century depicts a more permissive society than it has ever been.

[15]   Jagger's involvement in the movie business is highlighted by his most notable role as the cross-dressing club bodyguard in *Bent* from 1997. With his Jagger Films production company, he served as executive producer of *Tania*, while the script for *Enigma* is currently in progress at the time of writing.

[16]   This includes album tracks, singles and star-studded collaborations with Bono, Bowie, John Lennon, Lenny Kravitz, Peter Tosh, Ry Cooder, Dave Stewart and Jeff Beck.

Originally recorded while Jagger was working on his third solo album, *Wandering Spirit*, in 1992, 'Charmed Life' was shelved as not suitable for the album. With *Very Best* Jagger would commission English producer Ashley Beetle to remix the old demo, instructing him to come up with something rare. The result was a buoyant, feel-good dance track that contrasted with the other rock songs. Starting with an instrumental introduction (a slightly out-of-tune string quartet), there is little hint of the dance groove that suddenly enters and changes the mood (0:16). Driven by a crisp, jangly repeated guitar figure and pounding bass is Jagger's penetrative voice. Additional interest is supplied by the child-like backing vocals of his daughter, Karis Jagger, on the hook, 'charmed life', with the pervasive guitar-riffing – semiquavers are evenly played with up and down attack strokes by one hand, while two notes are controlled with the other hand. Heightened by the use of ghost notes at the end of the riff, the effect is produced by the guitarist holding one hand loosely over the fret while still maintaining the semiquaver movement over the strings. Processed with slap echo, the guitar riff shapes the timbre at the same time as adding to the overall rhythmic texture of the mix.[17] Other attractive features include a blatant reference to disco, captured by the regular four-on-the-floor beat, the rhythm guitar riff (discussed above), the strings and the synths. It is telling that Jagger, a quintessential rock artist, turns to a style that 'sucked' at a time when the Stones were building their career. While they had no issues with embracing African American styles such as R&B, veering away from the trappings of disco in the direction of cock-rock became the Stones' musical trademark. Even with the 1978 hit single 'Miss You' from the album *Some Girls*, with its suggestive disco flavour, it is revealing that Jagger would claim that the Stones did not really consider this as real disco despite the keyboardist Billy Preston's involvement in the dance scene.[18]

Disco's vengeance in the last decade of the twentieth century reconfigured its own aesthetics by putting right its previously vapid references: gay, silly, uncool, and artificial. Krims (2007) debates disco's revival in the 1990s. Still benefiting from the recordings and shows by artists such as Gloria Gaynor and the Bee Gees, this time round it was 'shorn of the dancing, the clothing, the fashion, the modes of social interaction' (ibid., p. 64) that had contextualized it in the 1970s. Hence, Jagger's safe and acceptable embrace of disco in 'Charmed Life'. This speaks volumes about stylistic reinvestment and subcultural appropriation. Furthermore, his deployment of disco elements spotlights the commercial motives of the music industry and the portability of the dance scene in and out of fashion. Most notably, Jagger's slick, upbeat dance approach in 'Charmed Life', harnessed by a polished vocal performance, comes over as self-mocking and overplayed in a camp manner; similar to his version of 'Dancing in the Street' with Bowie from 1985, the aesthetics

---

[17]   I am grateful to Eirik Askerøi for not only clarifying this technique of guitar-playing to me, but also demonstrating it by playing it.

[18]   Thanks to Helge Klungland, an avid Stones fan, for this and other useful indicators.

of the mix are over-the-top and in-yer-face. This is also discernible in the ecstatic vocal tone, consistently kneaded into the melodic phrases that build up in tension through inflections, dynamics and textural colouring. Vocally, his upward and downward tessitura dissolve into long sustained notes, foregrounding a virtuosic singing technique. Added to this are the characteristic shouts of 'yeah', yowls and occasional grunts associated with his fun-loving musical signature. Supported by a throbbing bass line that gels with the kit's tight control of the groove, Jagger's voice is beefed up by the brazen obstinacy of the rhythmic structures. One moment that stands out is the short respite from the groove in the C section (2:28–2:45), where Jagger embellishes the melody in an exaggerated blues-style, 'ooh, I like to keep my head way down in this town'. Here his tone comes over disdainfully flippant, situated in the low register. With little delay, though, the mood changes with a register shift upwards, as he informs us that he is going to walk tall with head up high. In passages such as these, vocal obstinacy marks a positivity that is conveyed through the rasping of vocal tones that connote great exertion. As Jagger's voice ascends from chest to head register, his technical control is more challenged, and with the complex ornamentation on cadential notes, he releases all his pent-up emotions. Jagger's attribute of axial pitching (by this I mean notes that encircle a central pitch rather than hitting it spot-on) is an appropriation of African American scatting that characterizes many of the climactic moments in his songs. In such instances his 'normal' singing voice is marked by a *sotto voce* (under the voice) manner. Parodying the 'charmed man' in this character song, he once again turns to aspects of flashiness and artifice in musical display, as evident in the extremities of vocal timbre, register and dynamic control. Musically, Jagger takes risks by interjecting melodic phrases with shouts and screams, all of which are part and parcel of a showmanship that traverses a range of emotional possibilities. It is these stylistic codes that foreground the submissive side of his temperament.

Lest we forget, Jagger's imagery is formed by the media conditions that standardize his musical style. And returning to Korsyn's point, musical performance functions as an imitative process, dependent on specific mannerisms of symbolic meanings that are constituted in media hype.[19] While ascribing to a pop aesthetic, Jagger's performances connote desire through his sexualized representation. Middleton (2006) has theorized such strategies through vocal display, whereby, codified in their own specific ways, singers 'stand naked, their bodies not mediated by external instruments'. In gender terms, as Middleton puts it, this occurs in an 'already sexualized site, heavily coded feminine (which means that men who sing, especially in live situations when their bodies are on display, are already in danger of being seen as feminized or queer)' (Middleton 2006, p. 94). Also at issue here is vocal nuance (in live performance or visual recording format), and the ambivalence produced by notions of Otherness:

---

[19]   See Wicke (1990) for an in-depth discussion of symbolic meaning, mythology and imagery in rock music, and Scott (2003) for a critique of eroticization within Western classical and popular music.

The female body is fixed in its place – as too are the bodies of feminized racial and class groups, such as *dandified blacks* and working-class teddy boys – through a technology of adornment, which maintains a central, albeit ambivalent role for the imaginary, vivifying presence of voice (Middleton 2006: pp. 94–5, my emphasis).

Toying with the term 'technological adornment', Middleton considers the sexualized role of the male performer and the physical source of human sound. This returns us to the question of vocal masking.[20] In terms of imaginary presence and its masking effect, what is it that enables Bowie and Jagger to pull off their acts across a number of styles and genres? And how are their gendered mannerisms and virtuosic control mediated within the technosphere? I now turn to the production team backing the artist.

## The Dandy-behind-the-dandy

The producer's relation to an artist varies considerably. This is why approaches to recording range from an ad-lib manner to a fully calculated plan prior to the artist entering the recording space. Over time artists develop techniques and skills in recording, and much of this is based upon a close alliance with producers. When it comes to the recorded song, the transition from the basic elements to the polished end result signifies a shift from what Virgil Moorefield has described as 'the 'illusion of reality' (mimetic space) to the 'reality of illusion' (a virtual world in which everything is possible)' (Moorefield 2005, p. xiii).

Today's recording studio is suited to reproducing any sound imaginable, and this alone has implications for the way in which composition and performance has developed. Middleton has made the point that the record is finished in a way the oral performance never can be. And, paradoxically, the recording is an 'extreme form of reified abstraction' (Middleton 1990, p. 83). In this sense, the spontaneity of musical expression is fossilized into the digital codes of finite documentation. However, an argument for the recording as a flexible artefact that alters in appearance according to what is being played could be made. In a sense, the rise of

---

[20]   Not unlike the male artists I have looked at, numerous female performers play around with stereotypical categorizations. Kylie Minogue, with a voice that has a high-pitched, thin, throaty timbre with a weakish low range, moulds into a visual representation that holds great appeal for a number of reasons not just based around her good looks. In applying Middleton's point, I would suggest that Minogue's fixed identity is generically predicated upon queered fantasies across the board as her voice is non-challenging and fastens effortlessly onto the authoritative positioning of gender stereotypes. However, seldom does her voice stand alone, and one needs to consider why Minogue's performing style is directed to the queer gaze not only through her biography, but also through the way she masks.

the pop dandy owes everything to his recorded documentation aurally and visually, where the fashionable display of sartorial desire provides a source of entertainment. Cicolini maintains that the twenty-first century dandy has conjoined Wildean matters of political, sexual and social resistance within 'the urban marketplace' (Cicolini 2005, p. 15) And, just as with fashion design, pop stars stand out because of a team of collaborators who support them, contributing to every step along the way in terms of songwriting, recording and visual production. One could say that the production team's task is to position the mask. This assertion, I realize, raises a number of problematic issues concerning the role of the *auteur* (Frith 1996; Toynbee 2000; Moy 2007; Shuker 2008). Indeed, the authorial scope of an artist is down to the division of labour and creative relationships that result in the final production of a song. While space does not permit me to go into all the intricacies of what lies behind the production, I will single out a few examples that shed light on this process.

Starting with Williams's stylization and musical characteristics, I am keen to hone in on those who help construct him – the team of producers, songwriters and musicians that help realize his act. Verified by a kaleidoscope of different pop acts, Williams's cooperation with numerous producers and musicians account directly for his success, foregrounding all the objectifying elements that go into his spectacular performances. Take his collaboration with British singer-songwriter Stephen Duffy, founder of Duran Duran in 1978 (with Nick Rhodes and John Taylor).[21]

Reforming his band, The Lilac Time, and releasing the album *Looking for a Day in the Night* (1999), Duffy caught the attention of Williams, who promptly enlisted his services. In a flattering interview, Duffy would boost Williams's credibility by claiming that he possessed 'an in-depth knowledge of New Order and Joy Division, and a real appreciation of Morrissey'.[22] Within a short while Duffy had co-written over 60 songs with Williams, venturing into all forms of experimentation, albeit carefully paced. Success came with Williams's single 'Radio', co-written and produced by Duffy, which made it to number one in the UK charts in 2004. *Intensive Care* was released in 2005, and on this album, Duffy's

---

[21]    Following a few demos and local gigs, Duffy left Duran Duran to start his band Only Five Believers, who evolved into The Hawks. Their single, 'Words of Hope', released in 1980, would eclipse Duran Duran's first single by one year. Later Duffy would go on to form the synth-based band Tin Tin, who recorded 'Kiss Me', which became a hit both in the UK and USA. Later, launching himself as a solo artist known as Stephen 'Tin Tin' Duffy, he issued a remix of 'Kiss Me' in 1985, followed by the single 'Icing on the Cake', and finally the album *The Ups And Downs*. He recorded three more singles and an album, *Because We Love You*, under the name Stephen AJ Duffy, before he ended his pop phase. Throughout the 1990s Duffy continued to be prolific, recording under many names, as well as working with numerous artists and bands, such as R.E.M., Mitch Easter, Nigel Kennedy, Alex James, Stephen Page and Nick Rhodes.

[22]    'Radio daze: Stephen Duffy' in *Guardian Unlimited*, 15 October 2004.

input was not only as co-writer, but also sole producer and multi-instrumentalist (including programming). By 2005 Duffy was Williams's musical director and live on-stage guitarist for a major world tour, and, undoubtedly, a great source of inspiration for the material on *Intensive Care*. Significantly, the song 'Radio', consisting of numerous stylistic traits that verify Duffy's sonic imprint, was most reminiscent of his background in New Wave bands.

Williams's musical style is down to his productions and, moreover, his stage personality, which relies on the assistance of others who author him. Like Madonna, his choice of tip-top producers and musicians enables him to maintain sufficient stylistic diversity that reaches a huge catchment area (Hawkins 2007b; Moy 2007). Take the earlier collaboration with another producer/songwriter, Guy Chambers, on his first five solo albums. This led to 40 million sales worldwide, with each album reaching number one in the UK. In pop, however, *auteur* feuds frequently arise when the stakes are high. Chambers would claim that the division of work with Williams was at least 50/50, even though he wrote most of the music. An acrimonious disagreement over royalties finally led to their split. Following the release of the fifth solo album *Escapology* in 2002, Chambers left, disgruntled. Authorship always rests upon the shoulders of the collaborator as much as the artist, and this is a contentious point that warrants attention when it comes to artistic input and ownership (Moy 2007, p. 82).

Reiterating my starting point in this discussion, the key to the success of the pop dandy depends on collaboration, and this is evident in documentaries that include footage from performances in the making. The DVD of *Rock DJ* is a fine example, where Williams is filmed rehearsing, writing and performing. Soon, though, *his* creative input in this songwriting process becomes questionable. Much attention is afforded to him 'arsing around', getting irritated by the rigour of the recording process and petulantly emphasizing his super-ego in the form of quips and jabs at those working with him. Of course, everyone smiles and chuckles along with the so-called maestro. But notwithstanding the tensions that arise from close collaborations, the matter of agency and control appears to be in the hands of the studio jester. The implication of this is that the star performer works his authorship in 'proprietorial terms' (ibid., p. 87); the individual filmed at work masks the relegation of collaborative creative input.

Indubitably, the producer's own ego and musicality impact the recording and styling of music, and in British pop there is a long tradition of this, stretching from George Martin to contemporary figures such as Stephen Hague, another dandy-behind-the dandy. The producer of many of the artists taken up in this book – Marc Almond, the Pet Shop Boys, Blur and the Sex Pistols – Hague came into production as a musician rather than an engineer. Claiming this as an advantage, he says: 'As a producer, I've worked with several excellent engineers who've struggled with things like, "Can you take it from bar three of the chorus?" and things like that' (in Massey 2000, p. 252). Considering recording vocals and what goes into a 'great vocal take', Hague emphasizes the abstract nature of the recording process, drawing attention to how subjective this really is: 'it's sort of organic on one level, where what's right for the track is not necessarily the most blazing over-the-top vocal performance' (ibid., p. 254). Describing his work with certain English artists (he avoids mentioning names) in the mid-1980s, he points out that they were not 'really' singers:

> There was a really charming English thing – you know, that kind of 'pretty boy who can't quite sing' thing – and I would often work really hard to get those sounding confident and upfront from somebody who's not actually confident or upfront (ibid.).

From this statement alone, evidence of constructing the voice is apparent: manipulating, enhancing, transforming and disguising its flaws are a prime goal. Studio production techniques are the equivalent to audio make-up: 'That's a case where you do lots of vocal takes and not worry about pitch and all that stuff, because I could alter the pitch later on certain lines when the *moment was there* but the pitch wasn't' (ibid. – my emphasis). Technically, the task of getting the mike set-up right and capturing the voice in the most creative way is tricky. Hague concedes that 'some singers sound better on some mics than others' (ibid., p. 255). Elaborating on this, he explains how using a Shure Beta 88, a hand-held mike, when recording Chrissie Hynde was a strategy specifically designed for the studio context. In Hynde's case, though, the mike was not that detailed as her abundance of expression compensated for all of that. Yet in many of the other cases the inverse would apply, as artists 'only came alive' through the most costly Telefunken mike.

Picture the following scenario. The start of a recording session when one sets up five or six mikes and then runs through a couple of things while 'switching between them'. Hague elucidates, 'You can usually tell pretty quickly' (ibid.) the qualities of singing. Another technical ploy of vocal enhancement is compression, something Hague uses sparingly. Once a voice is recorded with an abundance of compression, you cannot dispense with it; he stresses: 'Whereas if you just record it in such a way that you are not peaking out in your recording format, then you can add as much as you want at any point later in the process' (ibid.). Perhaps the most edifying dimension of Hague's production process is getting the artist into the mood, a vital part of the recording dynamic that involves coercion and ego-boosting. Not unlike the role of the fluffer,[23] the producer has to coerce the performer into performing at his best, and this happens through enhancing sound image. '(S)ome singers that I've worked with', Hague insists, 'like to hear a lot of compression in their phones while they're singing, but that's something you just

---

[23]    The term is mainly associated with a hired member of the crew on a porn set whose role is to sexually arouse male actors to erections prior to filming. Fluffing is also related to touching up an actress's hair and make-up prior to shooting. And, primarily used in the UK, this term can also refer to an aspect of acting when an actor misreads or loses their way and is said to have 'fluffed their lines'.

set up on a sidechain so that when they are getting their foldback it can be heavily compressed or really bright'. For the most part, then, are the deceptive strategies turned to when sitting behind the glass wall: 'Whatever they like to hear that gets them to do it, that's what I always try to give them' (ibid.).

From Hague's comments it is possible to conclude that recording techniques not only provide the producer with the know-how to control the studio space, but also the opportunity to mask the artist's vocal identity, turning it into an idealized and reconfigured performance. Yet, this does not necessarily imply 'sonic purity' or perfection, as style, as a determinant of temperament, has the last say. That is to say, there are countless instances in popular music where the aesthetic needs to be rough-edged, unpolished and amateur in order to convince (Bannister 2006). At any rate, the role of the producer is to record a performance in a way that individualizes the artist's persona by colouring it in. Attempting to understand (and then technologically harness) the star's personality is the greatest challenge, and, as Hague insists, the technological attention paid to vocal recording ensures that the image of the 'self' is disseminated in a way that literally sells. Hence, the voice is masked through a transformation process that translates into an object of appeal.

Pertinent in this regard is the construction of Britishness through sound recording. Culturally defined through language, ethnicity and nationality, voices are received according to their origins, which explains the differences between an American and a British voice, and all the subtleties that sometimes go amiss. While many British artists hold onto their local accents, others get it on by sounding American (one of the best cases being George Michael). In this study of the pop dandy, the majority of the artists I have covered are identifiable by their accent as much as their 'contrariness'. On this basis, then, the typologies of what sounds British are of central importance. Hague insists that sounding British is down to cultural and historical phenomena, such as the role of the radio in Britain, especially in the case of national stations such as BBC1. These tend to be more freewheeling than in the US: 'It can be a real cross section of things – there's everything from Cliff Richard's Christmas prayer to French dance acts, which can be side by side on the charts – and that would be an extremely unusual situation in the US' (Massey 2000, p. 256). From this we can see that many things distinguish a British recording from an American.

Although somewhat generalized, Hague's remarks are revealing: 'English musicians don't want to sound like somebody else, and they never had to experience themselves sounding like somebody else. That actually translates into the sound of the records' (ibid.). A crucial point is that British record companies have different demands from their American counterparts, where there are a lot of musical reasons to 'do the right thing by the artist's label' (ibid., p. 257) in Britain. With the role of engineers in the recording process, they play 'less by the book': 'If you have a mentor, oftentimes in the States, the protégé will carry on the tradition, whereas in England, the protégé can't wait until they can prove that they can do it better or cooler than the guy who taught him!' (ibid., p. 257).[24]

Taking punk as an example, Hague stresses how US punk is significantly different from British punk as British punks were allowed to 'dumb themselves down' for the market (ibid.).

Such insights reveal the skills of the producer in shaping the artist's temperament, assisting them to 'play out themselves'. If nothing else, the producer's role is an individualizing one. Whatever the stylistic differences, be it Adam Ant's enactment in 'Prince Charming', Ray Davies's parody in 'Dandy', David Bowie's wry retort in 'Fashion' or Mick Jagger's relishing of a dandified existence in 'Charmed Life', the recorded performance recreates, fetishizes and masks subjectivity. In the music industry, 'change a word, claim a third' is a catchphrase commonly coined for songwriting relationships, where just a few trivial changes provide an artist with access to ownership. Because authorship is collective, it is not what it necessarily seems. That an artist might be most engaged in the frontmanship of the performance space does not necessarily mean he is an equal partner when it comes to the creative processes of songwriting, production and compositional practice. In other words, the role of the *auteur* can be a delusion.

## Language, Spoof and Characterization

Masking as a concept is also applicable to the mechanisms of language in musical style. Aspects of innuendo, spoof and *double entendre* in performance involve dialogue and characterization.[25] Singers, as I pointed out in Chapter 5, are central characters who employ a range of techniques they know will access their fans. As a rule, the 'successful performance' hinges on carefully measured responses that take place through the communicative entities of musical gesture and language, where the control of tension that goes into structuring a performance is tied up with conventions that draw on linguistic sources and musical codes in specific ways. Crafting a performance, let us say, extracts situations that not only relate to the narrativity of a song, but also to personal biography. Further, the juxtaposing of words and music in song form are largely determined by the staged performance.

In popular music studies writers have theorized vocal norms when it comes to music analysis.[26] Generalizing strategies, though, are not without their problems. Moore argues this when elaborating on the complexities of vocal style in Bill Haley, Little Richard, Fats Domino and Elvis Presley (2001, pp. 44–9). Consider the gradual alteration in the pronunciation of English adopted by rock

---

[24]   Also see Morris (1999) for an enlightening study of US voices in British radio.

[25]   Although *double entendre* is a French expression, it is not used in the same way in French. The French turn to the phrase *double sens* (double meaning) in this case.

[26]   Walser (1993); Whiteley (1997); Fast (2001); Griffiths (2003); Auslander (2006); Middleton (2006).

singers over time, and its implications for legitimating new styles and musical directions. Identifying norms lies in understanding the interaction of musical elements (rhythm, harmony, melody, instrumental timbre) with language, and how they contribute to a style. Part of this are affected mannerisms and the relationships between vocal style, word usage and individuality. Vocality not only mirrors national characteristics, but also relates directly to social class. This is because music functions as a narrative that defines desire, purpose and belonging. Hence, an artist's choice of lyrics is a justification of not only where they come from and who they are, but also how they speak.

Arguing that class is not only a British disease, but also a British obsession, Simon Elmes has uncovered what he believes bonds the British together. More than common political and religious beliefs, it is 'similarity of style, whether in choosing designer labels, or music to listen to, or simply where to go for entertainment' (Elmes 2000, p. 60) that groups people together. Tracing the ways we speak and the reasons for this, Elmes turns to Dr Johnson's Dictionary (1755) – published 23 years before Beau Brummell was born. Elmes discovers the reasons for why new standards for 'good English' were advocated, and where correctness of speech was aligned to breeding, high class and refinement. In 1791 John Walker's 'Critical Pronouncing Dictionary' was so acclaimed that the author assumed the affectionate title 'Elocution' Walker, while by the dawn of the Victorian era purity of accent was considered the noblest feature of the educated gentleman, in stark contrast to the urban masses of the Industrial Revolution and the wealthy classes.

On a number of counts, Elmes's study illuminates the tendencies of speech and accent in the mid-nineteenth century, when an industry based on self-help manuals for 'speaking properly' emerged. Running into 40 editions, a sixpenny guide, 'Poor Letter H – Its Use and Abuse' written by Henry Sweet (an authority on Anglo-Saxon ethnicity and the English language), became the precursor for a flood of literature that told people how to mind their 'aiches' and take care of their 'ars'. This would be the precursor of the model for Professor Higgins in George Bernard Shaw's *Pygmalion* (1913).[27]

The 1950s and 1960s saw BBC radio contesting its own policy of using standard spoken English (a London accent that was accepted as 'Received Pronunciation' (RP)) with its obvious historical ties to Dr Johnson. Thanks to the efforts of the well-known radio producer Charles Parker, the voices of 'ordinary people' would be represented and taken more seriously. From the mid-1960s numerous British pop artists started sounding less American, and as Peter Trudgill (1983) has pointed out, a new generation gained a new confidence in regional accents, where the desire to sound working-class, or rather British urban working-class, became

---

[27]     *Pygmalion* led to a series of successful adaptations: the film *Pygmalion* (1938), the Broadway musical by Lerner and Loewe, *My Fair Lady* (1956), the film version *My Fair Lady* (1964) and the modern film update of *Pygmalion*, *She's All That* (1999). Not surprisingly, Shaw's play and the incessant swearing of Eliza Doolittle in lines such as, 'not bloody likely' shocked Edwardian audiences!

prevalent. All this coincided with the emergence of popular culture and British working-class bands, and in 1967 one of Britain's most celebrated radio DJs, John Peel, would nurture an entire generation of working-class dandies. Overwhelmed by the Beatles' *Sergeant Pepper* and the British underground scene, Peel introduced hippy culture to British youth, being the first DJ to play the Sex Pistols' 'God Save the Queen' in 1976. Peel's impact on British pop is inextricably tied to social class and language, not least through the convergence and acceptance of regional accents in the public sphere, and the breakthrough of a large group of unsigned artists who would go on to be mainstream artists.

Perceived more as a 'social handicap' than an asset (Elmes 2000, p. 74) by most by young Britons, RP would, in the end, become quite undesirable. Trends in English pronunciation at the onslaught of the twenty-first century reflect this, and, as Elmes ascertains, this is down to the media:

> The media seeks out and exposes every aspect of style, particularly different language styles. Fashions in expression, as in everything else, change increasingly swiftly and fame and fortune depend on catching those fashions. It is no longer necessary to speak with a certain sort of accent to become successful and wealthy, nor does a broad accent of any sort debar people from becoming glamorous and famous. Energy and self confidence are now as important as a knowledge of what is correct. Style is everything. Life is fuller and faster and spoken English gains from the variety this brings (Elmes 2000, p. 75).

Another aspect that is commonplace in British culture is 'mouthing off'. Nowhere is this more rife than in public spaces: on the train, on the bus, on the high street or down the pub. Peculiarly, disorder comes about through swearing, the reason being that swear words are '*energetic* bits of language' (ibid., p. 79, author's emphasis)[28] that immediately affect the listener. The discourse around the choice of words and bad language, be it in the form of defiance or conformity, suggests a condition of possibility stating or masking one's social class. Swear words used in punk, for example, challenged the politeness and niceties of the dominant culture. Yet what is considered as 'good taste' by one class could be opposed by that taken for 'poor taste' by another (Barnard 1996, p. 131). Accent also plays a big role in this process. In Blur's case, they turned to an English spoken in the area of the Thames and its estuary in the South East and East of England (especially in London, Kent and Essex), distinguishing themselves from the Northern- ness of Oasis and Suede. Rather than comprising a single form of English, Estuary English includes various phonetic characteristics of working-class London speech. Studies have shown that such features have gradually seeped into middle-class speech, as well as into other accents of south-eastern England. Moreover, qualities of Cockney pronunciation found in Estuary English include diphthong shifts – 'I' becomes the diphthong in

---

[28]   In 1965 critic Kenneth Tynan's utterance of the f-word on live TV literally caused a national scandal and a breakthrough for broadcasting.

words like 'brown', a broad 'A' is found in words like 'bath', 'grass', and 'laugh', while 'T'-glottalization is apparent in glottal stops, where the 'T' is articulated as a glottal occlusion instead of fully pronounced before a consonant or end of word, such as 'eight' or 'water'. By no means restricted to working-class groups, Estuary English has been widely used by the young since the 1990s. Indeed, masking one's original accent to sound like 'common people' has been so widespread in the UK that the term 'Mockney' was introduced derisively in the 1990s to refer to this. Awash with examples of this, British pop culture would be normalized via language trends that are potent forms for social commentary.

How then do speech patterns and language converge with sound to affect pop music? And what processes of transformation emerge from language when set to music? Frith makes the point that a 'pop song is ordinary language put to extraordinary use' (Frith 1996, p. 168); lyrics tell stories differently, also saying a lot about how musical style functions. Differences between character songs, love ballads, rap tracks and rock songs, after all, are as vast as the effect of singing and pronunciation. For perceiving words in music is linked to what we gain from the sung voice in recorded form; habitually, this is determined by glamorous intent. Talking of which …

**Seduction and Glamour: The Cover Song**

Being dandy involves a set of performance practices that entice the listener into a vibrant sound domain. The pop performance, after all, is about charming our visual and aural senses. In British popular song the 'character song' reveals various ploys that are underway. Referring to the link between music hall, cabaret and other forms that involve processes of acting, Frith has suggested that the seductive pull of the character song lies in the theatricalization of what the singer is singing about (Frith 1996, p. 171), and, in pop terms, the narrative function of this is to portray the artist as the song's protagonist. Accordingly, the singer enacts a part that makes public a high degree of self-consciousness. In considering this, I want to focus on stylistic appropriation through cover songs and why voices are glamorized according to their production in an arrangement, with very different intentions in mind.

Like many pop artists who precede him, Williams has fused pastiche with parody by turning to well-known standards. *Swing When You're Winning*, from 2001, is an album that represents a vaunted escape into the realm of nostalgia from the first track, 'I Will Talk and Hollywood Will Listen' to the last, 'Beyond the Sea'. In a respectful tribute to Frank Sinatra, Bobby Darin, Dean Martin, Sammy Davis Junior and others, Williams dons the tuxedo to seduce his fans into the golden age of dance hall. Throughout the album, aided by an 18-piece band (recorded, note, in the legendary Capital Records Studio, Los Angeles, formerly Frank Sinatra's turf), Williams redefines his persona. Performing these songs (most of them are covers) in a way that aspires to the swing era giants certainly paid off (thanks to all those karaoke sessions down the pub while growing up in Stoke-on Trent!). Brimming with emotion, Williams takes a trip down memory lane in an attempt to authenticate and spoof his musical versatility. Moreover, turning to a genre outside the domain of mainstream pop, and pulling it off, tells us much about the masking process. Williams's performance in *Swing* has been interpreted by Catherine Parsonage as a catharsis. For Williams appears as 'a figure separate from the politicized extremes of "star" or "real person", both of which were problematic identities for him at the time' (Parsonage 2004, p. 62). Embracing swing covers, Williams reconstructs his star status by further glamorizing it. Parsonage discusses how this album (and the subsequent live concert in the Royal Albert Hall) provided Williams with an opportunity to heighten his credibility as a musician and not just as an entertainer. And, with the assistance of recording technology, he would iron out any creases by emulating Sinatra's performance style.

Compromising technical demands through the studio recording means accosting difficulties when having to perform live. The concert at the Royal Albert had to be almost perfected with the support apparatus of an army of sound technicians, musicians, a voice coach, and not least solid backing singers. Almost managing to pull it off, Williams's performance at this event was luckily reinforced by his endearing vocal mannerisms and personal quips. Close inspection reveals that his interpretation of the covers on this album is little more than imitation of the original. Yet, as Parsonage claims, fans were more drawn to the extra-musical dimensions of this project than just the performance, where 'comedy and entertainment in a more general sense' (ibid., p. 78) were tied up with the endorsement of Williams's endearing characteristics.[29]

Much the same evaluation can be applied to Rod Stewart. Albeit with less self-parody than Williams, his regurgitation of covers from the 1930s and 1940s by Cole Porter, Irving Berlin, and George and Ira Gershwin led to huge success in the transition from rock star to ageing entertainer. Stewart's two album releases in this genre managed to rival the same success he had in the 1970s. *It Had to Be You...The Great American Songbook*, released in 2002, went to the top of the album charts in the USA, UK and Canada, while the second album in this genre, *As Time Goes By: the Great American Songbook Volume 2*, soared as high in the charts in these three countries in 2003. But things would not stop here. Now on a winning streak, Stewart would release *Stardust...The Great American Songbook Volume 3* in 2004, followed by the fourth and final in 2005,

---

[29]    Parsonage adopts a theoretical concept of 'middle of the road' (MOR) for referring to the canon of music that is marked by a convergence of jazz and pop, which she maintains is frequently subjected to scholastic derision. In particular, the role of jazz in MOR and the debates around easy listening raise interesting questions to do with the mainstreaming of jazz. Parsonage attributes the formation of the MOR canon to recording practices and technology, and its influence on enabling the type of performance we encounter in Williams's *Swing* album (Parsonage 2004, pp. 70–72). Also see Steve Bailey's study (2003) of the ironic cover album in rock culture.

*Thanks for the Memory... The Great American Songbook, Volume 4.* Falling under the category of British blue-eyed soul singers,[30] Stewart's contribution to soul and R&B is admittedly profound. Unlike Williams, though, Stewart expends more effort in sounding American, performing these ballads with a rock edge to his style. Of course resuscitating the 'great' American popular song tradition of the pre-rock era in itself is a daring task for any British artist that can easily backfire. But, as Barbey claimed, every true dandy 'dares, but he dares with tact', (D'Aurevilly 1988, p. 51), always knowing where to stop.

Scrutinizing the tactics of Williams and Stewart exposes numerous features concerning strategies of imitation in cover songs, which I will return to later in this section. In contrast to, say, Almond's covering of well-known songs such as 'Strangers in the Night', 'Happy Heart', and 'Dream Lover', or the Pet Shop Boys' covers of *West Side Story*, Williams's and Stewart's covers seem more safe and respectful, where the emphasis is placed on being true to the original. With Williams, this is borne out as he dubs over Frank Sinatra on the track 'It Was a Very Good Year'. Taking the first two verses (superimposed over the 1965 arrangement), it is Sinatra's original version that guides him through the rest of the track.

Sinatra's effect on other British artists, though, has not only always been plain sailing. During the 1970s his style of performance and glitzy band arrangements hardly reflected the sentiments of a large sector of the population in Britain, unemployed, disillusioned and fed up. In a time when going to college did not guarantee work, and when 'signing on' was more the norm, the sound of disco, big band standards and prog rock brought little solace to many. Put mildly, the elaborate productions of prog rock albums and sophisticated string arrangements in disco only trivialized the social conditions of the day, far removed from the emerging punk groups and their records. Typifying punk, distorted guitar sounds, with feedback and snarling vocals, created a splash of sound that was underpinned by frenetic bass lines. Fast and feverish, punk favoured the local accent over the transatlantic accent associated with many British rock artists. Predominantly London-based, much punk was a vernacular southern style, defiant and sneering in a way that subverted the rock and 'easy listening' establishment. In contrast to Williams's cover of Paul Anka's 'My Way', and indeed Frank Sinatra's, Sid Vicious's version could not have been further removed. That it reached number six in the UK charts in 1979 says everything about the social climate of the day.

---

[30] Blue-eyed soul is a dubious term employed in the 1970s and 1980s, referring to white artists who perform R&B and soul. Its use originates from the mid-1960s in association with white artists such as The Righteous Brothers, the Box Tops and The Rascals. While the term per se has nothing to do with referring to artists with blue eyes literally, it does describe white artists who are heavily influenced by music genres attached to soul: British artists include David Bowie, Robert Palmer, Lisa Stansfield, Annie Lennox, George Michael, Tom Fox and others.

Menacingly wrenched from its saccharine melodic strands, Vicious's version of 'My Way' is delivered in a manner that is stripped of all the pretensions of soulful outpouring and skilful vocal articulation associated with big band numbers. On all fronts his performance is confrontational as he alters the lyrics and music to suit his style. With more than just a touch of mischievous intent, the final refrain holds one finger up to Sinatra and all those bourgeois followers of big band schmaltz: 'For what is a brat, what has he got, When he wears hats and he cannot, Say the things he truly feels'. The effect of this legendary recording is a full-blown send up of conservative values, and, in retrospect, a moving ode to Vicious's own short life. Moreover, the song is a snapshot of a wretched existence brought to life by a crass arrangement and foul language, not only challenging the niceties of Sinatra's ballad, but also diverting one's attention to British social class matters. Vicious, probably Britain's premier punk dandy, was bold enough to turn to a standard swing number to highlight his disdain not only for a musical style, but also a specific type of masculinity. Summing up the frustrations of a generation sick and tired of mainstream rock and pop, Vicious made a scathing statement on musical styles of the day. Alas, the anarchy and rebellion that fuelled punk would burn so furiously that by 1979 it had petered out.

Aptly titled, 'Anarchy in the UK', another track by the Sex Pistols, relied on similar strategies. In stark contrast to The Damned's 'New Rose' (the first punk single), 'Anarchy in the UK' is a more polished production with multilayered guitars and vocals and an abundance of effects. Foregrounded in this recording, Johnny Rotten's visceral anger and acerbic lyrics are an antithesis to glam fashion. Powerful enough to bring the Sex Pistols national and international fame, this song is a glamorous anthem in its own right.[31] Hardly able to play bass when he replaced bassist Glen Matlock, Vicious made rehearsals and recording sessions all the more trying. Upon release of 'Anarchy in the UK', Vivienne Westwood, McLaren's partner at the time, had insisted that Vicious must be the lead singer rather than Rotten. That he should not have been bassist is borne out by most live performances, where Vicious's amplifier would be kept down or even turned off. In the band's later recordings bass parts would be taken by Matlock or Steve Jones.

Not uncoincidentally, the Queen's Silver Jubilee in 1977 coincided with the Pistols' second single, 'God Save the Queen', which reached number two in the UK charts; this was their heartfelt contribution to the national celebrations. On the main day of the Jubilee, a boat was hired to perform on while sailing down the

---

[31] Notably, EMI's gig series at Amsterdam's Paradiso would be the last live event with Glen Matlock – rumour has it he was sacked because he liked the Beatles. More plausible, though, is Matlock's own explanation that it was a conflict with Johnny Rotten that caused him to resign. Nonetheless his departure signified a momentous event in the Pistols' history as Vicious, former drummer of Siouxsie and the Banshees and The Flowers of Romance, was brought in by Malcolm McLaren to replace Matlock; a decision based less on his musical ability and more on the punk attitude he exuded.

Thames; this ended in strife as a police raid prevented them continuing. McLaren, the band members and some followers were duly arrested. It was during this period that assaults on the Pistols' fans became more frequent by band members, and soon things turned on them when Rotten was the victim of a violent attack by a knife gang outside the Pegasus pub, Islington, sustaining injuries to his hands. As a result their tour to Scandinavia was delayed by a few weeks, followed by a secret tour in the UK to avoid cancellation – this was called SPOTS (Sex Pistols On Tour Secretly). October 1977 saw the release of the album *Never Mind the Bollocks, Here's the Sex Pistols*, featuring Matlock again on bass with Vicious only playing on a small section of the record, his part dubbed to mask his flawed playing. After their split, Vicious would record one live album, *Sid Sings* in 1979, backed by The Idols. Five months later, following the death of his girlfriend Nancy Spungen and a short imprisonment, Vicious died of a heroin overdose, paradoxically during a party celebrating his release on bail for murder charges.

Numerous points of interest surface when considering the impact of Vicious on British popular music. One can hardly dispute his charisma on stage, his anti-establishment stance that accounted for his appeal. Popularizing a punk aesthetic, he would negotiate a performance strategy never witnessed before. Masking was for him distancing and self-effacement, where a do-it-yourself musicianship defied all conventions. With this aesthetic emerged a display of masculinity that would incite anger by projecting angst onto others.

Above all, Vicious showed up the pop dandy's rejection of mainstream values in original ways. Converting ordinariness into outrage, he would sneer in the face of the showbiz artists that Stewart and Williams would later politely imitate. Subjecting himself and others to violence, Vicious demonstrated that punk was confrontational, nasty and rebellious, and, moreover, a denial of the dominant social order and repugnant hegemonic masculinity. For its time, punk's enervation seemed more extreme than any other style, where the social conditions of its outcry sabotaged all around it, fashioning a protest against the uptightness of Britishness. Fashion designer Fraser Moss has claimed: 'Maybe it's because the British are so uptight that we always have something to rebel against' (Moss in Cicolini 2005, p. 51). With rebellion as its mission, punk certainly introduced a new male order, predicated on aggression and passivity simultaneously (Bannister 2006, p. 51). Much of this was orchestrated by the partnership between Westwood and McLaren, who picked up on the inextricable tie between music and fashion as they subverted traditions and pushed the boundaries of look and sound. Punk fashion, absurdly though, ended up as a glamorized rejection of corporate fashion and the desire to find one's individuality again.

Which brings to mind the extent to which pop stars tend to their physical appearance, attitude and stage presence – a prime source of entertainment. Creating the anarchic prototype by sound and look, Vicious mirrored a sector of British youth who were raw, emotional and transient in their identity. Vehemently, he epitomized the demonic male anti-hero by the power of a personality that exercised tremendous physical exertion and frenzied eroticism. Living up to his name, his expression was a brutal musical style that fed off the salacious voyeurism of performances, pushing fans right to the edge. Combining male aggression with an ambivalent attitude to gender, Vicious pitted himself against the prettiness of the rockers of the day, pouring scorn on the glossiness of their construction and heteronormativity (read: patriarchal order). Julia Kristeva has suggested that punk is an inverted form of dandyism that converts emasculation into style. Furthermore, Kristeva views the dandy's obsession with style as a reaction against the acceptable face of masculinity (regulated by the father), and, in the case of punk, this is taken to an extreme through intended debasement that converts into something effete and narcissistic (Kristeva 1987).

Worth considering, in summing up, is the refashioning of the original song as a new version through irony. Kurt Mosser interprets Vicious's cover of 'My Way' as ironic, and far more potent than 'mere parody'. By relating the way Vicious sings the first verse to Sinatra's own version, Mosser insists that in the latter there is a reverence for 'both life and the values with which one lives it' (Mosser 2008). The subversive nature of Vicious's performance cannot be overstated. Mosser's observations of renditions of covers suggest that concepts of 'respect' and 'authenticity' are a subset of a problematic conception of 'intention'. That 'My Way' is a narrative of someone reflecting on their life as they approach its end deserves an ironic reading in the case of Vicious, who died when he was only 21. Aspects of his performance picked up by Mosser include his 'lugubrious singing' in the first verse, and his 'drawing out syllables' in a way that reminds one of the 'stereotypical drunken guest singing at a wedding'. Features such as these need to be matched against the musical elements, such as the rapid beat and tempo that turns this cover into a 'frenetic, quasi-comic version'. As Mosser sees it, cover songs have been reliant on the artist's intention in much of the research undertaken in cover songs hitherto. Redefining the term 'cover song' as 'systematically ambiguous', Mosser goes on to suggest the need for identifying a range of different types of cover songs along a continuum. Accordingly, this raises the question of why an artist chooses to copy another's song, and what kind of assumptions might be drawn for evaluating this. Which returns us to the main point: how does the cover song mask the artist's intentions, and where might the origins of this be located? Entrenched in pop expression, dandyism concerns glamour and theatricality in very nostalgic ways. Into the twenty-first century a British sensibility is discernible in the emergence of a neo-modernist stylization; in the clean lines, subtle colours and sober attitudes towards performance. Can this be seen as a backlash against the turbulence of fashion and design, post-Sex Pistols, Galliano, Westwood et al.?

## And Finally … Derisions of Virtuosity

Agility, polish and proficiency are terms used to describe musical virtuosity in performance. In music-speak the pop artist requires an array of technical skills to showcase their performance. Virtuosity can be traced back to Baroque times when the performer would display mastery over instrumental performance and compositional practice. By the nineteenth century it is well documented that the virtuoso had evolved into a highly skilled musician, whose technical abilities would set out to dazzle by sight as much as sound. Lydia Goehr refers to Stravinsky's argument for visibility in the virtuoso performance; he claimed that the 'details an audience sees actually shape its understanding of performance' (Goehr 1998, p. 155). Overtly physical and visual spectacle in the nineteenth century certainly epitomized the performer-composer, such as dandy-composers Liszt, Chopin and Paganini. Goehr goes on to argue how the very sight of gestures and movements in these performers explained 'visibility's part in the musical affair' (ibid., p. 154). In pop music traditional ideas of virtuosity have been transferred to the domain of showmanship today, albeit in a very different staged form. Adroitness in playing or singing is to link musical originality to virtuosity albeit via recording techniques, media and technology (Waksman 1999; Fast 2001). Fitting into this mould is the concept of individuality, based upon musicianship that functions to authenticate the subject. Numerous ploys, as we have seen, are effectively used to this end. Consider mimicry and appropriation. Let us say crudely that pop artists regurgitate the styles of others to recreate something that becomes their own. Alterations of an original, however, are also attributable to, in Moore's words, 'the other musicians who take part in developing a performance, and by the engineers and producers who shape the physical product, such that its origins are normally utterly submerged' (Moore 2006, p. 334). Relevant to this debate is the reconstruction of earlier styles, in which compositional innovation stands for devices of appropriation, chance and elaboration. Mimicry, then, emerges from variations of imitation that can be construed as 'new', pastiche or downright musical forgery.

Take the genealogy of doo-wop songs from the 1950s, and their origins in popular songs from the 1930s and earlier, with traits of harmonic progression, vocal mannerism and instrumental accompaniment that resurfaced in the early 1970s.

The final track on Roxy Music's self-titled debut album from 1972, 'Bitters End', is a prime example of this. Tongue-in-cheek, this arrangement, a farcical take on the art of posing, employing a mid-1950s African American style (that started on the streets of New York and Philadelphia), frames Ferry's precise English diction.[32] All the way through the backing vocals punctuate the melodic phrases in a contrived 'white' manner, reaching a climax in the middle eight section where the word 'bizarre' is reiterated in a banal call and response to the narrative. Stylistically, I read the use of doo-wop as a nostalgic commentary on a bygone age, an antithesis to glam, and, moreover, a relic of a generation

---

[32]    Other British artists who turned to doo-wop in the 1970s were Bowie ('Drive-In Saturday' (1973)), Led Zeppelin ('The Ocean' (1973)), and Electric Light Orchestra ('Telephone Line' (1977)). Doo-wop was very popular in Britain during the early 1960s, up to the British Invasion in 1964.

whose musical preferences were worlds apart. The final phrase, a pointer to the song's main narrative, 'should make the cognoscenti think', concludes with a pseudo-intellectual jab at the pretentiousness of protest songs. Identifying quirkiness in 'Bitters End' opens up many avenues for considering stylistic borrowing, which, in this case, is remarkably contrived. As Ron Moy puts it, Ferry's vocal gestures on this track are 'pushed to the point of parody', with the overpronounced, 'clipped, exaggeratingly English tones of Noël Coward' (Moy 2007, p. 60). Curiously, this is in contrast to many other tracks where Ferry hides behind a European croon that is non-English.

Ferry's chameleon approach to switching voices on the first glam track ever is an instance of virtuosity in itself. This is not dissimilar to Almond's tendency to italicize his utterances through a camp voice that is smooth and suave. What I mean by this is that Almond's style is implicated in hyperbolic mannerisms. In this way, loaded meanings are solicited through citation, a technique that taps into the traditions of Brel, Aznavour and Judy Garland, as well as numerous pop stars such as Bolan, Bowie and Morrissey. Like Ferry's vocal approach in 'Bitters End' and Ray Davies' in 'All of My Friends Were There' (see Chapter 2), Almond's vocal sensibility consummates his own sanctioned desires as rhetorical and self-celebratory.

Spectacularly up-front, he addresses 'the plight of stars' (ironically *his* plight) in the track 'The Stars We Are', the title track from the album released in 1988. Towards the end of the song, a heart-wrenching moment occurs when Almond soars above the orchestra with the lines, 'for stars we are, and stars we'll be, just you and me' (2:31–3:13). During this chorus hook, an unleashing of powerful emotions takes place in a *bel canto* style, skilfully executed by phrasing that gives way to full-throated sonority. All the way through the song a long crescendo works up to this moment as he forcefully pelts out all his welled-up sentiments. Riding the swell of orchestral sweeps, Almond tells us that we can also be stars. Delivered with sheer physical exertion, he grabs hold of specific notes in the high register, embellishes them, and then dissolves into the glittering arrangement. Peaking musically in this manner is, mildly put, as melodramatic as it gets; this is virtuosity, underpinned by burlesque. What one derives from such moments is the normalization of something exaggerated and 'unnatural'. Evoking the clichéd details of an unusually poignant ballad style, Almond expertly refashions these codes in a scintillating arrangement, transforming the blandness of simple song into a large-scale carnivalesque affair.

Contingent on a mannered way of projecting his persona, Almond's coded performance is part of a calculated package. As I have already suggested, pop artists are set apart by the style of their clothes, their looks, their voice and their mode of performance. For being dandy is the outcome of a meticulously developed and rehearsed performance routine, which, on first encounter, is not necessarily that obvious. Then there is temperament; this is integral to music production. Baudelaire conferred the accolade of dandy only on those who he sensed as *esprit de caste*, in terms of intellectual heroism and single-minded determination. As subjects of a particular cast of mind, pop dandies are symbols of *the* moment in history in which they are caught up, whose emergence is symptomatic of a mass-consumer and globalized age. Baudelairean, in this sense, the pop dandy exists only when eyes are upon him: his own, ours and, of course, the media's. For the purpose of dandifying a performance lies in the signifying practice of imprinting oneself on the memories of others in the name of fame.

This tactic is borne out by Neil Hannon of the group The Divine Comedy. When the song 'Something for the Weekend', from the album *Casanova*, became a huge success in 1996, Hannon caught the public eye as an immaculately dressed, foppish man on the cusp of the Britpop wave. Following an appearance on Chris Evans's TFI Friday television show, Hannon was soon splashed across the cover of *Melody Maker*. From this point on his impersonations of the modern dandy would be verified by interviews, live performances, videos and record sleeves. 'Something for the Weekend' is pop dandyism at its best: its superficiality radiates through the leering, tongue-in-cheek lyrics (that recount the protagonist's lover deceiving him, and then her mates beating him up), which are arranged with strings, brass, woodwinds, guitars, bass and kit. Set to a disco-like march groove, the song worms its way to the final tag (4'02"), 'He went down to the woodshed, They came down hard on his head, Gagged and bound and left for dead'. Not only is the sound overproduced, but, melodically, the forceful repetition of the tonic affords Hannon the chance to exaggerate the extended cadence point in an ever-so-camp manner.

Humorous intent, as I read it, is multilayered, as the macabre lyrics are trivialized through the promise of a party weekend. And with this comes ironic distancing, worked through by the music giving no clue to the morbid lyrics. The fanfare brassiness of the arrangement is very affected, and in the Pet Shop Boys-like disco middle section, the musical style is reminiscent of the kind of radio song played to the nation just before the weekend starts. Compressed, Hannon's voice is transported by a wave of textures that are jubilant, up-tempo and swishy.

By choice of title alone, there is every chance that Hannon might have been familiar with the cultural-linguistic satire in the phrase, 'Something for the weekend, sir?' – a euphemism for purchasing condoms. Widely used by British barbers during the second half of the twentieth century, the phrase is thought to have originated from Monty Python's *Wonderful World of Sounds* (1972): 'A herd of zebras visiting the same chemist to ask for something for the weekend'. Later albums by The Divine Comedy, however, would attempt to ditch the frivolity and silliness of the *Casanova* period, encapsulating Hannon at his most dandy. On the album sleeve of *Casanova*, Hannon is shot leaning over the deck of a flashy, brown polished boat, arms folded with a tilt of the head towards the right and cigarette in mouth. Black-oiled hair, suntan, stylish jacket and ornate cravat exoticize his appearance as suave, Italianized and gigolo-like. Such stereotypical iconography has its parallel in the musical coding, returning us to the question of individual agency through masking. How does the virtuosic control of style work through parody and pastiche? And, to what extent does a cultivated temperament rely on listening/viewing competence?


**Conclusion**

With all these matters in mind, I want to return to role-playing and music's function in this operation. Crafting the pop performance is about music expressing the body, contributing with an intensity that shapes the flow of emotions of those who experience it. Performing, however, entails different activities that are constrained by the imaginative conventions of listening that register feelings and preferences. Music-making is a unique manifestation, and, as Alan Lomax has argued, it is one of great human adaptation: various levels of 'symbolic behaviour' are congruent and 'epitomize some singular and notable aspect of a culture' (Lomax 1968, p. 8). This helps explain why members of one social group identify and express their feelings quite differently from another. Style is a matter of cultural and social identity, and for Lomax this means that '(h)uman beings are constantly evaluating and recalibrating their experiences' (ibid., p. 12) according to what they 'feel' must be right for social exchange: 'The most important thing for a person to know is just how appropriate a bit of behaviour or communication is and how to respond to it appropriately' (ibid., p. 12).

So whether we are talking of African song and dance, Bollywood film music or British indie pop, musical communication demands intricate processes of social interaction. The pop performance is a mass of subjectivities that usher in the fantasy of the body in time and space, and, in the case of the dandy, this is mediated by a playfulness that is defined by social class, history, nationality, gender and sexual orientation. In all the artists I have looked at, there is something in the spectacle of musical genres that criss-crosses artifice and realism, sentimentality and sensuality in original ways. Personal style is therefore central to understanding the mechanics of authorship, and the ways by which the author entertains musically.

Something as minute as the effect of close-miking the voice, and compressing it with added effects, displays the traits of the genre to which the performance belongs. But there are limits to identifying genre, and, as Toynbee suggests, genres 'may be *inherently* unstable' (Toynbee 2000, p. 104 – author's emphasis) because musicians are wary of aspects of definition and self- identification. Such is the paradox of the pop performance. Pop music profiles stardom through transformative and reflexive modes of performance. And, on this note, recorded expression releases the voice in a context where the artist is compelled to reinvent themselves as 'real'. If this is the case, then the virtuosic antics of performing cannot be relegated to the final result. For the fantasies we hear in a voice and see in an image, and the enjoyment derived from such identification, make the performance thrilling and memorable. This is how the pop dandy springs to life.

# Conclusion

# 'Let the boys all sing and the boys all shout …'

Dandyism is a complete theory of life. And its material is not its only side. It is a way of existing, Made up entirely of shades.

D'Aurevilly[1]

In the 77 pages of his analysis of 'Yankee Doodle', Oscar Sonneck points out that this air had little sign of dwindling in popularity. Every nation has its 'humorous, even burlesque, patriotic airs' (Sonneck 1909, p. 79), he would claim, and, in order to survive, a tune must have its redeeming features. Through the wealth of facts presented by Sonneck there is a subtext of national ownership, and in an account so rife with anecdotes, chronological sources, and ethnological reflections, curiously enough, there is only one fleeting reference to the 'dandy'; the author rather chooses to dwell on the 'macaroni'[2] (ibid., pp. 127–9). Sonneck's outline of the comic appearance of yankee doodle and his link to the British and the New England 'country bumpkins' (ibid., p. 129) concludes that 'Yankee Doodle' is so full of provincialisms, slang expressions, and allusions to American habits, that 'no Englishman could have penned these verses' (ibid., p. 141). Further to this, other assertions persist. Had the text been British, Sonneck surmises, it would have certainly found its way to England, which he asserts was not the case. And had 'Yankee Doodle' been a British satire on 'the unmilitary appearance of provincial American troops', then 'the verses would have to be derisively satirical, which, they are not' (ibid.).

Sonneck's oversight of 'Yankee Doodle's' popularity in Britain during the mid-1830s is cause for commentary. Strangely enough, he neglects the resounding success of African American bandleader Francis Johnson, whose visit to London included performances of this air to packed houses. Also there were the Hutchinson Family Singers, one of the best-known musical ensembles of mid-nineteenth century America, who visited Britain in 1845 with 'Yankee Doodle' high up on

---

[1]    D'Aurevilly (1988, p. 31).

[2]    My thanks to Steve Sweeney-Turner for elaborating on the etymology of macaroni, and for pointing out that it was used in Edinburgh in the eighteenth century to signify the persona or style of one affecting an Italianate aesthetic, particularly in the contexts of male youth expression.

their concert programme.[3] It would be redundant to pursue Sonneck's omission of the popularity of 'Yankee Doodle' in Britain any further, or, for that matter, to labour over his disregard for the dandy. Yet his omissions are telling. Dandies have historically destabilized the status quo when it comes to appearance and presence in society, and Sonneck might well have deemed this too trivial a detail to expound upon.

Dressing up says who you are; for 'clothes maketh the man', don't they? But who is the dandy in 'Yankee Doodle'? Somebody affected? Possibly. Unwise? Hardly. One thing that leaves us in little doubt is his peculiarity and survival tactics. My point is that the dandy probes at things that intrigue if not unsettle. In the numerous instances considered in this book, dandified performativity is a homosocial enactment, fraught with the fear of failure and spurred on by a burning urge to compete and succeed. Interpreting music's role through this form of characterization, a line can be drawn from the first impulses of compositional thought to the full-blown studio production.

Experiencing musical events is about a participatory situation, albeit often passive, whereby the listener is positioned as voyeur. The uniqueness of being engaged in a performance involves various forms of identification. For the rituals of the musical experience create powerful empathic response, measurable by gain and fame. As we saw in Chapter 6, the function of masking, of faking it, is to access an audience from within. In this way, masking prompts us to rethink the constituencies of reception and the kinds of musical practices that not only mobilize our emotive responses, but also shape our convictions.

In the categories of Britishness and the dandy I have identified stylistic traits that shape the artist's performance. Offering up perspectives on the interpretation of masculinity, my study attempts a reappraisal of a few of the many identities that dominate our cultural landscape. Pop subjectivity, after all, includes countless junctures of extra-musical and musical expression, drawing attention to cultural authority; what, then, are the lineages between the performer and the listener, how are they constructed, and why are they negotiated across a range of texts and practices? Crucially, the characteristics of the pop dandy are conceived in the recorded space and transported down the production line. Pop dandyism therefore occasions a colourful spectrum of cultural practices, prompting a range of ontological consideration points.

In sum, here are the main outcomes of this study:

1.  Dandified characteristics in pop entail a set of attitudes, norms and conditions of self-aestheticization that lead to social elevation and commercial gain.
2.  British pop dandies are products of a post-industrialized society with intricate social, political and cultural genealogies. Their peculiarity is

---

[3]   I am grateful to Derek Scott for pointing out these details, and drawing my attention to two different arrangements of 'Yankee Doodle' by Brinley Richards (1861) and J. Levy (1878), both published by London firms.

governed by intricate practices that are transmitted through media hype. On this basis, the media not only constructs but also contextualizes the dandy.

3.   Down the ages dandyism has been assigned specific social roles that account for the performance strategies found in pop music, traceable back to Beau Brummell, George Gordon Byron, Oscar Wilde, Noël Coward, Quentin Crisp, and others.

4.   A collusion of styles and idioms in the 1950s and 1960s that gave rise to pop dandyism are in debt to the profound effect of the art school tradition in Britain. Andy Warhol's aesthetic of passive voyeurism, emphasizing the division of female passivity and masculine passivity, created new opportunities for male representation in popular music – the performative element of disembodiment, as well as the idea of the subject as disengaged, questioned the structures of cultural politics in the art world of the time.

5.   Modelled on a Warholian aesthetic, British pop artists have recreated codes of sexuality and gender display. Challenging through stereotypes, numerous artists refuse to play out one single identity. Rather they open a space for redefining masculinity and contesting gender norms, which generations of British bands and artists have pursued.

6.   Eccentricity converts musical style into dandyism, whereby the British individual becomes mythologized through the idiosyncrasies of performance practices, such as those emanating from music hall, operetta, pantomime, and so on.

7.   Paramount to understanding the pop persona is visual and sonic spectacle. Baudelaire's discourse on the body, and its temperament, includes a conceptualization of naivety, which, in pop, is an arbitration of the 'natural' as much as the cultural. Representations in pop regularly disclose the qualities of a 'fake naivety' that can be linked to male subjectivity.

8.   Fashion is a structuring tool, working socially and politically in the construction of the pop dandy. In tandem with music, fashion exposes class identities and positions. Historically, the shaping of masculinity through a Mod sensibility signifies a major development in the British pop scene in London during the swinging Sixties. This had repercussions for all the trends that ensued.

9.   Pop texts – music videos, song recordings, television appearances, Internet and live performances – reveal the disciplining of masculinity. What is more, they show up the spectacle of the body as desire-inducing and contingent upon public display. Theatricalizing the body embodies the dandy in fascinating ways.

10.  Many dandies queer their performances, and the valorization of masculinity through homosocial behaviour accents gender anxiety in a variety of ways. British pop is rife with a queer sensibility, both as a marker of opposition and compliance. Camp contributes to this significantly in the form of

political intent.

11. Because the pop voice designates narrativity, it relies on strategies that involve authorship. Vocal address can therefore account for the peculiarities of performance, while the staged voice suggests a polysemic text for multiple identification.

12. Musical performance fuels tropes of behaviour; this corresponds to how the performer mediates his or her personality. In this respect, recorded corporeality is about vocal masking, entailing not only the produced sound, but also a transformation of this via the listener's own experience. Strategies of masking differ vastly from one artist to the next, illustrating the flexibility and appeal of the dandy as a social and cultural phenomenon.

One of the main tasks of this book has been detailing the artist's performance strategies aesthetically, and questioning the recording's role in this construction. Pop artists are embodiments of contemporary ideas, situated according to the stylistic categories to which they pertain. In spite of everything, they are part of the public domain. And conceding their own constructedness, they confess to their 'real' selves in interviews and media reporting. Commonly, the pop artist tells us what lies behind a video performance, a song, a concert or an album, which contributes to the holistic text.

Vulnerability, confirmed as much off-stage as on-stage, discloses countless confessionals; it is a prerequisite of stardom to appear to bare all. Such public display sparks off any type of emotional reaction, from outrage, condemnation and protectiveness to heightened empathy with the star. This is why biography forms an integral part of the pop text, as the artist is the property of the public fan. I have addressed this phenomenon as a vital component in working out the popularity of the star, especially through iconography. Pop dandyism repeatedly highlights the Baudelairean anti-hero, predicated upon realism and creativity at the same time. A historical figure, with variations found in all sorts of social and cultural contexts, the dandy is produced and 'enjoyed' on a global scale.

Dwelling on this specific point one last time, I draw to a close some of my thoughts on the Britishness of dandyism. By today's standards the dandy looms larger in British culture than in any age before, now that stardom intensifies and overwhelms the imagination. Continuously reinventing himself, the pop star nevertheless remains a predominantly white male, class-based institution figure, aspiring to commercial success. As we have seen, bands and artists, in drawing on bygone styles, reconstruct their notions of Britishness. Rewinding for a moment to the start of the 1980s, I turn to my last example, The Jam, who drew on distinct African American influences (soul, R&B, Chuck Berry, Little Richard and others). Yet all along they would uphold a sense of Britishness through their Mod style. In the wake of the pop-punk revival in the late 1970s and early 1980s, The Jam furnished a style that was openly in debt to the Sex Pistols (especially Johnny Rotten), The Who, The Kinks and others. Headed by The Jam, the Mod revival embraced the original 1960s Mod subculture, recreating a look and musical flavour that was melancholy. Pop dandy Paul Weller, lead singer of The Jam, turned to a style that borrowed directly from the guitar style of The Who's Pete Townshend, and Wilko Johnson of Dr Feelgood.

'Going Underground', the Jam's first number one, released in March 1980, is a fitting coda for this book. Spokesman for a generation of disillusioned youth in the early 1980s, Weller pelts out, 'I want nothing society's got, I'm going underground'. With all the ardour he can muster up, he delivers this song with the most passionate determination. Musical intensity is conveyed through features such as a fast tempo, jangly guitar riffs, splashing cymbals and a jerky bass line, all contributing to sonic textures that accompany Weller's voice. Working up into a frenzied climax, and assisted by brilliant lyrics, Weller provides a cynical narrative on the British government's policy on arms trading at the time.[4]

In the video for this song, The Jam are depicted as Mods in every conceivable way. Weller's look, enhanced by the vitality of his singing and guitar-playing, is striking: black tailored suit, elegant Italian shoes with white socks, tidy hairstyle and sporting a large, fancy gold and black braided scarf, worn as a cravat with a gold brooch as tie stud. The finishing touch is a shiny gold star on his left lapel, symbolizing solidarity as much as his camp attire. What does the 'look' say about Weller, The Jam, and the revival of a dandified style? Journalist John Harris claims The Jam is a good place to start 'if you want to understand the mixture of worry, confusion and national sclerosis that defined the years between 1978 and 1982'.[5] Against the backdrop of Thatcherism, Weller's Mod sensibility and undisguised tribute is to musical legends from the 1960s, such as Ray Davies, Steve Marriott, Pete Townshend, and soul icons Curtis Mayfield and Marvin Gaye.

The anti-star aspect of punk would metamorphose into a performer with a literary consciousness, inflamed by style and delivery. The middle section of 'Going Underground' reflects this in the aggressive delivery of 'la la la la', developing into a shattering final refrain, 'let the brass bands play and feet start to Pow! Pow! Pow! Pow!' (2:38–2:40). A host of stylistic referents illustrate The Jam's great affinity with the golden age of British bands: guitar flourishes, frenetic drumming and the overall controlled feedback and reverb in the mix. The poignancy of this song is located most in an ending that refuses any neat or finite closure. That is to say, instead of resolving to the tonic (D flat), as one might expect, the final cadence involves a subtle shift from the dominant chord (A flat) to a subdominant sixth (G flat 6) on the last phrase, 'the boys all shout for tomorrow'. The effect of this is anarchic. Heavily reverbed and lingering, Weller's final melodic note, the sixth (E flat) of the G flat major, establishes a despondency that comes about through an avoidance of both musical and narrative closure; for going underground is no longer an option, as the singer refuses the temptation of resolving to a perfect

---

[4]   In Moore's analysis of this song he points out the characteristic use of the Ionian progression (I–VI–IV–V), which is set to a 'lyrical redolent of punk' (Moore 2001, p. 143).

[5]   'The Jam? They were a way of life', *The Guardian*, 3 February 2006.

cadence (read: masculine ending). In the aftermath of the final chord, an atom bomb is heard and seen going off at the close of the video.

Musically, the texture in 'Going Underground' is dominated by a dirty, scratchy sound, shaped by brash guitar lines, with a harsh treble frequency and a pounding bass part played with a plectrum that creates a raw grind.[6] This is The Jam's sonic signature. The solo guitar, panned to the left with overdrive, complements the rhythm guitar to the right, regulated by a rhythmic drive with the use of 'pedals' merged into the vocals as a wash of sound. Masking is evident in the video, as the guitar solos remain absent from what we see – rather than the second guitarist, on the right-hand side of Weller, it is the bass player, Bruce Foxton, we see. This visual detail makes for an unusual presence of musical tension.

The guitar-playing in The Jam, like their singing, is unhinged pitchwise, and rhythmically it is indicative of a punk aesthetic. The Jam's idiom in 'Going Underground', as in many of their other songs, is characterized by the sounds of the Rickenbacker guitars, popular in British bands of the 1960s – John Lennon played a semi-acoustic Rickenbacker up until the mid-1960s.[7] Authenticity lies in the visual details as much as in the marked out-of-tuneness in the guitar sound, an effect that arises from pressure being exerted on the fretboard. All along Weller's shouting style gives the impression of coming directly from the heart. Energetic, aggressive, sublime unbridled passion – the emotive qualities of Weller's performance – fuse in unison with the instruments in a headrush on 'pow, pow, pow, pow!' A torrent of emotions unleashed at this final plateau are steered by a modulation up a major second (C flat to D flat) on the hook 'going underground'. Provocatively, this unexpected turn in tonal activity eases Weller into the final lap (2:26), the exertion of which is marked by loud dynamics in a frenzied climax; the effortful force of his straining in the high register drives the snide slice-of-life message home.

Loaded with insinuation, 'Going Underground' is about resistance, its musical heritage being in the cultural movement of the 1960s and 1970s, inspired by French existentialists such as Albert Camus and Jean-Paul Sartre. Weller, dandified Modfather, provides a stirring tribute, drawing on pop melodies and a political conscience to produce an inner force that is raw and compelling. A figure of our age, postmodern and confrontational, he is a veteran of sophistry who makes everything he performs a novelty. He is the dandy bending the rules on an ego-trip, who flaunts his subjectivity as vain yet vulnerable. Walden argues that what matters to today's dandy 'is "attitude", "life-style", iconic status, and a platform from which he or she can flaunt their persona' (Walden 2002, p. 55). This rings true in the Wellerian dandies, whose 'notional insurrection' rubs up against their social environment where 'they are seen (and see themselves) as glittering adornments'

---

[6]   Thanks to Eirik Askerøi for pointing out the details of guitar techniques used in this song and various aspects of production.

[7]   It was Cláudia Azevedo who drew my attention to the type of guitars being used by The Jam, and the matter of referencing too earlier British bands.

(ibid.). Pop dandyism is relevant to sounding the way one looks. (The British attitude to dress is much like the approach to music; it is coded by sartorial subtlety and twisted self-ridicule.) A prime element in dandyism, then, is the link between fashion and music, dependent on an embarrassment invested into the subversive act of expressing oneself. David Piper, who launched the vaudeville entertainment Modern Times Club at the Great Eastern Hotel, Liverpool Street, London in 2003, claimed that the seminal relationship between Westwood and McLaren was a 'pivotal factor in British style'. This is because they were subversive 'within the boundaries of what you would wear' (Cicolini 2005, p. 45). Piper goes on to suggest that maybe this is because the British are so inhibited, and, as a result, need something to protest about. British pop music, like fashion, is street-tailored to be subversive and free. Inhibitions removed, the performer undrapes all the clichés of splendour, the pre-emptive strategy in catering *for the fans*.

Pop dandies are the outcome of what Baudelaire called 'the rising tide of democracy, which invades and levels everything' (Baudelaire 1964, p. 29). Following in the footsteps of Beau Brummell, the dandy satirizes his socio-political context through the extravagance of his display. Half-joshingly, his revolt is also Wildean, where just the right dose of eccentricity assures celebratory status. The aim is to create a subjectivity that harnesses attitude, bodily, in most peculiar ways. It is as if style is about being effortless and never appearing to try too hard.[8]

The main thesis of this book affirms that the 'pop' part of the dandy is a generic marker: not because of epistemological weight, but because this marker refers to the expressive power of a collective identity that is strongly rooted in traditions. There's a reason that pop is dandified and that the artist has evolved as the true *prince of the world*. One thing remains certain: British pop music has acquired a global profile by the glamorizing of the individual before the masses. After all, we only listen to those we have an affinity to, and being entertained is the emotional state of identifying with stars who appear and then fall. Barbey claimed that constant perpetual change characterizes those who produce a cult, and that the existence of the dandy is based on more than an illusion. I don't think I have ever been in doubt of the incongruities of temperament found in pop expression, a persistent source of enthralment, that is governed by the traditions of our culture. It is this quality that the pop dandy expresses so perfectly.

---

[8]   The appeal of the dandy lies in those feelings of at-oneness we, as fans, have with the pop performer. It is worth stressing that the performer's rebuttal of critics' jibes and scorn contributes to an empathic relationship with the fan. What matters in pop is moving the listener, and, as Carl Wilson puts it, the pop artist needs to be a 'convincing fake' in a way that a 'lie feels true' (Wilson 2007, p. 123).

# Discography

**Albums**

Adam and the Ants: *Kings of the Wild Frontier*, Epic Records (1980)
___: *Prince Charming*, Epic Records (1981)
Adams, Bryan: *Reckless*, A&M Records (1984)
Almond, Marc: *Stardom Road*, Sequel (2007)
Antony and The Johnsons: *I Am A Bird Now*, Secretly Canadian (2005)
Babyshambles: *Down in Albion*, Rough Trade (2005)
Beatles: *Sergeant Pepper's Lonely Hearts Club Band*, Parlophone (1967)
Bowie, David: *Hunky Dory*, RCA (1971)
___: *Aladdin Sane*, RCA (1973)
___: *Low*, RCA (1977)
___: *'Heroes'*, RCA (1977)
___: *Let's Dance*, EMI (1983)
___: *Lodger*, RCA (1979)
___: *Scary Monsters (and Super Creeps)*, RCA (1980)
___: *Heathen*, Sony (2002)
Collins, Phil: *No Jacket Required*, Virgin (1985)
Coward, Noël: *Twentieth Century Blues: The Songs of Noel Coward*, Ichiban (1998)
Cure, The: *Three Imaginary Boys*, Fiction (1979)
___: *Seventeen Seconds*, Fiction (1980)
___: *Pornography*, Fiction-Elektra (1982)
___: *The Top*, Fiction (1984)
___: *Kiss Me, Kiss Me, Kiss Me*, Fiction (1987)
Darkness, The: *The Darkness – Permission to Land*, Atlantic (2003)
Dire Straits: *Brothers in Arms*, Vertigo (1985)
Divine Comedy, The: *Casanova*, Setanta (1996)
Duran Duran: *Rio*, Capitol/EMI (1982)
Ferry, Bryan: *Boys and Girls*, Virgin (1985)
___: *Slave To Love: Best of the Ballads*, EMI (2000)
Jagger, Mick: *Wandering Spirit*, Atlantic/WEA (1993)
___: *Goddess In The Doorway*, Virgin (2001)
___: *The Very Best of Mick Jagger*, WEA/Rhino (2007)
Japan: *Adolescent Sex*, Hansa Records (1977)
Kinks, The: *Face to Face*, Pye NPL (1966)
___: *The Kinks Are The Village Green Preservation Society*, Pye (1968)
___: *Lola versus Powerman and the Moneygoround, Part One*, Pye (1970)

Lilac Time, The: *Looking for a Day in the Night*, Spin Art (1999)
Mansun: *Attack of the Grey Lantern*, Parlophone (1997)
Morrissey, Steven: *Ringleader of the Tormentors,* Sanctuary (2006)
Oasis: *Be Here Now*, Creation (1997)
Palmer, Robert: *Riptide*, Island (1985)
Pet Shop Boys: *Nightlife*, Parlophone (1999)
___: *Pet Shop Boys: Pop Art – The Hits*, Parlophone (2003)
Pink Floyd: *Dark Side of the Moon*, Harvest (1973)
Rolling Stones, the: *Some Girls*, Virgin (1978)
Roxy Music: *For Your Pleasure*, E.G. Records (1973)
___: *Stranded*, Polydor (1973)
___: *Avalon*, Virgin (1982)
Sex Pistols: *Never Mind the Bollocks, Here's the Sex Pistols*, Virgin (1977)
Spice Girls: *Spiceworld*, Virgin (1997)
Stewart, Rod: *It Had to Be You ...The Great American Songbook*, J-Records (2002)
___: *As Time Goes By: the Great American Songbook Volume 2*, J-Records (2003)
___: *Stardust ...The Great American Songbook Volume 3*, J-Records (2003)
___: *Thanks for the Memory ...The Great American Songbook 4*, J-Records (2005)
Sting: *The Dream of the Blue Turtles*, A&M (1985)
Tears for Fears: *Songs From the Big Chair*, Mercury (1985)
T. Rex: *Dandy in the Underworld*, EDSEL Records (1977)
Vicious, Sid: *Sid Sings*, Alex (1979)
Wham: *Make It Big*, Columbia (1984)
Williams, Robbie: *I've Been Expecting You*, Chrysalis (1998)
___: *Sing When You're Winning*, Chrysalis (2000)
___: *Swing When You're Winning*, EMI (2001)
___: *Escapology*, EMI (2002)
___: *Intensive Care*, Chrysalis (2005)

## Songs

Adam and the Ants: 'Prince Charming', *Prince Charming*, Epic Records (1981)
___: 'Stand and Deliver', *Prince Charming*, Epic Records (1981)
Almond, Marc: 'The Stars We Are', *The Stars We Are*, Parlophone (2002)
___: 'Dream Lover', *Stardom Road*, Sequel (2007)
___: 'Happy Heart', *Stardom Road*, Sequel (2007)
___: 'Kitsch', *Stardom Road*, Sequel (2007)
___: 'Strangers in the Night', *Stardom Road*, Sequel (2007)
Antony and The Johnsons:'I Fell in Love with a Dead Boy', Durtro (2001)
___: 'For Today I Am a Boy', *I Am A Bird Now*, Secretly Canadian (2005)

Babyshambles: 'Albion', *Down in Albion*, Rough Trade (2005)
___: 'A Rebours', *Down in Albion*, Rough Trade (2005)
___: 'Fuck Forever', *Down in Albion*, Rough Trade (2005)
___: 'La Belle et la Bete', *Down in Albion*, Rough Trade (2005)
Beatles: 'Yellow Submarine', *Revolver*, Parlophone (1966)
___: 'All You Need Is Love', Parlophone (1967)
___: 'Hey Jude', Apple Records (1968)
___: 'Come Together', *Abbey Road*, Apple Records (1969)
Beyoncé: 'Green Light', *B'Day*, Sony (2005)
Blur: 'Girls & Boys', *Parklife*, EMI (1994)
___: 'Country House', *The Great Escape*, EMI (1995)
Bowie, David: 'Slip Away', *Heathen*, ISO (2002)
___: 'Space Oddity', Philips (1969)
___: 'The Man Who Sold the World', *The Man Who Sold the World*, Mercury (1970)
___: 'Andy Warhol', *Hunky Dory*, RCA (1971)
___: 'Moonage Daydream', B&C (1971)
___: 'Heroes', *'Heroes'*, RCA (1977)
___: 'Ashes to Ashes', *Scary Monsters (and Super Creeps)*, RCA (1980)
___: 'Fashion', *Scary Monsters (and Super Creeps)*, RCA (1980)
Coward, Noël: 'Twentieth Century Blues' (1931)
___: 'Mad about the Boy' (1932)
___: 'A Marvellous Party' (1939)
___:'Sail Away' (1950)
Cure, The: 'Boys Don't Cry', *Boys Don't Cry*, Fiction (1980)
___: 'Jumping Someone Else's Train', *Boys Don't Cry*, Fiction (1980)
___: 'Let's Go to Bed', Fiction (1982)
___: 'The Lovecats', Fiction (1983)
___: 'The Walk', Fiction (1983)
___: 'Catch', *Kiss Me, Kiss Me, Kiss Me*, Fiction (1987)
___: 'Hot, Hot, Hot', *Kiss Me, Kiss Me, Kiss Me*, Fiction (1987)
___: 'Just Like Heaven', *Kiss Me, Kiss Me, Kiss Me*, Fiction (1987)
___: 'Why Can't I Be You', *Kiss Me, Kiss Me, Kiss Me*, Fiction (1987)
___: 'Lovesong', *Disintegration*, Fiction-Elektra (1988)
___: 'Friday I'm in Love', *Wish*, Fiction (1992)
Damned, The: 'New Rose', *Damned Damned Damned* (1976)
Darkness. The: 'I Believe in a Thing Called Love', *Permission to Land*, Atlantic (2003)
Divine Comedy, The: 'Something for the Weekend', *Casanova*, Setanta (1996)
Ferry, Bryan: 'Let's Stick Together', *Let's Stick Together*, E.G. Records (1976)
___:'Don't Stop The Dance', *Boys and Girls*, Virgin (1985)
___: 'Slave To Love', *Boys and Girls*, Virgin (1985)
___: 'Windswept', *Boys and Girls*, Virgin (1985)
___: 'Kiss and Tell', *Bête Noire*, Virgin (1987)

___: 'Limbo', *Bête Noire*, Virgin (1987)
___: 'Help Me', *Ultimate Collection*, EMI (1993)
___: 'Is Your Love Strong Enough?', *Slave to Love*, EMI (2000)
Gorillaz: 'Clint Eastwood', *Gorillaz*, Parlophone (2001)
Hendrix, Jimi: 'Purple Haze', Track (1967)
Jagger, Mick: 'Hide Away', *Goddess In The Doorway*, Virgin (2001)
___: 'Visions of Paradise', *Goddess In The Doorway*, Virgin (2001)
___: 'Charmed Life', *The Very Best of Mick Jagger*, WEA/Rhino (2007)
___: 'Dancing in the Street', *The Very Best of Mick Jagger*, WEA/Rhino (2007)
___: 'God Gave Me Everything', *The Very Best of Mick Jagger*, WEA/Rhino (2007)
___: 'Joy', *The Very Best of Mick Jagger*, WEA/Rhino (2007)
___: 'Lucky in Love', *The Very Best of Mick Jagger*, WEA/Rhino (2007)
___: 'Old Habits Die Hard', *The Very Best of Mick Jagger*, WEA/Rhino (2007)
___: 'Too Many Cooks (Spoil the Soup)', *The Very Best of Mick Jagger*, WEA/Rhino (2007)
Jam, The: 'Going Underground', Polydor (1980)
Jamiroquai: 'Virtual Insanity', *Travelling without Moving*, Sony BMG (1996)
Japan: 'Adolescent Sex', *Adolescent Sex*, Hansa Records (1977)
Kinks, The: 'You Really Got Me', Pye (1964)
___: 'Dandy', *Face to Face*, Pye NPL (1966)
___: 'Dedicated Follower of Fashion', Pye (1966)
___: 'I'm Not Like Everybody Else', Pye (1966)
___: 'David Watts', *Something Else*, Pye (1967)
___: 'Two Sisters', *Something Else*, Pye NPL (1967)
___: 'All of My Friends Were There', *The Kinks Are The Village Green Preservation Society*, Pye (1968)
___: 'Village Green', *The Kinks Are The Village Green Preservation Society*, Pye (1968)
___: 'Lola', *Lola versus Powerman and the Moneygoround, Part One*, Pye (1970)
Loc, Tone: 'Wild Thing', Delicious Vinyl (1988)
Mansun: 'Wide Open Space', *Attack of the Grey Lantern*, Parlophone (1997)
Minogue vs. New Order: 'Can't Get Blue Monday Out Of My Head', Not On Label (2002)
Morrissey: 'At Last I Am Born', *Ringleader of the Tormentors*, Sanctuary (2006)
___: 'You Have Killed Me', *Ringleader of the Tormentors*, Sanctuary (2006)
Nirvana: 'Smells Like Teen Spirit', *Nevermind*, DGC (1991)
Oasis: 'Fade Away', Creation Records (1994)
___ 'Some Might Say', *(What's the Story) Morning Glory?*, Creation Records (1995)
___: 'All Around the World', *Be Here Now*, Creation Records (1997)
Palmer, Robert: 'Addicted to Love', *Riptide*, Island (1985)
___:'I Didn't Mean to Turn You On', *Riptide*, Island (1985)

___: 'Change His Ways', *Heavy Nova* (1988)

___: 'Simply Irresistible', *Heavy Nova* (1988)

Pet Shop Boys: 'Can You Forgive Her', *Very*, Parlophone (1993)

Prince: '1999', *1999*, Warner Bros (1982)

Pulp: 'Common People', *Different Class*, Polygram (1995)

___: 'Sorted for E's & Wizz', *Different Class*, Polygram (1995)

R.E.M: 'Man on the Moon', *Automatic for the People*, Warner Bros (1992)

Rolling Stones: 'Come On', Decca (1963)

___: 'Get Off of My Cloud', *December's Children*, Decca (1965)

___: '(I Can't Get No) Satisfaction', *Out of Our Heads*, Decca (1965)

___: 'We Love You', Decca (1967)

___ 'Jumpin' Jack Flash', Decca (1968)

___: 'Miss You', *Some Girls*, Virgin (1978)

Roxy Music: 'Bitters End', *Roxy Music*, E.G. Records (1972)

Ryan, Barry: 'Love is Love', Polydor (1969)

Ryan, Paul and Barry: 'Don't Bring Me Your Heartaches', *The Best of Paul & Barry Ryan*, Repertoire (1998)

___: 'Have Pity on the Boy', *The Best of Paul & Barry Ryan*, Repertoire (1998)

___:'Missy Missy', *The Best of Paul & Barry Ryan*, Repertoire (1998)

___: 'Magical Spiel', *The Best of Paul & Barry Ryan*, Repertoire (1998)

___: 'The Hunt', *The Best of Paul & Barry Ryan*, Repertoire (1998)

___: 'Zeit Macht Nur Vor Dem Teufel Halt', *The Best of Paul & Barry Ryan*, Repertoire (1998)

Scissor Sisters: 'Take Your Mama', Jive Records/Nonesuch (2004)

Scorpions, The: 'Rock You Like A Hurricane', *Love at First Sting*, Mercury (1984)

Sex Pistols: 'God Save the Queen', *Never Mind the Bollocks, Here's the Sex Pistols*, Virgin (1977)

___: 'Anarchy in the UK', *Anarchy in the UK: Live at the 76 Club*, Brilliant (1985)

Simon, Carly: 'You're So Vain', *No Secrets*, Elektra (1972)

Smiths, The: 'This Charming Man', *The Smiths*, Rough Trade (1983)

___: 'Panic', *Louder Than Bombs*, Rough Trade (1987)

Springsteen, Bruce: 'Atlantic City', *Nebraska*, Columbia (1982)

Suede: 'The Drowners', *Suede* (1993)

___: 'Stay Together', Sony (1994)

Sylvian, David and Ryuichi Sakamo: 'Bamboo Houses/Bamboo Music', Victor (1982)

T. Rex: 'Hot Love', Fly/Reprise (1971)

___: 'Children of the Revolution', EMI/Reprise (1972)

Twain, Shania: 'Man! I Feel Like a Woman', *Come on Over*, Mercury Nashville (1999)

U2: 'Where the Streets Have No Name', *The Joshua Tree*, Island (1987)

Vicious, Sid: 'My Way', *Sid Sings*, Alex (1979)

*THE BRITISH POP DANDY*

Williams, Robbie: 'Angels', *Life Thru A Lens*, EMI (1997)
——: 'Let Me Entertain You', *Life Thru A Lens*, EMI (1997)
___: 'Millennium', *I've Been Expecting You*, Chrysalis (1998)
___: 'Rock DJ', *Sing When You're Winning*, Chrysalis (2000)
___: 'It Was A Very Good Year', *Swing When You're Winning*, EMI (2001)
___: 'Somethin' Stupid', *Swing When You're Winning*, EMI (2001)
___: 'Radio', *Greatest Hits*, Chrysalis (2004)

# Bibliography

Alibhai-Brown, Yasmin (2000), *Who Do We Think We Are? Imagining the New Britain* (London: Allen Lane).

Ant, Adam (2007), *Stand & Deliver: The Autobiography* (London: Pan Books).

Auslander, Philip (2006), *Performing Glam Rock: Gender and Theatricality in Popular Music* (University of Michigan Press).

Bailey, Steve (2003), 'Faithful or Foolish: The Emergence of the "Ironic Cover Album" and Rock Culture' in *Popular Music and Society*, 26.2, pp. 141–59.

Bannister, Matthew (2006), *White Boys, White Noise: Masculinities and 1980s Indie Guitar Rock* (Aldershot: Ashgate).

Barnard, Malcolm (1996), *Fashion as Communication* (London: Routledge).

Barthes, Roland (1967/1990), *The Fashion System*, trans. M. Ward and R. Howard (Berkeley, CA: University of California Press).

Barthes, Roland (1977), *Image Music Text*, trans. S. Heath (London: Fontana).

Baudelaire, Charles (1964), *The Painter of Modern Life and Other Essays*, trans. and ed. J. Mayne (London: Phaidon Press).

Baudelaire, Charles (1986), *Fusées* (Paris: Editions Flammarion).

Baudrillard, Jean (1981a), *Simulacres et Simulation* (Paris: Editions Galilee).

Baudrillard, Jean (1981b), *For a Critique of the Political Economy of the Sign*, trans. C. Levin (St Louis, MO.: Telos Press).

Baudrillard, Jean (2005), *The Conspiracy of Art: Manifestos, Texts, Interviews (Foreign Agents)*, ed. S. Lotringer and trans. A. Hodges (Cambridge, MA: MIT Press).

Benveniste, Emile (1971), *Problems in General Linguistics*, trans. Mary E. Meek (Coral Gables: University of Miami Press).

Biddle, Ian and Jarman-Ivens, Freya (2007), 'Introduction: Oh Boy! Making Masculinity in Popular Music' in F. Jarman-Ivens (ed.), *Oh Boy! Masculinities and Popular Music*, (London: Routledge), pp. 1–17.

Biddle, Ian and Knights, Vanessa (eds) (2007), *Music, National Identity and the Politics of Location: Between the Global and the Local* (Aldershot: Ashgate).

Booth, Mark (1999), '*Campe-toi!*: On the Origins and Definitions of Camp' in F. Cleto (ed.), *Camp: Queer Aesthetics and the Performing Subject: A Reader* (Edinburgh: Edinburgh University Press), pp. 66–79.

Bracewell, Michael (1998), *England is Mine: Pop Life in Albion from Wilde to Goldie* (London: Flamingo).

Bradby, Barbara (1993), 'Sampling Sexuality: Gender, Technology, and the Body in Dance Music', *Popular Music*, 12/2, pp. 155–76.

Brett, Philip and Wood, Elizabeth (2002), 'Lesbian and Gay Music' in C. Palombini (ed.) *Revista Eletronica de Musicologia*, Volume VII.

Brett, P., Wood, E. and Thomas, G. C. (eds) (1994), *Queering the Pitch* (London: Routledge).

Breward, Christopher (2002), 'Style and Subversion: Postwar Poses and the Neo-Edwardian Suit in Mid-Twentieth-Century Britain' in *Gender & History*, Vol. 14, No.3, pp. 560–83.

Bronski, Michael (1998), *The Pleasure Principle: Sex, Backlash, and the Struggle for Gay Freedom* (New York: St. Martin's Press).

Buckley, David (2000), *Strange Fascination. David Bowie: The Definitive Story* (London: Virgin Books).

Buckley, David (2004a), *David Bowie: The Complete Guide to his Music* (London: Omnibus Press).

Buckley, David (2004b), *The Thrill of It All: The Story of Bryan Ferry and Roxy Music* (London: André Deutsch Ltd).

Burns, L. and Lafrance, M. (2002), *Disruptive Divas: Feminism, Identity & Popular Music* (London: Routledge).

Burston, Paul (1993), 'As Tears Go By', interview with Marc Almond, *Gay Times*, April 1993.

Burston, Paul (1995) 'Just a Gigolo? Narcissism, Nellyism and the "New Man" Theme' in P. Burston and C. Richardson (eds), *A Queer Romance: Lesbians, Gay Men and Popular Culture* (London: Routledge), pp. 111–22.

Butler, Judith (1990), *Gender Trouble: Feminism and the Subversion of Identity* (London: Routledge).

Butler, Judith (1993), *Bodies That Matter: On the Discursive Limits of 'Sex'* (London: Routledge).

Campbell, Sean (2007), '"Pack Up Your Troubles": Politics & Popular Music in Pre- & Post-Ceasefire Ulster', Issue 4, *Popular Musicology Online*.

Cicolini, Alice (2005), *The New English Dandy* (London: Thames & Hudson).

Citron, Marcia J. (1993), *Gender and the Musical Canon* (Cambridge).

Cleto, Fabio (ed.) (1999), *Camp: Queer Aesthetics and the Performing Subject: A Reader* (Edinburgh: Edinburgh University Press).

Cohn, Nick (1969), *WopBopaLooBopLopBamBoom* (London: Paladin).

Colls, Robert (2002), *Identity of England* (Oxford: Oxford University Press).

Cook, Nicholas (1998), *Analyzing Music Multimedia* (Oxford: Oxford University Press).

Craig, Steve (1993), 'Selling Masculinities, Selling Femininities: Multiple Genders and the Economics of Television' in *The Mid-Atlantic Almanack*, Vol. 2, pp. 15–27.

Cubitt, Sean (2000), 'Maybellene: Meaning and the Listening Subject' in *Reading Pop*, ed. R. Middleton (Oxford: Oxford University Press), pp. 141–59.

D'Aurevilly, Jules Barbey (1988), *Dandyism*, reprint of 1897 edition of *Of Dandyism and of George Brummell* by J.M. Dent & Company, London (New York: PAJ Publications).

Décharné, Max (2006), *King's Road: The Rise and Fall of the Hippest Street in the World* (London: Phoenix).

Docker, John (1994), *Postmodernism and Popular Culture: A Cultural History* (Cambridge: Cambridge University Press).

Doggett, Peter (2004), *Jimi Hendrix: The Complete Guide to his Music* (London: Omnibus Press).

Dotson, Edisol Wayne (1999), *Behold the Man: The Hype and Selling of Male Beauty in Media and Culture* (New York: Harrington Park Press).

Drukman, Steve (1995), 'The gay Gaze, Or Why I Want My MTV', in P. Burston and C. Richardson (eds), *A Queer Romance: Lesbians, Gay Men and Popular Culture* (London: Routledge).

Dyer, Richard (2004), *Heavenly Bodies: Film Stars and Society* (London: Routledge).

Edwards, Tim (2006), *Cultures of Masculinity* (London: Routledge).

Elmes, Simon (2000), *The Routes of English 2* (London: BBC Education Production).

Fast, Susan (2001), *In the Houses of the Holy: Led Zeppelin and the Power of Rock Music* (Oxford: Oxford University Press).

Foucault, Michel (1980), *The History of Sexuality: Volume 1: An Introduction* (New York. Vintage Books).

Fouz-Hernández, Santiago and Jarman-Ivens, Freya (2004), *Madonna's Drowned Worlds: New Approaches to her Cultural Transformations, 1983–2003* (Aldershot: Ashgate).

Fraser, Mariam (1999), 'Classing Queer: Politics in Competition' in V. Bell (ed.), *Performativity and Belonging* (London: Sage).

Frith, Simon (1983), *Sound Effects* (London: Constable).

Frith, Simon (ed.) (1990), *Facing the Music* (London: Mandarin).

Frith, Simon (1996), *Performing Rites: On the Value of Popular Music* (Oxford: Oxford University Press).

Frith, Simon (2007), *Taking Popular Music Seriously: Selected Essays* (Aldershot: Ashgate).

Frith, Simon and Horne, Howard (1987), *Art Into Pop* (London: Methuen).

Frith, Simon and McRobbie, Angela (1978), 'Rock and sexuality', in S. Frith and A. Goodwin (eds), (1990), *On Record*, (London: Routledge), pp. 371–98.

Garnett, Liz (2005), *The British Barbershopper: A Study in Socio-Musical Values* (Aldershot: Ashgate).

Gelder, Ken and Thornton, Sarah (1997), *The Subcultures Reader* (London: Routledge).

Gill, John (1995), *Queer Noises: Male and Female Homosexuality in Twentieth-Century Music* (London: Cassell).

Goehr, Lydia (1998), *The Quest for Voice: Music, Politics, and the Limits of Philosophy* (Oxford: Oxford University Press).

Grant, Alexander and Stringer, Keith (eds) (1995), *Uniting the Kingdom?: The Making of British History* (London: Routledge).

Green, Lucy (1997), *How Popular Musicians Learn: A Way Ahead for Music Education* (Aldershot: Ashgate).

Green, Lucy (2002), 'Gender Identity, Musical Experience and Schooling' in G. Spruce (ed.), *Aspects of Teaching Secondary Music: Perspectives on Practice* (London: Routledge).

Griffiths, Dai (2003), 'From Lyric to Anti-lyric: Analyzing the Words in Pop Song' in A.F. Moore (ed.), *Analyzing Popular Music* (Cambridge: Cambridge University Press), pp. 39–59.

Halberstam, Judith (2006), 'What's That Smell? Queer Temporalities and Subcultural Lives' in S. Whiteley and J. Rycenga (eds), *Queering the Popular Pitch* (London: Routledge), pp. 3–25.

Hannaford, Alex (2006), *Last of the Rock Romantics: Pete Doherty* (London: Ebury Press).

Harris, John (2004), *The Last Party: Britpop, Blair and the Demise of English Rock* (London: Harper Perennial).

Hawkins, Stan (1996), 'Perspectives in Popular Musicology: Music, Lennox and Meaning in 1990s Pop', *Popular Music*, 15/1, pp. 17–36.

Hawkins, Stan (1997), 'The Pet Shop Boys: Musicology, Masculinity, and Banality', in S. Whiteley (ed.), *Sexing the Groove: Popular Music and Gender* (London: Routledge), pp. 118–33

Hawkins, Stan (2001), 'Musicological Quagmires in Popular Music: Seeds of Detailed Conflict' in *Popular Musicology Online*, Issue 1.

Hawkins, Stan (2002), *Settling the Pop Score: Pop Texts and Identity Politics* (Aldershot: Ashgate).

Hawkins, Stan (2003), 'Feel the Beat Come Down: House Music as Rhetoric' in A.F. Moore (ed.), *Analyzing Popular Music* (Cambridge: Cambridge University Press), pp. 80–102.

Hawkins, Stan (2004), 'Dragging out Camp: Narrative Agendas in Madonna's Musical Production' in Santiago Fouz-Hernández and Freya Jarman-Ivens (eds), *Madonna's Drowned Worlds* (Aldershot: Ashgate), pp. 3–21.

Hawkins, Stan (2006), 'On Male Queering in Mainstream Pop' in S. Whiteley and J. Rycenga (eds), *Queering the Popular Pitch* (London: Routledge), pp. 279–94.

Hawkins, Stan (2007a), 'Aphex Twin: Monstrous Hermaphrodites, Madness and the Strain of Independent Dance Music' in J. Richardson and S. Hawkins (eds), *Essays on Sound and Vision* (Helsinki: Helsinki University Press), pp. 27–53.

Hawkins, Stan (2007b), '[Un]*Justified*: Gestures of Straight-Talk in Justin Timberlake's Songs' in F. Jarman-Ivens (ed.), *Oh Boy! Masculinities and Popular Music* (London: Routledge), pp. 197–212.

Hawkins, Stan (2007c), 'Those Norwegians: Deconstructing the Nation-State in Europe through Fixity and Indifference in Norwegian Club Music' in I. Biddle and V. Knights (eds), *Music, National Identity and the Politics of Location* (Aldershot: Ashgate), pp. 179–89.

Hawkins, Stan (2008), 'Temporal Turntables: On Temporality and Corporeality in Dance Music' in S. Baur, R. Knapp, and J. Warwick (eds), *Musicological*

*Identities: Essays in Honor of Susan McClary* (Aldershot: Ashgate), pp. 121–33.

Hawkins, Stan and Richardson, John (2007), 'Remodeling Britney Spears: Matters of Intoxication and Mediation' in *Popular Music and Society*, Vol. 30, No. 5, pp. 605–29.

Hearn, J. (1992), *Men in the Public Eye: The Construction and Deconstruction of Public Men and Public Patriarchies* (London: Routledge).

Heasley, Robert (2005), 'Crossing the Borders of Gendered Sexuality: Queer Masculinities of Straight Men' in C. Ingraham (ed.), *Thinking Straight: The Power, the Promise, and the Paradox of Heterosexuality* (London: Routledge), pp. 109–21.

Hebdige, Dick (1979), *Subculture: On the Meaning of Style* (London: Routledge).

Hemmings, Clare (1995), 'Locating Bisexual Identities: Discourses of Bisexuality and Contemporary Feminist Theory' in D. Bell and G. Valentine (eds), *Mapping Desire* (London: Routledge), pp. 41–55.

Hennion, Antoine (1983), 'The Production of Success: An Anti-musicology of the Pop Song', *Popular Music*, 3, pp. 32–40.

Hoeckner, Berthold (2002), *Programming the Absolute: Nineteenth-Century German Music and the Hermeneutics of the Moment* (Princeton, NJ: Princeton University Press).

Hopkins, Harry (1964), *The New Look: A Social History of the Forties and Fifties* (London: Secker & Warburg).

Howells, Bernard (1996), *Baudelaire: Individualism, Dandyism and the Philosophy of History* (Oxford: Legenda).

Jarman-Ivens, Freya (ed.) (2007), *Oh Boy! Masculinities and Popular Music* (London: Routledge).

Kallioniemi, Kari (1998), *'Put The Needle on the Record and Think of England'* – Notions of Englishness in the Post-War Debate on British Pop Music (Academic Dissertation: Cultural History, School of History, University of Turku, Finland).

Kaplan, E. Ann (1987), *Rocking Around the Clock: Music Television, Postmodernism, and Consumer Culture* (London: Routledge).

Kassabian, Anahid (2001), *Hearing Film: Tracking Identifications in Contemporary Hollywood Film Music* (New York: Routledge).

Katz, Bob (2002), *Mastering Audio: The Art and the Science* (Oxford: Focal Press).

Koch, Stephen (1974), *Stargazer: Andy Warhol's World and His Films* (London: Calder and Boyars).

Koestenbaum, Wayne (1993), *The Queen's Throat: Opera, Homosexuality and the Mystery of Desire* (New York: Da Capo Press).

Kopelson, Kevin (1994), 'Tawdrily, I Adore Him' in *Nineteenth-Century Music*, Vol. 17, No. 3, pp. 274–85.

Korsyn, Kevin (2003), *Decentering Music: A Critique of Contemporary Musical Research* (Oxford: Oxford University Press).

Krafft-Ebing, Richard von (1965), *Psychopathia Sexualis*, trans. F.S. Klaf (London: Staples Press).

Krims, Adam (2000), *Rap Music and the Poetics of Identity* (Cambridge: Cambridge University Press).

Krims, Adam (2007), *Music and Urban Geography* (New York: Routledge).

Kristeva, Julia (1987), 'Baudelaire, or Infinity, Perfume and Punk' in *Tales of Love*, trans. Léon Roudiez (New York: Columbia University Press), pp. 318–40.

Lacasse, Serge (2000), *'Listen to My Voice': The Evocative Power of Vocal Staging in Recorded Rock Music and Other Forms of Vocal Expression* (PhD dissertation, University of Liverpool).

Lance, Mark Norris and Tanesini, Alessandra (2005), 'Identity Judgements, Queer Politics' in I. Morland and A. Willox (eds), *Queer Theory* (Basingstoke: Palgrave Macmillan), pp. 171–86.

LeVay, S. (1994), *The Sexual Brain* (Cambridge, MA MIT Press).

Lhamon, Jr., W. T. (1998), *Raising Cain: Blackface Minstrelsy and the American Working Class* (Cambridge, MA: Harvard University Press).

Lindvig, Kyrre Tromm (2008), '"Wir Fahren auf der Autobahn": Kraftwerk and Constructions of Germanness' (doctoral thesis, University of Oslo).

Lomax, Alan (1968), *Folk Song Style and Culture* (New Brunswick: Transaction Books).

Maddison, Stephen (2000), *Fags, Hags and Queer Sisters: Gender Dissent and Heterosocial Bonds in Gay Culture* (New York: St. Martin's Press).

Marcus, Greil (1989), *Lipstick Traces: A Secret History of the Twentieth Century* (Cambridge, MA: Harvard University Press).

Marsh, Dave (1999), *The Heart of Rock and Soul* (New York: Da Capo).

Massey, Howard (2000), *Behind the Glass: Top Record Producers Tell How They Craft The Hits* (San Francisco: Backbeat Books).

Maus, Fred (2001), 'Glamour and Evasion: The Fabulous Ambivalence of the Pet Shop Boys' in *Popular Music*, 20/3, pp. 379–93.

Maus, Fred (2004), 'The Disciplined Subject of Music Analysis' in A. Dell'Antonio (ed.), *Beyond Structural Listening? Postmodern Modes of Hearing* (Berkeley: University of California Press), pp. 13–43.

McClary, Susan (1991), *Feminine Endings: Music, Gender, and Sexuality* (Minnesota: University of Minnesota Press).

McClary, Susan (1994), 'Same As It Ever Was: Youth Culture and Music' in A. Ross and T. Rose (eds), *Microphone Fiends: Youth Music, Youth Culture* (London: Routledge), pp. 29–40.

McClary, Susan (2000), *Conventional Wisdom: The Content of Musical Form* (Berkeley, CA: University of California Press).

McLeod, Ken (2003), 'Space Oddities: Aliens, Futurism and Meaning in Popular Music', in *Popular Music*, 22/3, pp. 337–55.

Meisel, Perry (1999), *The Cowboy and the Dandy: Crossing Over from Romanticism to Rock and Roll* (Oxford: Oxford University Press).

Middleton, Richard (1990), *Studying Popular Music* (Milton Keynes: Open University Press).

Middleton, Richard (ed.) (2000), *Reading Pop: Approaches to Textual Analysis in Popular Music* (Oxford: Oxford University Press).

Middleton, Richard (2006), *Voicing the Popular: On the Subjects of Popular Music* (London: Routledge).

Middleton, Richard (2007), 'Mum's the Word: Men's Singing and Maternal Law' in F. Jarman-Ivens (ed.), *Oh Boy! Masculinities and Popular Music* (London: Routledge), pp. 103–24.

Miller, Edward D. (2003), 'The Nonsensical Truth of the Falsetto Voice: Listening to Sigur Rós' in *Popular Musicology Online*, Issue 2.

Moers, Ellen (1978), *The Dandy: Brummell to Beerbohm* (London: University of Nebraska Press).

Moore, Allan F. (2001), *Rock: The Primary Text: Developing a Musicology of Rock*, 2nd edition (Aldershot: Ashgate).

Moore, Allan F. (ed.) (2003), *Analyzing Popular Music* (Cambridge: Cambridge University Press).

Moore, Allan F. (2006), 'What story should a history of popular music tell?' in *Popular Music History*, pp. 329–38.

Moorefield, Virgil (2005), *The Producer as Composer: Shaping the Sounds of Popular Music* (Cambridge, MA: MIT Press).

Morris, Nancy (1999), 'US Voices on UK Radio', *European Journal of Communication*, Vol. 14(1), pp. 37–59.

Mort, Frank (1997) *Cultures of Consumption: Masculinities and Social Space in Late Twentieth-Century Britain* (London: Routledge).

Mosser, Kurt (2008), '"Cover Songs": Ambiguity, Multivalence, Polysemy', *Popular Musicology Online*, Issue 2.

Moy, Ron (2007), *Kate Bush and Hounds of Love* (Aldershot: Ashgate).

Mulvey, Laura (1975), 'Visual Pleasure and Narrative Cinema', *Screen*, 16/3, Autumn.

Negus, Keith (1992), *Producing Pop. Culture and Conflict in the Popular Music Industry* (London: Edward Arnold).

Niblock, Sarah (2005), *Prince: Negotiating the Meanings of Femininity in the Mid-1980s* (unpublished PhD dissertation, Middlesex University).

Paglia, Camille (1990), *Sexual Personae: Art and Decadence from Nefertiti to Emily Dickinson* (New Haven, CT: Yale University Press).

Parsonage, Catherine (2004), 'The Popularity of Jazz – An Unpopular Problem: The Significance of *Swing When You're Winning*' in *The Source: Challenging Jazz Criticism*, Issue 1 (Leeds), pp. 59–80.

Petersen, Alan (1998), *Unmasking the Masculine: 'Men' and 'Identity' in a Sceptical Age* (London: Sage).

Pountain, Dick and Robins, David (2000), *Cool Rules: Anatomy of an Attitude* (London: Reaktion Books).

Reynolds, Simon (1989), 'Against Health and Efficiency', in A. McRobbie (ed.), *Zoot Suits and Second-Hand Dresses* (Basingstoke: MacMillan), pp. 244–55.

Reynolds, Simon and Press, Joy (1995), *The Sex Revolts: Gender, Rebellion and Rock 'n' roll* (London: Serpent's Tail).

Richardson, John (2005), '"The Digital Won't Let Me Go": Constructions of the Real in Gorillaz' "Clint Eastwood"' in *Journal of Popular Music Studies*, 17:1, pp. 1–29.

Richardson, John (2006), 'Intertextuality and Pop Camp Identity Politics in Finland: The Crash's Music Video "Still Alive"' in *Popular Musicology Online*, Issue 2.

Richardson, John (2007), 'Double-voiced Discourse and Bodily Pleasures in Contemporary Finnish Rock: The Case of Maija Vilkkumma' in J. Richardson and S. Hawkins (eds), *Essays on Sound and Vision* (Helsinki: Helsinki University Press), pp. 401–41.

Richardson, John and Hawkins, Stan (eds) (2007), *Essays on Sound and Vision* (Helsinki: Helsinki University Press).

Rimmer, Dave (2003), *New Romantics: The Look* (London: Omnibus Press).

Robins, Stephen (2001), *How to Be a Complete Dandy: A Little Guide for Rakes, Bucks, Swells, Cads and Wits* (London: Prion Books Limited).

Ross, Andrew (1999), 'Uses of Camp' in F. Cleto (ed.), *Camp: Queer Aesthetics and the Performing Subject: A Reader* (Edinburgh: Edinburgh University Press), pp. 308–29.

Rycenga, Jennifer (2006), 'Endless Caresses: Queer Exuberance in Large-Scale Form in Rock' in S. Whiteley and J. Rycenga (eds), *Queering the Popular Pitch* (London: Routledge), pp. 235–247.

Savage, Jon (1996), *Time Travel: Pop, Media and Sexuality 1976–96* (London: Chatto & Windus).

Scott, Derek (1989), *The Singing Bourgeois: Songs of the Victorian Drawing Room and Parlour* (Milton Keynes: Open University Press).

Scott, Derek (2003), *From the Erotic to the Demonic: On Critical Musicology* (Oxford: Oxford University Press).

Sedgwick, Eve Kosofsky (1986), *Between Men: English Literature and Male Homosocial Desire* (New York: Columbia University Press).

Segal, Lynne (1990), *Slow Motion: Changing Masculinities, Changing Men* (London: Virago Press).

Seidman, S. (ed.) (1996), *Queer Theory/Sociology* (Cambridge, MA: Blackwell).

Shneer, David (2007), 'Queer is the New Pink: How Queer Jews Moved to the Forefront of Jewish Culture', *Journal of Men, Masculinities and Spirituality*, Vol. 1(1), pp. 55–64.

Shuker, Roy (2008), *Understanding Popular Music Culture* (third edition) (London: Routledge).

Small, Christopher (1977), *Music – Society – Education* (London: John Calder).

Solie, Ruth (ed.) (1993), *Musicology and Difference: Gender and Sexuality in Music Scholarship* (Berkeley, CA: University of California Press).

Sonneck, Oscar George Theodore (1909), 'Report on "The Star-Spangled Banner", "Hail Columbia", "America", and "Yankee Doodle".' (Washington, D.C.: Government Printing Office). Reprint, 1972 (New York: Dover Publications).

Sontag, Susan (1966), *Against Interpretation and Other Essays* (New York: Farrar, Strauss & Giroux).

Steinskog, Erik (2008), 'Voice of Hope: Queer Pop Subjectivities', *Trikster: Nordic Queer Journal*, Issue 1 (http://trikster.net/1/index2.html).

Stevenson, Nick (2006), *David Bowie: Fame, Sound and Vision* (Cambridge: Polity Press).

Sullivan, Nikki (2003), *A Critical Introduction to Queer Theory* (New York: New York University Press).

Summers, Claude J. (ed.) (2004), *The Queer Encyclopedia of Music, Dance & Musical Theater* (San Francisco: Cleis Press).

Tagg, Philip (1981), *Fernando the Flute* (Gothenburg: University of Gothenburg Press).

Tagg, Philip (1982), 'Analysing Popular Music: Theory, Method and Practice', *Popular Music*, 2, pp. 37–67.

Tarasti, Eero (1997), 'The Emancipation of the Sign: On the Corporeal and Gestural Meanings in Music', *Applied Semiotics/Sémiotique appliquée* 2:4, pp. 15–26.

Terman, L.M. and Miles, C.C. (1936), *Sex and Personality: Studies in Masculinity and Femininity* (New York: McGraw-Hill).

Thomas, Calvin (ed.) (2000), *Straight with a Twist: Queer Theory and the Subject of Heterosexuality* (Champaign, IL: University of Illinois Press).

Tinkcom, Matthew (1999), 'Warhol's Camp' in F. Cleto (ed.), *Camp: Queer Aesthetics and the Performing Subject: A Reader* (Edinburgh: Edinburgh University Press), pp. 344–54.

Tosh, John (1999), *A Man's Place: Masculinity and the Middle-Class Home in Victorian England* (New Haven, IL: Yale University Press).

Toynbee, Jason (2000), *Making Popular Music: Musicians, Creativity and Institutions* (London: Arnold).

Trudgill, Peter (1983), *On Dialect: Social and Geographical Perspectives* (Oxford: Basil Blackwell).

Turner, Graeme (2004), *Understanding Celebrity* (London: Sage).

Visconti, Tony (2007), *Tony Visconti – The Autobiography: Bowie, Bolan and the Brooklyn Boy* (London: Harper Collins).

Waksman, Steve (1999), *Instruments of Desire: The Electric Guitar and the Shaping of Musical Experience* (Cambridge, MA: Harvard University Press).

Walden, George (2002), *Who Is A Dandy?* (London: Gibson Square Books).

Walser, Robert (1993), *Running with the Devil: Power, Gender and Madness in Heavy Metal Music* (Hanover, NH: Wesleyan University Press).

Warner, Timothy (2003), *Pop Music – Technology and Creativity: Trevor Horn and the Digital Revolution* (Aldershot: Ashgate).

Webb, Barbara L. (2001), 'The Black Dandyism of George Walker: A Case Study in Genealogical Method', *TDR/The Drama Review*, Vol. 45, No. 4 (Winter), pp. 7–24.

White, Shane and White, Graham (1998), *Stylin': African American Expressive Culture from Its Beginnings to the Zoot Suit* (New York: Cornell University Press).

Whitehead, Stephen M. and Barrett, Frank J. (eds) (2005), *The Masculinities Reader* (Cambridge: Polity Press).

Whiteley, Sheila (1997), *Sexing the Groove* (London: Routledge).

Whiteley, Sheila (2000), *Women and Popular Music: Sexuality, Identity and Subjectivity* (London: Routledge).

Whiteley, Sheila (2007), 'Which Freddie? Constructions of Masculinity in Freddie Mercury and Justin Hawkins' in F. Jarman-Ivens (ed.), *Oh Boy! Masculinities and Popular Music* (London: Routledge), pp. 21–37.

Whiteley, S and Rycenga, J. (eds) (2006), *Queering the Popular Pitch* (London: Routledge).

Whiteley, S., Bennett, A. and Hawkins, S. (eds) (2004), *Music, Space and Place: Popular Music and Cultural Identity* (Aldershot: Ashgate).

Wicke, Peter (1990), *Rock Music* (Cambridge: Cambridge University Press).

Wilson, Carl (2007), *Let's Talk About Love: A Journey to the End of Taste* (New York: Continuum).

Wilson, Elizabeth (2007), 'A Note on Glamour', *Fashion Theory*, Vol. 11/1, pp. 95–108.

Woods, Paul A. (ed.) (2007), *Morrissey in Conversation: The Essential Interviews* (London: Plexus Publishing).

Yates, N. and Samson, P. (2005), *Pete Doherty: On the Edge – The True Story of a Troubled Genius* (London: John Blake).

## Websites

http://www.blender.com/guide/articles.aspx?id=515
http://www.iht.com/articles/2006/11/24/features/jagger.php
http://www.marcalmond.co.uk/
http://www.concertlivewire.com/interviews/bowie.htm
http://www.carlysimon.com/vain/vain.html.

## Newspaper and magazine articles

'Ray Davies: I Don't Mean To Be Cruel To My Pals', *NME*, 4 November 1967.
'Bryan Ferry: Putting On The Style', *Melody Maker*, 12 July 1975.
'Robbie Williams: Royal Albert Hall, London', *The Observer*, 14 October 2001.

'Radio daze: Stephen Duffy' in *Guardian Unlimited*, 15 October 2004 (http://arts.guardian.co.uk/fridayreview/story/0,1327037,00.html).

'Pete Doherty and the New Decadence', in *The Independent on Sunday*, 6 February 2005.

'Kate Moss' Prince Alarming: Pete Doherty' in *Vanity Fair*, July 2005.

Jamiroquai, Clapham Common, London' by Ben Walsh, *The Independent (Music)*, Tuesday, 5 July 2005.

'Jay Kay: Surviving Paradise' by Dan Gennoe, *The Independent (People)*, Saturday, 6 August 2005.

'The Jam? They were a way of life' in *The Guardian Unlimited*, 3 February 2006 (http://arts.guardian.co.uk/filmandmusic/story/0,1700386,00.html).

'Bryan Ferry's Nazi gaffe', *The Independent*, 15 April 2007.

'Roll Up for a Magical Mystery Tour', *The Times*, 5 May 2007.

# Index

(References to illustrations and music examples are in **bold**)